Performance Instrumentation and Visualization

ACM PRESS

Editor-in-Chief:

Peter Wegner, *Brown University*

ACM Press books represent a collaboration between the Association for Computing Machinery (ACM) and Addison-Wesley Publishing Company to develop and publish a broad range of new works. These works generally fall into one of four series.

Frontier Series. Books focused on novel and exploratory material at the leading edge of computer science and practice.

Anthology Series. Collected works of general interest to computer professionals and / or society at large.

Tutorial Series. Introductory books to help nonspecialists quickly grasp either the general concepts or the needed details of some specific topic.

History Series. Books documenting past developments in the field and linking them to the present.

In addition, ACM Press books include selected conference and workshop proceedings.

Performance Instrumentation and Visualization

Edited by

Margaret Simmons
Rebecca Koskela

ACM Press
New York, New York

Addison-Wesley Publishing Company
The Advanced Book Program
Redwood City, California • Menlo Park, California • Reading, Massachusetts
New York • Don Mills, Ontario • Wokingham, United Kingdom • Amsterdam
Bonn • Sydney • Singapore • Tokyo • Madrid • San Juan

ACM Press Frontier Series
Performance Instrumentation and Visualization

First printed 1990

Library of Congress Cataloging-in-Publication Data

Performance instrumentation and visualization / edited by
 Margaret L. Simmons, Rebecca Koskela.
        p.   cm.
    Based on the Workshop on Parallel Computer Systems:
 Instrumentation and Visualization sponsored by Los Alamos
 National Laboratory and the Santa Fe Institute in May 1989.
    Includes index.
    1. Computer graphics—Congresses.   2. Parallel processing
 (Electronic computers)—Congresses.   I. Simmons, Margaret.
 II. Koskela, Rebecca.
 T385.P46   1990   004' .35—dc20   90-738
 ISBN 0-201-50937-7

ABCDEFGHIJ-MA-943210

CONTRIBUTORS

Bill Appelbe
Georgia Institute of Technology

William Bohm
University of Manchester

William C. Brantley
IBM Thomas Watson Research Center

David Callahan
Tera Computer Company

Robert J. Carpenter
National Institute of Standards and Technology

Henry Y. Chang
IBM Thomas Watson Research Center

Frederica Darema
IBM Thomas Watson Research Center

Blaine Gaither
Amdahl Corporation

Dieter Haban
University of Kaiserslautern

Jeff Hardy
Gould/Encore Computer Company

Harry F. Jordan
University of Colorado

Ken Kennedy
Rice University

Doug Kimelman
IBM Thomas Watson Research Center

Laura Bagnall Linden
Massachusetts Institute of Technology

Allen D. Malony
Center for Supercomputing Research and Development, University of Illinois

Alan Mink
National Institute of Standards and Technology

Kathleen Nichols
Apple Computer Corporation

Allan Porterfield
Tera Computer

Melvin Prueitt
Los Alamos National Laboratory

Daniel A. Reed
Department of Computer Science, University of Illinois

David C. Rudolph
Department of Computer Science, University of Illinois

Jeff Saltzman
Los Alamos National Laboratory

Shreekant Thakker
Sequent Computer

Dieter Wybranietz
University of Kaiserslautern

Jerry Yan
Sterling Federal Systems

PREFACE

Performance evaluation of parallel computer systems is a complicated process and a lively field of current research. This process is much more than mere benchmarking of the performance of parallel computers; it also involves an essential feedback mechanism for the design and implementation of hardware and software for the complex supercomputers of tomorrow. Effective evaluation of these systems based on their performance will require new kinds of data. In addition, the complexity and quantity of data from performance measurements are so overwhelming that new techniques are needed to allow efficient and timely analysis to take place. One such a technique is visualization, a method of computing that transforms symbolic data into geometric form thus allowing researchers to observe their simulations and measurements. Once the primary province of the entertainment industry, visualization is becoming a mainstay in the computer scientist's toolbox.

To address these issues, a "Workshop on Parallel Computer Systems: Performance Instrumentation and Visualization" co-sponsored by the Los Alamos National Laboratory and The Santa Fe Institute, was held May 8-10, 1989, in Santa Fe, New Mexico. This workshop was a successor to "Workshop on Instrumentation for Future Parallel Computing Systems" held in 1988. The goals of this year's workshop were to clarify features of performance instrumentation for current and future parallel computer systems and to determine which visualization techniques and tools would be appropriate for performance measurement of parallel computer systems. The availability of integrated basic hardware and software for the collection of performance data, coupled with the tools to enable graphical observation of the measurements, would not only teach us how to program such systems more effectively, but would lead to the design of more effective systems. To accomplish these two goals, selected designers, researchers, and users were brought together to exchange ideas on the role of visualization in the design of methods and tools for measuring the performance of tomorrow's supercomputers. This book includes the papers and descriptions of the demonstrations presented at the workshop, plus summaries of the working group discussions.

It is ironic that, as the computational power and performance of high-end supercomputing increases, it becomes harder to comprehend the complex results of the computational models. To that end, visualization has become a powerful, almost indispensable mechanism for the scientific user. Interactive visualization combines computer graphics and, imaging with user interfaces to aid understanding of complex computation. As a tool, visualization provides a time-efficient method for testing and debugging ideas as well as a gauge for performance. Gone are the days when batch jobs produce a thick stack of line printer output to be poured over in hopes of understanding a complex system. The ultimate goal of this effort is to enable the user to concentrate on science not computers.

One of the major limitations of the supercomputers of today is the providing enough data to processing units to keep them busy; thus placing the burden of increasing bandwidth between memory and processing units on the computer architect. As less bandwidth per processor is available, it becomes important to understand how the bandwidth is used and how to improve the memory performance. Chapter 1 describes a new tool, **PFC-Sim**, that allows dynamic measurement of FORTRAN programs using compiler techniques for improving memory performance.

Chapter 2 describes the hybrid tool for the on-line monitoring and measurement of parallel and distributed systems currently under development at the University of Kaiserslautern. There, a test and measurement processor (TMP) and monitoring software are being integrated into a graphics-oriented programming environment that supports program animation and visualization of algorithms.

Scientists are using images generated by computer as a fast method of assimilating large amounts of information from complex research problems. Most of the phenomena that occur in the universe transpire out of the reach of human senses. Our senses were designed to help us survive in a limited environment but were not designed to perceive the fundamental laws of the cosmos. By using computers to shift unobservable aspects of nature into the small window of our senses, we can begin to understand a larger fraction of the universe. Techniques from Los Alamos National Laboratory used to enhance this understanding are outlined in Chapter 3.

Supercomputing has entered the realm of three or more dimensions with the current generation of machines. Datasets generated from large-scale simulations or hardware instrumentation can be enormous. More importantly, the data are not as easily seen as two-dimensional data. Chapter 4 examines several techniques to look at three-dimensional data sets. These techniques include surface contouring and volumetric rendering. In addition, animation techniques that allow the examination of four-dimensional data are discussed.

Research is being conducted to determine how concurrent computations can be mapped onto multicomputers so as to minimize execution time. One of the most difficult issues to be addressed involves choosing an appropriate level of abstraction for modelling concurrent program execution without resorting to lengthy instruction-set level simulations or general stochastic models. The AXE experimentation environment was designed to facilitate such investigations at the operating system level using discrete-time simulation. Chapter 5 describes the visualization facilities of AXE, a rapid prototype environment for modelling concurrent systems.

The lack of tools to observe the operation and performance of parallel architectures limits the user's ability effectively to optimize application and system performance. Chapter 6 describes an integrated performance environment being developed for the Intel iPSC/2 hypercube. Included in this environment is a machine independent visualization tool, based on the X window system, that permits the performance analyst to browse and explore interesting data components of a system dynamically. Chapter 7 discusses the visualization system for this integrated performance environment.

The support environment of the performance monitor of IBM's RP3, a massively parallel multiprocessor machine is described in Chapter 8. Chapter 9 presents the analysis of parallel program performance on a bus-based, shared-memory multiprocessor.

Ideally, performance data should be visualized using high-level models and algorithm representations. Unfortunately, such models are specialized, and hence need to be customized using knowledge of the application. Alternatively, simple timeline displays of trace data events are difficult to relate to the program source. An effective compromise is to display trace data in terms of the program flowgraph, and the synchronization graph. Chapter 10 describes a simple mechanism for 'program performance replay', that can concurrently display performance data such as blocked processes, processor utilization, and block execution times, for a single trace, and performance 'averages and comparisons' over sets of traces for different input data and runtime scheduling parameters.

Parallel computers are inherently more difficult to program than traditional von Neuman machines. In addition to worrying about program correctness within a single computation thread, the programmer must worry about communication between concurrent tasks. Even if synchronization is done correctly so that the program executes without error, the program may be written in such a way as not fully to utilize the available processors due to bottlenecks of one kind or another. Thus, it is important to provide tools to assist in program understanding. Traditional program analysis tools provide only aggregate information, such as tools which plot the total number of processors in use over time. Chapter 11 describes ParVis (PARallel VISualization), a tool that gives detailed information on individual tasks. ParVis is designed to work with Multilisp, a parallel Lisp dialect.

Reflective memory is a mechanism for providing shared memory communications at high speed between homogeneous or heterogeneous systems, at
distances of up to 120 feet. As the demand for shared memory parallel processing exceeds the capacities of a single bus systems, interconnection schemes
like reflective memory will be important. Chapter 12 discusses instrumentation
issues for reflective memory implementations: how reflective memory fits within
the parallel processing taxonomy and how it is used in real-time applications.

The interpretation of performance of programs for parallel computers is
of considerable interest. It can be used to compare different architectures and
to determine the efficiency with which a given architecture is exploited. The
reasons for a given performance measure, however, are often not related to the
architecture. Chapter 13 discusses examples in which features of performance
probes, such as execution time as a function of number of processors, are determined by widely different issues. The examples demonstrate how easy it is
for one performance influence to mask or masquerade as another.

In Chapter 14, Mink and Carpenter describe a hybrid performance measurement tool for MIMD multiprocessors. The tool uses software (embedded
code) triggers and hardware sampling, thus introducing a minimal amount of
perturbation to the executing program.

Thakkar presents the results of his study of the effect that different coherence policies can have on the performance of parallel programs on the Sequent
Symmetry Series in Chapter 15.

In addition to the interesting mix of papers described above, the workshop
participants were divided into four discussion groups to explore in detail problems of the performance of parallel programs and the role of visualization in
performance analysis. The four discussion groups were:

1. Monitoring the Performance of Parallel Programs

   This group focused on their experiences in analyzing the performance of
   parallel programs and the role of instrumentation in the analysis.

2. Graphical Aids to Constructing Parallel Programs

   The first goal of this group was to gather together a list of existing tools
   available for constructing and measuring the performance of parallel programs. The group then discussed the limitations of these tools and put
   together a description of an effective parallel computation monitoring tool.

3. Standards in Performance Instrumentation and Visualization

   This group discussed the feasibility of standards in the area of performance
   instrumentation and visualization. The group was also interested in determining those areas of performance and visualization that would make good
   candidates for standardization.

4. Dataflow and Hybrid Dataflow Architectures.

Pure dataflow machines and the newer von Neumann/dataflow hybrids represent a class of multi-threaded machines that use hardware to support a *virtual* task namespace and extremely rapid context switching. This working group discussed the role of the dynamic execution tree in performance instrumentation and what kinds of processor performance data are required for hybrid architectures.

The last four chapters of the book are the summaries of these working group discussions.

ACKNOWLEDGMENTS

We would like to thank our co-sponsor, The Santa Fe Institute, and our corporate sponsors, Cray Research, Inc., Digital Equipment Corporation, IBM, and Thinking Machines Corporation for their support of our workshop. We would also like to thank our advisory committee, Arvind of MIT, Raul Mendez of Supercomputer Research Institute in Tokyo, Dan Reed of the University of Illinois, and Karl-Heinz Winkler of Los Alamos for their efforts on our behalf.

Once again, the workshop has been judged a success. Those who helped contribute to that success through their support include Ann Hayes, Andy White, and Norm Morse; we thank them for their support. Thanks also to Yvonne Martinez, Debbie Martinez, Sheila Girard, Andi Sutherland, Marcella Austin, and Jan Hull for their help with the organization of the workshop.

Once again, Yvonne Martinez has done an excellent job in the preparation of this manuscript.

CONTENTS

CHAPTER 1   **Analyzing and Visualizing Performance of
             Memory Hierarchies**   1
             David Callahan   Ken Kennedy   Allan Porterfield

             1.1   Introduction   1

             1.2   PFC-Sim   2

             1.3   Rice Compiler Evaluation Program
                    Suite   6

             1.4   Cache Performance   7

             1.5   Program Transformations   13

             1.6   Effectiveness   18

             1.7   Conclusions   23

CHAPTER 2   **Monitoring and Measuring Distributed
             Systems**   27
             Dieter Wybranietz   Dieter Haban

             2.1   Introduction   27

             2.2   Problems with Monitoring and
                    Measuring   28

             2.3   Design Objectives of the TMP
                    Monitoring System   29

             2.4   TMP Principles   30

             2.5   The TMP Monitoring System   31

2.6   Instrumentation of the Host System   32

2.7   Event Generation   32

2.8   Hardware Implementation   33

2.9   Evaluation and Display of
       Measurement Data   35

2.10   Current Work: User-controlled
       Evaluation and Display   38

2.11   Conclusions   41

CHAPTER 3   **Scientific Visualization at Los Alamos**   47
             Melvin L. Prueitt

3.1   Introduction   47

3.2   Molecular Structures   48

3.3   Three-Dimensional Contour Surfaces   49

3.4   Chemistry   49

3.5   Earth Sciences   50

3.6   Physics   51

3.7   Biology   51

3.8   Mathematics   52

3.9   Conclusion   52

CHAPTER 4   **Visualization Techniques for High
             Dimensional Data Sets**   55
             Jeffrey Saltzman

4.1   Introduction   55

4.2   Higher Dimensional Data Sets   56

4.3   Visual Tools   57

4.4   Software   59

4.5   Examples   60

4.6   Conclusions   61

CHAPTER 5   **Performance Instrumentation and**
             Visualization Using AXE   63
             Jerry C. Yan

             5.1   Research Background   63

             5.2   AXE — An Experimentation
                    Environment   64

             5.3   Hardware Monitor   66

             5.4   Software Monitors   69

             5.5   Experimental Usage   71

             5.6   Conclusions and Future Research   71

CHAPTER 6   **Integrating Performance Data Collection,**
             Analysis, and Visualization   73
             Allen D. Malony   Daniel A. Reed   David C. Rudolph

             6.1   Introduction   73

             6.2   Intel iPSC/2 Description   75

             6.3   Environment Organization   77

             6.4   Software Instrumentation   79

             6.5   Hardware Monitoring   81

             6.6   Data Analysis and Visualization   85

             6.7   Summary   95

CHAPTER 7   **JED: Just An Event Display**   99
             Allen D. Malony

             7.1   Introduction   99

             7.2   Target Environment   100

             7.3   Organization   101

             7.4   Top-Level Interface   102

             7.5   Trace Control   103

             7.6   Event Control   105

	7.7	Task Groups	108
	7.8	Task Display	110
	7.9	Event Display	112
	7.10	Conclusion	114

CHAPTER 8   **Support Environment for RP3 Performance Monitor**   117
William C. Brantley   Henry Y. Chang

	8.1	Introduction	117
	8.2	Overview of RP3 Performance Monitor	118
	8.3	User Mode Access to PMC	121
	8.4	Virtual PMC	121
	8.5	VPMC System Interface	122
	8.6	Example Uses	123
	8.7	Discussion	125
	8.8	Summary	129

CHAPTER 9   **Environments for Visualization of Program Execution**   135
Doug Kimelman

	9.1	Introduction	135
	9.2	One View of Program Visualization	136
	9.3	The RP3 Environment	137
	9.4	A Prototype Visualization System	138
	9.5	A Visualization Environment	143
	9.6	Conclusion	145

CHAPTER 10   **Software Tools for Visualization of Performance**   147
Bill Appelbe

| | 10.1 | Introduction | 147 |

10.2	Taxonomy	150
10.3	VIPER — a Source Level Performance Visualization Tool	151
10.4	Implementation	154
10.5	Conclusion	154

CHAPTER 11 Parallel Program Visualization Using ParVis   157
Laura Bagnall Linden

11.1	Introduction	157
11.2	Multilisp	158
11.3	Events: The Link Between Multilisp and the Display	160
11.4	The ParVis Display	161
11.5	A List-Processing Example	164
11.6	The Filter Facility	170
11.7	Limitations to ParVis	180
11.8	Related Work	181
11.9	An Integrated Parallel Programming Environment	184
11.10	Conclusion	185

CHAPTER 12 Reflective Memory Instrumentation Issues   189
Blaine Gaither   Jeff Hardy

12.1	Applications	189
12.2	NP1 Overview	190
12.3	Reflective Memory	190
12.4	Performance Issues	191
12.5	Instrumentation	191
12.6	Application Level Monitoring	192

12.7   Conclusions   192

CHAPTER 13   **Performance: The Need For An In-depth
View**   195
Harry F. Jordan

13.1   Introduction   195

13.2   Levels of the Computation Influencing
Performance   196

13.3   Parametrized Execution Time   198

13.4   Multiprocessor Examples   201

13.5   Conclusions   211

CHAPTER 14   **A VLSI Chip Set For A Multiprocessor
Performance Measurement System**   213
A. Mink   R. Carpenter

14.1   Introduction   213

14.2   Measurement System Design   215

14.3   uTRAMS Data Capture Section   217

14.4   FIFO   222

14.5   Output Section   222

14.6   uREMS Data Capture Section   224

14.7   Testing   226

14.8   Conclusions   228

CHAPTER 15   **Performance of Parallel Applications on a
Shared-Memory Multiprocessor System**   235
Shreekant S. Thakkar

15.1   Introduction   235

15.2   Symmetry Multiprocessor Systems   236

15.3   Symmetry Cache Coherence and Bus
Protocols   236

15.4   Performance Monitoring   240

15.5   Performance Evaluation   241

15.6   Conclusions   255

CHAPTER 16   **Graphical Aids to Constructing Parallel**
              Programs Summary   259
              David Bailey

CHAPTER 17   **Standards Working Group Summary**   263
              Allen D. Malony   Kathleen Nichols

17.1   Introduction   263

17.2   Background   265

17.3   User Interfaces to Data Collection   267

17.4   Performance Data Exchange   268

17.5   Hardware Performance Instrumentation   270

17.6   OS Instrumentation   272

17.7   Performance Visualization   274

17.8   Performance Environment Architecture   275

17.9   Conclusions   277

CHAPTER 18   **Dataflow and Hybrid Dataflow**
              Architectures Summary   281
              A.P.W. Bohm

18.1   Introduction   281

18.2   Dataflow Languages   282

18.3   Intermediate Forms   283

18.4   Models of Computation   284

18.5   Architecture   286

18.6   Realization   286

18.7   Conclusion   287

CHAPTER 19   **Performance Analysis of Parallel**
Applications and Systems Summary   289
Frederica Darema   Shreekant Thakker

Performance
Instrumentation and
Visualization

1

Analyzing and Visualizing Performance of Memory Hierarchies

David Callahan
Ken Kennedy
Allan Porterfield

1.1 Introduction

A major limitation of supercomputers today is the inability to get data to the processing units fast enough to keep the units busy. Vector and parallel processors replicate arithmetic units, dramatically increasing the number of operations that can be performed during any time period. Vector and shared memory multiprocessors, however, still have (at some point in the memory hierarchy) a single memory to support the increase in computational power. This has placed a substantial burden on computer architects to increase bandwidth between the memory and the processing units. Doubling the number of processing units is much easier than doubling the amount of data that main memory can supply during a given time period. As less bandwidth per processor is available, it becomes increasingly important to understand how the bandwidth is used and to define mechanisms to improve its effectiveness.

To analyze and improve the memory performance of a program, tools that relate the hardware performance to the high level program that is being executed are required. Existing memory performance tools were designed to test memory

1

performance, not to allow users to improve performance of specific programs. These tools provide no mechanism to relate memory performance to identifiable parts of the executing program.

Motivated by a desire to explore compiler techniques for improving memory performance, we have developed a new tool, **PFC-Sim** that allows dynamic measurement of FORTRAN programs. The first use of **PFC-Sim** was to examine cache performance and the effects of a variety of program transformations on performance. Using the execution statistics generated during execution, several tools to display and summarize the performance of the program have been developed.

The remainder of this chapter presents the design and implementation of **PFC-Sim** along with some examples of how it has been used to study memory performance.

1.2   PFC-Sim

PFC-Sim is a program-driven event tracing facility consisting of three parts: a preprocessor, run-time routines, and visualization tools. **PFC-Sim** runs on long programs in a limited amount of space and creates a map between actions in the trace and the corresponding events in the source program. To eliminate the need for an enormous trace file, the simulation of memory occurs during program execution. Unique marking of each event in the program source allows a simple mapping between the source program and actions during execution.

The basic structure of **PFC-Sim** can be used to measure any dynamic value that results from events that can be identified during compilation (memory performance, vector performance, dynamic instruction frequency, to name a few possibilities). It is particularly well suited to problems where normal techniques generate excessively long trace files.

A one hour program accesses the cache billions of times. Even with very small trace entries, this easily exceeds available disk storage on most systems. In a typical tracing simulation, a single execution of the program is traced, the trace file is compacted in some manner, and then many simulations are run on the resulting compacted trace file. **PFC-Sim** runs on programs where the original trace file is too long to store, by running the simulation concurrently with the program being traced, eliminating the need to have all of the trace entries available at one time.

Computing only the hit ratio of a program would not aid a programmer in determining whether a particular section of code is getting adequate memory performance. To improve a program's memory performance, some means of determining the reference or set of references causing the majority of the misses is needed. By marking loads and stores in the program source, a simple mapping between events and source program statements is derived; every event has a unique number. By relating performance of the program to locations in the source, the programmer has knowledge about where to start efforts to improve the performance. What **PFC-Sim** does not do is give the programmer some ideas about methods of modifying the program that would likely lead to faster programs.

The **PFC-Sim** preprocessor accepts as input a FORTRAN program to be simulated and inserts instrumentation code into it. The **PFC-Sim** simulator consists of three externally-linked FORTRAN calls which can simulate a wide variety of memory structures. The set of visualization tools present the information from the simulation in ways that allow quick identification of important events. Each of the three parts are more fully explained in the following sections.

1.2.1   PFC-Sim Preprocessor

The **PFC-Sim** preprocessor is embedded inside a powerful vectorizing and parallelizing source-to-source translator developed at Rice University, the Parallel FORTRAN Converter (PFC). PFC builds and uses a dependence graph to transform a FORTRAN77 program (possibly with vector and parallel extensions) into an equivalent FORTRAN program with vector and/or parallel constructs. The output of **PFC-Sim** does not use any non-FORTRAN77 constructs that were not present in the original program.

To simulate memory usage on the original input program, **PFC-Sim** marks the tree immediately after parsing, scanning for memory events. A memory event is either a LOAD or a STORE. The **PFC-Sim** preprocessor inserts two types of calls, namely LOAD and STORE, in front of ordinary statements. Calls to LOAD and STORE are treated by the simulator in the same way that hardware would treat the equivalent instructions. Each call passes the address being accessed, the length of the element, current simulation time and a unique identifier for the particular reference.

The default handling of scalars is to ignore the references that they generate. The number of blocks occupied by scalars will normally be very small, and preliminary testing showed that they cause very few additional misses to occur. A second reason to ignore scalars is that many will be kept in registers between uses when a good global register allocator is available. Ignoring scalar references is also practical. The simulator requires three times as long to run when scalars are included.

All statistics about memory performance are kept in the simulator. When program execution completes, the statistics must be saved. Every FORTRAN RETURN or STOP statement in the main routine of a program is preceded by a call to SIMFNL. SIMFNL builds a data set with the information that was gathered on that particular run.

Besides inserting statements for memory references, the preprocessor also divides the program into basic blocks. During execution, profiling data are generated, and simulated execution time is kept. The simulation slows the program down, but event frequency can be determined from the simulated time. An accurate estimate of the execution time of a single basic block is possible in the absence of any memory delays. By incrementing the simulation time at the beginning of any basic block and adding a miss penalty when appropriate, an accurate clock is maintained.

One effect of the preprocessor is to approximately double the size of a program. Figure 1.1 shows matrix multiply before and after the preprocessor. Most of the changes are straightforward. (The second parameter is the length of the value being loaded in bytes.) The addition of a subroutine call for every subscripted array access increases the execution time of the program between 10 and 20 times. (A one and half hour program takes about one day for the cache to be simulated on a IBM 3081-D.)

```
DO I = 1, N
      DO J = 1, N
            A(I,J) = 0
            DO K = 1, N
                  A(I,J) = A(I,J) + B(I,K)*C(K,J)
            ENDDO
      ENDDO
ENDDO
```

becomes
```
DO I = 1, N
      DO J = 1, N
            CALL STORE(A(I,J),4,TIME,1)
            A(I,J) = 0
            DO K = 1, N
                  CALL LOAD(A(I,J),4,TIME,2)
                  CALL LOAD(B(I,K),4,TIME,3)
                  CALL LOAD(C(K,J),4,TIME,4)
                  CALL STORE(A(I,J),4,TIME,5)
                  A(I,J) = A(I,J) + B(I,K)*C(K,J)
            ENDDO
      ENDDO
ENDDO
```

FIGURE 1.1
Matrix multiply—before and after **PFC-Sim**.

1.2.2 Memory Simulation

The run-time package for memory simulation consists of five routines. The three mentioned in the previous section and two that are called internally from LOAD and STORE. An initialization routine is called the first time that the memory simulator is activated to set up all of the control structures. The initialization routine reads in the specifications for the requested memory and performs the appropriate actions. The second internal routine is an automatic prefetch mechanism that can be used to simulate hardware prefetching. Almost any memory structure can be modeled by the package.

The initialization routine reads in a file that contains seven parameters. The first five specify the type of memory to be modeled, the sixth gives the frequency of trace entries for one of the visualization tools, and the last activates hardware prefetching. The five memory parameters are

- number of memory blocks;

- size of each memory block;

- associativity — direct mapped, set or fully associative;

- replacement algorithm — LRU, FIFO, Random, or OPT; and

- write policy — Write-back or Write-though.

These options cover most caches and main memories available in present architectures. The OPT replacement algorithm is a useful tool in detecting when transformations could have a noticeable impact on performance, although it requires a lot of space to implement.

After the initialization routine has identified the memory to be simulated, the memory control structure is initialized. The initial cache contains no values. After memory initialization, LOAD and STORE calls perform almost identical actions. Both routines emulate the memory lookup function and increment the arrays that count either hits or misses for the unique identifier passed with the call. The difference between the calls is that STORE marks the block as dirty and may require that the block be immediately written out. Besides the arrays to count hits and misses, a traffic array counts the number of bytes that are moved between memories due to each reference.

To provide a means for the programmer to examine memory performance during execution, a compact trace file can be generated which profiles the hit ratio over time. Instead of providing a reference by reference summary, a single entry is generated for every time interval. The entry provides the hit ratio for the previous time quantum and the location of the program at the end of the time quantum. The interval is a parameter and is in microseconds (of simulated time). Trace entries are also generated every 5000 misses, giving more detailed information about the location of large numbers of memory misses.

1.2.3 Visualization Tools

Many different visualization tools can be developed using compact trace and statistics files. Two have already been developed. The first is a browser (on a color IBM 3279) that allows a user to color every reference in the program according to the hit ratio of that reference. For example, by coloring all of the low hit ratios red, while leaving the remaining references green, references that have the greatest possibility of being improved are easy to locate.

This identification eliminates between 50 and 95% of the references in most programs. Of the remaining references, simple profiling tools can pinpoint the typically small number of references that cause the majority of the misses. The quick identification of misses allows the programmer to focus on the task of improving memory performance in the portion of their program that memory delays can be reduced.

The second tool uses the trace file to graph the miss rate as a function of execution time. The trace file may be viewed at any magnification from the interval between the compact trace file entries to a level which allows the entire program to be viewed. To allow the programmer to locate portions of the code that have poorer memory performance than expected, the tool provides a means of moving from a particular trace file entry to the point in the program which is currently being executed.

Most programs move though at least three stages, initialization, computation, and output. The computation may itself consists of multiple stages. By generating a compact trace file **PFC-Sim** allows the memory bandwidth requirements of various phases to be displayed. In addition, the performance of each phase can be examined in detail to determine peak bandwidth required during subphases. Using this display tool, the programmer gets a detailed view of the cyclic nature of the memory requirements of his program.

These tools are useful to the expert programmer. They allow him to pinpoint sections of the code and individual data structures that should be the targets of optimization. The tools do not provide help in deciding what changes would be most effective at reducing the number of memory misses. Performance tools for the majority of programmers would need to provide additional information about the effect of various possible changes. One method of providing memory performance information to the average user, is for the compiler to automatically improve the performance of a program by blocking (or other transformation).

1.3   Rice Compiler Evaluation Program Suite

PFC-Sim was used to examine the cache performance of a new supercomputer benchmark set. The Rice Computer Evaluation Program Suite (RiCEPS) is being gathered to address the lack of a publicly accessible set of computationally intensive programs. RiCEPS is a group of programs culled from production supercomputers. Each program was selected to be representative of a group of applications. The programs are substantial in size and require a significant amount of execution time.

Work on the benchmark set is progressing in parallel with this study. The benchmark set is to grow to about twenty programs. Each program in the benchmark set includes, in addition to the FORTRAN program, a brief description of what the code does (what it solves/what algorithms it uses) and at least one set of data to run the program. Some of the programs — having been previously packaged as benchmarks — generate their own data and do not use any explicit data sets.

The experiments reported used a preliminary version of the benchmark set containing twelve programs. The programs' execution times range from one minute (MATRIX) to several hours (SIMPLE, BARO, BOAST) on an IBM 3081D. While most programs are 1 to 3 thousand lines, they range in size from 15 lines to over 23,000 lines. All of the programs compiled with the IBM VS2 FORTRAN compiler and ran on an IBM 3081D.

The benchmark programs used for this work included:

□ **MCMB** - a microbial biodegradation program;

□ **MATRIX** - a 100 × 100 matrix multiply;

□ **BARO** - weather simulation code;

□ **SIMPLE** - a hydrodynamics program from LLNL;

□ **EFIE304** - calculates the current distribution on an arbitrary body;

□ **BOAST** - a black oil reservoir simulator;

□ **EULER1** - a solver for one dimensional unsteady Euler equations;

□ **SHEAR** - three dimensional turbulent fluid dynamics simulation;

□ **MHD2D** - solves 2D MHD equations with periodic boundary conditions;

□ **ONEDIM** - one dimensional Schroedinger equation solver;

□ **LINPACKD** - standard LINPACK benchmark [1]; and

□ **WANAL1** - boundary control of wave equations program.

1.4   Cache Performance

PFC-Sim was used to study the effectiveness of many types of caches. A full report is in [2]. Rather than try to present all of the cache performance results, only a sample of the kinds of tests that **PFC-Sim** allows will be presented. First, the effect of cache size on performance of supercomputer programs is measured.

This is the type of memory performance study that has been carried out in the past, but **PFC-Sim** allows the study of much longer programs than the previous studies. The second study examines the hit ratios of individual references in a program, rather than whole programs. This task could not be done by previous cache simulation techniques.

1.4.1   Cache Size

When describing a cache, the first characteristic given is normally its size. During the design of a computer, the selected cache size is often the largest that can fit in a reasonable fraction of the available physical space and that will not represent an unreasonable fraction of the total machine cost. Within the physical and practical constraints, a larger cache results in a higher hit ratio. A series of cache simulations examines the effect of increasing cache size from 16K to 256Kbytes.

As shown in Figure 1.2, all of the programs' hit ratios increased as data cache size increased. An average 16K cache hit 70.8% of the time, a 32K cache hit 75.9% of the time, and the hit ratio continued to rise smoothly to a peak of 90.9% for a 256K cache. The average hit ratio line is nearly straight. Each doubling of the data cache size increased the hit ratio by approximately 5%. The average hit ratios of the larger caches are dominated by a few programs with very large working sets. For 256K caches, only four of the eleven programs[1] had a significant percentage of misses. Over 50% of the misses were generated by a single program WANAL1.

Overall, the average effect of doubling the cache size was to reduce the miss ratio by about 21% for each doubling of cache size. This was lower than the 27% that Alan Smith found with his sample group [3]. The average improvement as cache size increased was lower for this set of programs due to differences in the programs used in the two studies. The larger working sets of the RiCEPS programs increased the probability that a program's working set does not fit into a given cache size. This decreased the effectiveness of each doubling of the cache size.

The programs did not react uniformly to the increasing cache size. Some, like EFIE304, hit ratios increased dramatically at both 32 and 64K and very few misses occurred with a 128K data cache. Others, like MATRIX, hit ratios increased less than 5% between 16 and 32K, but the misses were almost non-existent with a 64K cache. SIMPLE showed improvement when the cache size increased from 16 to 32K, but few additional hits occurred if the cache was increased to 256K. WANAL1's hit ratio increased less than 0.1% when the cache was increased from 16K to 128K (and only 6% at 256K).

---

[1] Hit Ratios are not available for MCMB above 64K because the 16Mbyte virtual address space available under the IBM VM Operating system will not contain both the program's data space and the larger cache data structure required.

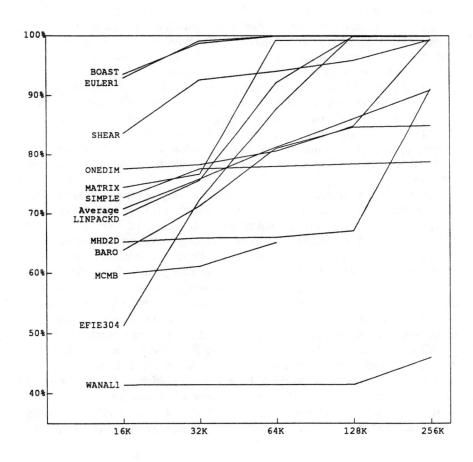

FIGURE 1.2
Effects of cache size—hit ratios.

For a programmer to understand how cache size affects a program's performance, the programmer needs to understand why the programs use the larger caches with such differing effectiveness. To understand why programs react so differently, let us consider the performance of MATRIX in detail. The first doubling in cache size had little effect (hit ratio increased by 2%), and the second was very effective (hit ratio increased by 22%). MATRIX only has 5 array accesses, the first when the result element is initialized to zero and the remaining four inside the main loop ($A = A + B * C$). The number of misses produced by four of the references did not change between any of the simulations. The only value that changed is the number of misses that occur when loading an element from the C array. When only a 16K cache existed, the load of C missed 100% of the time (1,000,000 misses, 0 hits). Increasing the cache size to 32K caused the hit ratio for the C reference to increase slightly, (8.74% with 912,576 misses, 87,424 hits). Increasing the cache size further to 64k caused the hit ratio for C to jump to 99% (10,000 misses, 990,000 hits) where it remained for 128K and 256K caches. The radical difference can be explained by computing working set sizes.

A 100 × 100 single precision FORTRAN array occupies 40,000 words. In the naive implementation of matrix multiplication that was used, the entire C array is referenced before any element in C is accessed a second time. This causes a perfect LRU mechanism to remove every element before it is ever reused. The only way that an element can still be present in caches smaller than 40,000 bytes is if the LRU replacement is less than perfect. When the number of words in the array exceeds the amount of storage needed for the entire array (and the active column of B), the hit ratio rises very quickly. The hit ratio, graphed as a function of size, is not a smooth function, but a series of steps that occur whenever the working set size of a particular reference is exceeded.

Overall, increasing the cache size is sporadically very effective at reducing cache misses and memory traffic between the cache and the main memory. When the cache size exceeds the working set size for a portion of the program, the increase is very effective; otherwise, the increase has very little effect on the hit ratio. The working set size of a program will be a difficult value to identify during compilation since it can depend both on the program and the input data.

1.4.2 Hit Ratios of Individual References

In the previous section, the performance of MATRIX was examined in detail. Three of the references were almost always hits (> 99%), one reference was always a miss and the last reference was a miss when the cache had smaller than 40K. Except for a very small range of cache sizes around 40K, every reference in MATRIX could be viewed as either a hit or a miss. If references generally demonstrate this behavior, then the information can be used to improve the performance. The only references whose hit ratio can be improved are those that generate misses.

The cache hit ratio reported by **PFC-Sim** for complete programs is actually the total of the hits and misses counted for each individual reference in the program. By looking at the hit ratios of individual references (Figure 1.3), references are divided into two groups (hits and misses).

Figure 1.3 graphs the individual hit ratio for every reference in the benchmark programs for a 32K LRU 4-way set associative cache. It clearly demonstrates two preferred ratios. Over 94% of the references had individual hit ratios above 95% or below 5%. No other region had even 1% of the references. The approximately one-third of the references that miss over 95% of the time account for over 96% of the misses in all of the RiCEPS programs,

The bimodal nature of individual references' hit ratios and the overwhelming percentage of the misses that occur for references that miss on almost all references suggest that, for each program reference, the minimum working set size required to prevent misses is constant between references during execution. If a programmer or compiler can make an estimate of the working set size required for each variable, and knows the cache size, then the program references that degrade overall machine performance can be identified and improved.

1.4.3 Processor Performance

Previous sections have measured the cache performance in absolute numbers. The effectiveness of hiding the CPU from the main memory and the communications costs involved in that hiding were given. More important is the overall impact of the cache on processor performance. The overall performance can be broken into two categories: delays from cache misses and peak performance as dictated by memory bandwidth considerations.

For the test programs, reducing the cache misses can significantly improve performance. As supercomputers have become faster in recent years the speed differences between caches and main memories has increased. Cray now has computers (early versions of the Cray-2 [4]) in which accessing the main memory requires 57 cycles. When the delays to memory reach this level, reducing the misses can improve performance by 20 to 30%. In this environment, improving cache performance can be a very profitable optimization.

Miss Delays. **PFC-Sim** generates profile data counting the number of times that every basic block is executed. Since a basic block has no control flow, it is possible to estimate the execution time (ignoring any memory delays) of each block. An estimate of the total execution time, in cycles, is easily generated during execution. The total execution time for a program would be this estimate plus any delays caused by memory misses.

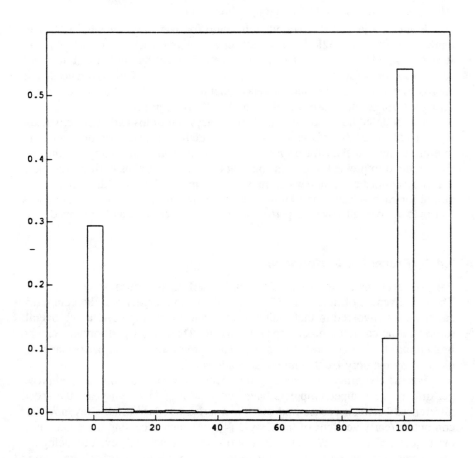

FIGURE 1.3
Individual hit ratio distribution.

In this study, we have assumed that loads, stores, and integer addition instructions, all take 1 cycle, floating-point addition takes 10 cycles, and a floating-point multiply takes 20 cycles.

Using the estimate for total execution time and the number of misses in each program, the amount of time spent waiting on cache misses can be computed for various distances to main memory. Figure 1.4 graphs the cost of memory performance for each program with a 32K, LRU, 4-byte line, write-back, no prefetching cache. Even when a cache miss takes 50 cycles to return, programs with high hit ratios (BOAST, EULER1) spend less that 1.5% of execution time waiting on the main memory. Any effort to improve the cache performance of these programs will have a minimal (or counterproductive) effect.

Most of the programs fall into a second category. They spend between 2 and 5% of the time waiting on the cache when the main memory takes 5 cycles to return a value. Thus, effort spent on improving cache performance will have little effect on execution time when the memory requires very few cycles to access. As the number of cycles to memory increases, optimization of cache performance could bring noticeable benefits. When the cache is 20 cycles away, elimination of cache delays would result in 7% to 16% faster programs. If main memory is distant (50 cycles), the improvement can be as much as 32%. For this group of programs, attempts to remove cache delays can significantly improve performance when a substantial delay occurs every time main memory is accessed.

One program tested, WANAL1, did not fit into the two groups. WANAL1's cache performance was substantially poorer than any other program tested. Even when main memory was only 5 cycles away, WANAL1 would execute 9.1% faster with no cache misses. When main memory was 50 cycles away, half of the execution was spent waiting for memory references.

1.5 Program Transformations

A number of transformations can effect the memory performance of a program. In conjunction with the cache performance study, we looked at the effect of a large number of well known transformations on memory performance [2]. Among others examined were loop fusion, loop interchange, strip mine and interchange, and unroll and jam. Two new transformations were also examined, peel and jam and wavefront blocking. The effectiveness of transformations will be shown by examining the two new transformations.

1.5.1 Peel and Jam

Peel and jam is a transformation that fuses loops with certain kinds of fusion preventing dependence edges. Fusion-preventing edges are dependences that

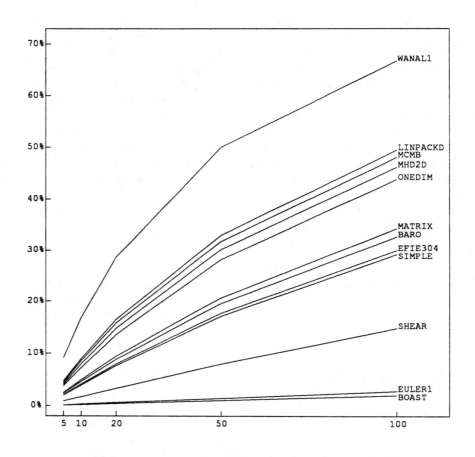

FIGURE 1.4
Percentage of execution time spent in miss delays.

would be reversed by fusion. An example is when the first loop defines a value on the second iteration and the second loop uses it in its first iteration. The two loops could not be fused because the value would be used before it was defined. By peeling the correct number of iterations from the first loop body, the correct relationship between the references in the two loop bodies is maintained after fusion.

In peel and jam, the first loop of a pair of loops has a small number of iterations unrolled into a prologue. The majority of the iterations are left in a loop that can be fused with the second loop body (see template in Figure 1.5). Peel and jam can be viewed as aligning the loop nest. The peel step causes a number of iterations of the first loop to be executed prior to execution of the fused loop nest and the fusion step aligns the loop bounds of the two loops.

Peel and jam is very similar to loop alignment [5-7]. In these papers, loop alignment is used to bring all accesses of a memory location to the same iteration of a loop. Peel and jam just attempts to guarantee that the dependences are not reversed when fusion is performed. Peel and jam does require that all dependences after fusion be from a reference originally in the first loop body to a reference originally in the second loop body.

Example.   There is at least one important group of problems that are amenable to peel and jam. This is the set of grid-based partial differential equation (*pde*) solvers. A typical *pde* code makes numerous passes over a grid, successively smoothing the function. Each individual pass uses the old or new values of adjoining points to compute its new value. Since each iteration uses only nearby values, the dependences have very small maximum distances. Also, since the induction variables tend to be easily recognizable, the compiler can accurately compute the distances.

To obtain a better idea of how peel and jam will work in practice, the following example shows part of a program in RiCEPS. The example illustrated in Figure 1.6 is taken from the one-page inner loop that accounts for well over 99% of WANAL1's execution time.

```
DO I = 1, M+1                   loop body#1(1)
     loop body#1(I)             DO I = 1, M
ENDDO                                loop body#1(I+1)
DO I = 1, M                          loop body#2(I)
     loop body#2(I)             ENDDO
ENDDO
```

FIGURE 1.5
Peel and Jam.

In the WANAL1 example in Figure 1.6, three copies of the FI and SI arrays are maintained, namely the current, old, and oldest arrays. Each iteration of the outer loop recomputes the arrays. The first loop nest copies the values of the old array into the oldest array, and the current array into the old array, in preparation for recomputing the current values. The second loop nest computes the new value of FI. The computation of each element of FI involves references to six other elements (its old and oldest values and together the old values of the four adjacent points up, down, left and right).

The two loop nests use the same arrays. Fusing the loop nests increases the locality of reference. Moving the K loop inside the first loop nest is straightforward. The J loop cannot be fused because the nth iteration of the second loop uses the n+1st value of the old array, which has not yet been properly modified. The second loop's access would incorrectly use the oldest value instead of the old value.

The fusion preventing anti-dependence between the two statements has a known distance of one. By peeling the first iteration of the upper loop (J), we can safely fuse the two J loops to improve the memory locality.

Exactly the same method will allow the I loops to be fused. This eliminates the data cache misses for three of the references in the second loop nest. When the resulting program was tested with **PFC-Sim**, peel and jam eliminated 200 million misses during a single execution of the program. Performing the transformation on other loops, the total reduction approached 500 million data cache misses. This is well over 20% of the total misses in the program (2.35 billion).

One interesting aspect of peel and jam is that it works on the two programs that have the lowest cache hit ratios for the largest cache size examined. This is probably not completely coincidental. Each smoothing iteration accesses each element in the array a small number of times. The grids tend to be large to improve the accuracy of the solution. This causes very large working sets and poor data cache performance when the working sets exceed the data cache size.

1.5.2 Wavefront Blocking

The previous blocking techniques both use non-reordering transformations to block data accesses into groups that a second transformation reorders in order to improve the data cache performance of the processor. The resulting memory accesses reuse a square block of data, and hopefully reuse each element before it is pushed from the cache.

Two other combinations of transformations were discussed earlier, namely, peel and jam and loop skew and interchange. Peeling and skewing are non-reordering transformations that allow loops with dependences that would otherwise prevent fusion or interchange to be transformed. By merging the sets of transformations, a very powerful pair of blocking transformations is produced, *strip mine, skew and interchange* and *unroll, peel and jam*. Both of these trans-

```
        DO 30 N = 1,NT
            DO 35 J = 0, M+1
                DO 35 I = 0, M+1
                    DO 35 K = -1, 0
                        FI(I,J,K) = FI(I,J,K+1)
                        SI(I,J,K) = SI(I,J,K+1)
35              CONTINUE
C      Solutions for FI
            DO 40 J = 1, M
                DO 40 I = 1, M
                    FI(I,J,1) = 2*FI(I,J,0)-FI(I,J,-1)+P*(FI(I+1,J,0)
                        +FI(I-1,J,0)+FI(I,J+1,0)+FI(I,J-1,0)-4*FI(I,J,0))
40              CONTINUE
30      CONTINUE
```

FIGURE 1.6
Application of Peel and Jam to WANAL1.

forming combinations access the data in a pattern that resembles the hyperplanes (or wavefronts) that Lamport described in [8], for parallelization. For parallelization, every element in the wavefront must have all of its inputs computed before the wavefront is executed (since there is no guaranteed order of computation). For blocking, the wavefronts are executed sequentially. Thus, dependences that lie along the wavefront are allowed. Due to the similarity with wavefronts, this class of transformations is called *wavefront blocking*.

Figures 1.7 and 1.8 show the two wavefront blocking transformations. The profitability of the two wavefront blocking methods can be found using the same methods as their square blocking counterparts.

By performing a loop skew in the middle of strip mine and interchange, the block being accessed is no longer square. Computing the bounds of the resulting trapezoidal region is more complicated than for blocking transformations. Taking vertical slices out of the trapezoid, results in slices of increasing length until the maximum width is achieved. As various columns are completed the slices will decrease in length. Strip mine, skew and interchange accomplishes the changing slice length by intersecting two regions. The first region is the iteration space of the original outer loop (I in the example). The second region is the tilted iteration space of the loop created by the strip mine transformation. Computing the intersection is done by taking the maximum value of the two lower edges and the minimum value of the two upper edges. Figure 1.7 shows a generic example of strip mine, skew and interchange.

Unroll, peel and jam also generates a trapezoidal access pattern. Unrolling the original outer loop (I in the example), produces a number of copies of the inner loop (J). To fuse the first copy with the second copy, one iteration of

```
                                    DO New = 2,N+(M/SM)
DO I = 1, N                           DO I = max(1,New-N),min(N,New-1)
   DO J = 1, M                           DO J = 1, SM
      loop body(I,J)                        loop body(I,J+SM*(New-I-1))
   ENDDO                                 ENDDO
ENDDO                                 ENDDO
                                    ENDDO
```

FIGURE 1.7
Wavefront blocking: strip mine, skew and interchange.

the first loop must be peeled. To fuse the first loop with the UF copy of the loop, UF - 1 iterations of the first loop must be executed before the fused loop. This produces the large prologue seen in Figure 1.8. Since the loops must all execute the same number of total iterations, an epilogue completing each copy's iteration is also generated. The amount of code generated grows rapidly as the unroll factor increases. The prologue and epilogues can be fused into the main loop by using guards to control the execution of the various loop bodies on each iteration. This substantially reduces the code explosion, but adds overhead to each loop body during execution. It may also reduce the opportunities for scalar optimization between the various copies of the loop body.

The wavefront blocking transformations allow us to block any loop nest where the dependence distances can be bounded from below. The transformations are tedious to implement correctly by hand, but can be done during compilation. The problems of implementing these transformations at compile time deal with the accuracy of the dependence graph and the presence of extraneous dependence edges introduced by the programmer.

1.6   Effectiveness

Using the programs in RiCEPS, a study of the effectiveness of the transformations was conducted. The profiler in **PFC-Sim** was used to identify the most frequently executed statements, since these basic blocks contain the references that dominate the overall memory performance. An automatic system should not restrict its focus on these basic blocks, but most of the improvement will occur from transformations to these inner loops.

The programs were first examined to see whether an automatic system built on a parallelizing compiler could be expected to noticeably increase the performance of supercomputer applications. For those programs where transformations could not reduce the number of data cache misses, the programs were

```
                                        DO I = 1, N, UF
                                            DO J = 1, UF-1
                                                loopbody 1
                                            ENDDO
                                                .
                                                .
                                                .
                                            DO J = UF-1, UF-1
                                                loopbody UF-1
                                            ENDDO
        DO I = 1, N                         DO J = UF, M
            DO J = 1, M                         loopbody 1
                loop body                        loopbody 2
                                                   .
            ENDDO                                  .
        ENDDO                                      .
                                                loopbody UF
                                            ENDDO
                                            DO J = M+1, M+1
                                                loopbody 2
                                            ENDDO
                                                .
                                                .
                                                .
                                            DO J = M+1, M+UF
                                                loopbody UF
                                            ENDDO
                                        ENDDO
```

FIGURE 1.8
Wavefront blocking: unroll, Peel and Jam.

analyzed to determine if the problem was inherent in the algorithm or if it was a function of the program itself.

Based on the success of automatic transformation in improving cache performance, the programs can be divided into three groups: the transformable, the semi-transformable, and the non-transformable.

1.6.1 Transformable Programs

Transformable programs are programs that a compiler could transform to improve cache performance with no changes by the programmer. This group includes two whole programs (MATRIX and WANAL1) and parts of two other programs (ONEDIM and SIMPLE).

The precision of interprocedural information did not affect the analysis of the tested programs since the transformations affected code segments that included no procedure calls. However, the presence of interprocedural array analysis is important for several of the semi-transformable programs.

The misses in MATRIX can be almost eliminated by strip mine and interchange of the outer two loops. If the middle loop is split in half and moved to the outside, the number of misses (for a 32K 4-byte line cache) falls from 932,576 to 40,000. Since the loop uses 30,000 different values, proper blocking almost completely eliminates values being pushed from the cache prematurely.

WANAL1 had 2.35 billion misses before transformations. Figure 1.6 shows the innermost loop. Loop interchange, moving the K loop inside the I and J loops, reduces the misses by 336 million. About 250 million more misses are removed by that one application of peel and jam. Another 250 million misses were removed by first distributing the top loop, and peeling and jamming the loop that initializes the SI array with the loop nest that computes the new values of SI. Variable renaming of a summation variable allowed fusion of three loops, eliminating another 200 million misses. Overall, almost half of the misses could be eliminated from the program giving the lowest hit ratio of the tested programs.

Peel and jam eliminated half of the misses that occurred in SIMPLE. Unfortunately, while almost all of the computation in WANAL1 was in the loops that could be fused, only a small fraction of SIMPLE's computation is contained in the jammed loop nests. Peel and jam still increased the hit ratio by 1%, from 77% to 78%.

Approximately 60% of the misses in ONEDIM occur in three matrix multiply operations. Strip mine and interchange of the three loop nests is identical to that used in the MATRIX program. This should allow the hit ratio (for a 32K cache) to increase from 79% to about 91%. The remaining misses occur in a loop nest that cannot be improved and will be discussed in the next section.

Overall, the results of applying transformations to improve memory performance are at best mixed and possibly even disappointing. Only about four programs (out of twelve) could be improved at all, and only three of those were improved significantly. The overall average hit ratio for a 16K cache increased by about 5% to 76%. The effect of transformations to increase memory performance is effectively to double the cache size provided by the hardware. The improved programs use an X K cache almost exactly as well as the original programs used a 2X K cache.

Effectively doubling the cache size of any computer is a worthwhile result, but the fact that only one-third of the programs could be modified was disappointing. The following two sections discuss the results of examining each program to determine why transformations were not possible.

1.6.2   Non-transformable Programs

Only two programs (LINPACKD and EFIE304) and part of a third (ONEDIM) have fundamental algorithmic reasons for their inability to be blocked into versions with better memory performance. In all three cases, the problem is pivoting for numerical stability.

Figure 1.9 is an example abstracted from LINPACKD that will serve as an example of pivoting. Some statements that do not affect the ability to apply

```
For k = 1 to n -1
        Determine l∈ { k, k+1, ..., n} = max_{k≤i≤n} |da(i,k)|
        r(k) = l
        Swap a(k,j) and a(l,j)
        w(j) = a(k,j)
        For i = k + 1 to n
                t = a(i,k) / a(k,k)
                a(i,k) = t
                For j = k + 1 to n
                                                a(i,j) = a(i,j) - t * w(j)
```

FIGURE 1.9
Gaussian elimination with partial pivoting.

transformations have been removed. Since l is computed in the loop, there is
no effective method to determine how a(l,*) interacts with a(k,*). This causes
dependences with distances that cannot be computed.

Algorithmically, the various rows can be interchanged at any time before
the Gaussian elimination is completed. The compiler is therefore correct in
its assessment of the dependences. The values are potentially reused and the
distance between the reuses is not computable.

Even with a system that automatically blocks the program, fusion does
not seem possible in these programs. Since the dependence distances between
the columns can be bounded, a future system may be possible to do some
transformations with this program. The variable l is limited in the range from
k+1 to n. This allows direction vectors to be accurately computed. By defining
the range of dependences to be a box that resembles the letter l, partial pivoting
may be divided into loops that access a specific amount of data.

Pivoting is most likely not the only algorithm that demonstrates a dependence nature that will prevent transformations. It is the only one in this initial
version of RiCEPS. In Gaussian elimination, the program could replace the
pivoting with a QR factorization, which is amenable to blocking, easier to par-
allelize, and demonstrates better stability. This kind of algorithm revision may be
very appropriate for programs that run on supercomputers. Any algorithm that
prevents parallelization at outer levels will probably severely limit performance
as the number of processors in a supercomputer increases.

1.6.3 Semi-transformable Programs

The largest group of the tested programs are semi-transformable. Automatic
techniques to improve memory performance of these programs do not work due

to the way that the program was written. The problems fall basically into two groups: code that is too unstructured for a compiler to analyze well, and code that contains a construct that inhibits transformation.

The best example of ugly code is found in a library routine, FTRVMT called by both MHD2D and SHEAR. Figure 1.10 shows a single loop nest taken from the subroutine FTRVMT. In both programs, a large fraction of the total references occur inside this routine. The programmer of the library routine linearized the references to the array DATA. Although linearization is one method suggested for dependence analysis of multiply-subscripted arrays [9], linearization, in this case, obscures the actual array access pattern. If other parts of the program are examined, it can be determined that neither NSKIP or MSKIP are constants during compilation.

Since the value of MSKIP is unknown, the distances that arise during dependence analysis are symbolic. The presence of symbolic distance values complicates the application of transformations. If the loop were written without linearization, it may be possible to determine that MSKIP is actually accessing a column of the array in a single step manner. With this knowledge, the loops could be blocked.

FTRVMT has been vectorized (the inner loop is preceded by a CRAY vector directive). Although it may perform as well as any other program written for the same machine and compiler, it can not effectively be ported. It is not only machine dependent, but it is also dependent on the intelligence of the compiler vectorization. When this program was first written (pre-1985), the CRAY compiler did not do a very good job of automatic vectorization. As the compiler has improved, and continues to improve, the linearization (and resulting symbolic distance vectors) inhibit any sort of transformation to the surrounding program.

```
        DO 109 JL = 1 ,I2K
            IF (JL-1) 102,102,104
102         EXJ = (1.,0.)
            DO 103 JJ = JL, NPTS,2*I2K
                DO 103   MM = 1,MTRN
                    JS = (JJ-1)*NSKIP + (MM-1)*MSKIP + 1
                    H = DATA(JS) - DATA(JS+I2K*NSKIP)
                    DATA(JS) = DATA(JS) + DATA(JS+I2K*NSKIP)
                    DATA(JS+I2K*NSKIP) = H
103         CONTINUE
            /* two more equivalent loops */
109         CONTINUE
```

FIGURE 1.10
FTRVMT—linearization preventing transformation.

A program that would require very precise interprocedural analysis to transform is BARO. The work in its inner loop is broken into three pieces. The smallest segment is contained in the procedure with the loops and the other two segments occur in separate subroutines. To block the loops, information about the access pattern of the arrays in the subroutines must be gathered.

Transforming BARO would be a difficult task. Rather than separating the boundary iterations of the grid from the other iterations, the main body of the loop is an intertwined jumble of checks to see if this iteration is on the boundary, followed by jumps to the appropriate code segments. After the boundary iterations are separated (by the compiler or by hand), the program still could not be parallelized. BARO is a partial differential equation program that needs to maintain both old and new values of arrays. Rather than copy an array from a current array into an old array at every iteration, an extra array dimension is declared. Every access to the array that wants an old value uses the variable JQ3, and every access to the current value uses the variable JQ4. When it is time to copy the current value into the old array and compute a new current value, JQ3 is set equal to JQ4 and JQ4 is set equal to 3-JQ3. This effectively copies the array with only two assignments and one subtraction. Compilers will have a difficult job determining that JQ3 is never equal to JQ4. More importantly for blocking, it is difficult to recognize that the values that were loaded into JQ4 on the previous iteration are being accessed on the current iteration using JQ3. BARO appears to use the values within two grid points to determine the next iteration. It appears that wavefront block angled by two iterations would successfully block the access, improving the memory performance significantly.

The programs in the semi-transformable group cannot be modified by a compiler, or probably even a programming environment, to improve the memory performance. However, they could be rewritten in a style that would make them amenable to transformation. After they are modified, the resulting code could be ported between machines without further modification.

1.7 Conclusions

1.7.1 PFC-Sim

PFC-Sim's basic structure is a powerful mechanism for developing a range of tools to examine program behavior. As it was designed for this research, **PFC-Sim** is both easy to modify and flexible.

The **PFC-Sim** front-end examines the source of a program, identifies and marks events of interest. During execution, each one of the events can be counted or otherwise noted. As implemented, the basic event is a memory reference and the dynamic action on each event is to model some type of memory hardware. The structure, however, can be easily modified for other applications. One graduate student, working part-time and having had no previous experience with the compiler (or the operating system environment it lives on), modified **PFC-Sim** to determine the dynamic vectorization percentage of floating point operations, in about two months. Developing new visualization tools for the back-end required less than a week each. Modifying the output into a form that could be accepted easily by a graphics tool was straightforward.

PFC-Sim can obviously be modified to gather any type of dynamic statistical information desired. More interesting modifications of **PFC-Sim** are for applications in debugging and performance analysis. By simulating the effects of a machine around the execution of a program, both data and program breakpoints are easy to implement. Other debugging activities can also be implemented. While **PFC-Sim** would not provide major debugging functionality over present sequential systems, it would provide benefits in parallel debugging. A careful implementation could maintain clocks for each parallel stream and duplicate actual event ordering for specific hardware. Duplication of actual event ordering may simplify debugging of race condition problems. Using **PFC-Sim** for performance analysis (or performance debugging) is already done to some degree. As a memory simulator, **PFC-Sim** generates profiling data for the basic blocks in each program. To determine the effectiveness of some transformations in this work, profiling data was used to limit examination of the programs to the most frequently executed basic blocks. Generating more sophisticated tools on top of the available data (and expanding the amount of data collected) would not be difficult.

Modifications to the basic structure of **PFC-Sim** can be used for a variety of program evaluation and debugging purposes. For some applications, like dynamic statistic gathering, it seems to be exceptionally well-suited to produce information in forms that can be used by other tools. For other applications, like debugging, the **PFC-Sim** structure is a new approach that could be very useful. While **PFC-Sim** was developed for this research, this paper uses just one of its many possible configurations to examine the performance of data caches on actual supercomputer applications.

1.7.2 Automatic Blocking (and Parallelization)

One of the goals of automatic vectorization and parallelization has been the transformation of "dusty deck" FORTRAN programs into equivalent vector or parallel versions. A number of vectorizing compilers do a good job of locating loops that can be vectorized. The success of "dusty deck" vectorization has suggested that automatic parallelization can eventually be achieved.

To be most effective at blocking or parallelization, transformations must be performed on large code segments. To manage memory, the compiler attempts to manipulate the entire program in such a way that a value is never pushed from cache until a computation using it has completed. To achieve minimum parallel computation time, the compiler examines whole programs and attempts to find maximal parallel sections. This contrasts with vectorization which normally examines smaller code segments.

Investigating the applicability of automatic blocking of supercomputer programs has uncovered a basic problem with whole program, automatic techniques. The problem is that nearly all large programs (such as RiCEPS) have some number of constructs that prevent transformations. Some of the constructs are included as performance tricks (like declaring a single array and using pointers to access it, so that only the pointers need to be swapped). Some constructs are attempts to generate fast code with mediocre compilers (linearizing the arrays for vectorization). Some constructs are unpredictable end conditions (programs that check for convergence after every iteration).

Although existing programs may be difficult to transform, the transformations could be applied to a program that implements the same algorithms without the use of transformation inhibiting constructs. The resulting programs could be optimized automatically for a wide class of processors. The present technique of program optimization for each new class of supercomputers requires the programmer to manually tune the program to the machine. This is a time-consuming process that may be avoidable as present-day state-of-the-art compiler techniques become widespread. Instead of tuning each program for each machine, the program could be modified a single time. The single modification would be aimed at removing the unnecessary constructs that inhibit the compiler from performing transformations. The compiler would then perform the required tuning for each new type of machine.

What does the transformable program look like? These studies have found that better structured programs are more likely to be transformable. Compiler technology has reached a level of sophistication where structured coding practices can be encouraged not only for readability and maintenance, but to reduce the effort involved in porting programs to a new supercomputer.

References

1. John Dongarra, "Performance of Various Computers Using Standard Equations Software in a Fortran Environment," in *Computer Architecture News*, 16(1), March 1988.

2. Allan Porterfield, "Software Methods for Improvement of Cache Performance on Supercomputer Applications," PhD thesis, Rice University, 1989. Technical Report Number Rice COMP TR89-93.

3. Alan Smith, "Cache Memories," *Computer Surveys*, 14(3), September 1982.

4. Margaret L. Simmons and Harvey J. Wasserman, "Performance Comparison of the Cray-2 and Cray-X-MP/416 Supercomputers," in *Supercomputing 88*, 1988.

5. Randy Allen and Ken Kennedy, "Vector Register Allocation," Technical Report Rice COMP TR86-45, Rice University, 1988.

6. Randy Allen, David Callahan, and Ken Kennedy, "Automatic Decomposition of Scientific Programs for Parallel Execution," Technical Report Rice COMP TR86-42, Rice University, 1986.

7. David Callahan, "A Global Approach to Detection of Parallelism," PhD. thesis, Rice University, 1987.

8. Leslie Lamport, "The Parallel Execution of DO Loops," *Communications of the ACM*, 17(2), February 1974.

9. Michael Burke and Ron Cytron, "Interprocedural Dependence Analysis and Parallelization," in *Proceedings of the SIGPLAN 86 Symposium on Compliler Construction*, 1986.

2

Monitoring and Measuring Distributed Systems

Dieter Wybranietz
Dieter Haban

2.1   Introduction

During the last years, increased activities to design, develop and construct new technologies for improved performance, reliability and availability have led to the investigation of new computer architectures. Due to the inherent limits of centralized approaches, systems with many processors executing in parallel are under construction. Two major directions can be distinguished: multiprocessor systems and distributed systems. We will focus on distributed systems in which processors at different nodes do not share memory and processes can only communicate by message passing. A few examples of those architectures are the Hypercube [1], the Butterfly [2], and the Transputer [3]. Despite the progress in hardware architecture, operating systems and programming languages, all of these systems demonstrate a significant lack in methods and tools for performance analysis, monitoring system behavior, debugging and tuning. Distributed systems feature several hundreds or thousands of processes running on different processors that are interconnected by (a) network(s). Due to the lack of global time, control and state it is very difficult to understand the behavior of these systems. The acceptance and wide use of new parallel and distributed architectures will depend heavily on adequate programming environments that include support of users and system engineers during monitoring, measuring and debugging activities.

In this paper, we describe the real-time hybrid monitor Test and Measurement Processor (TMP) that has been developed as part of the Incremental Architecture for Distributed Systems Project (INCAS). INCAS belongs to the wide class of research projects that investigate the capabilities of multicomputer architectures. A multicomputer is a locally concentrated set of loosely coupled autonomous nodes of identical structure each with local memory and local peripherals. Each node itself may consist of a tightly coupled multiprocessor system. In the INCAS Project, during the implementation of software – among others a small distributed operating system, two languages and some applications were developed – the availability of adequate debugging, monitoring and measuring support turned out to be very crucial for our future work and led to the construction of the TMP. See [4] for further details on INCAS.

The TMP approach does not interfere with the host system while causing a negligible performance degradation of less than 0.1%. Unlike pure hardware monitors, the TMP improves performance measurements and the understanding of the behavior of distributed systems by providing information in a user-oriented, high-level manner. The TMPs are transparently integrated into the hardware and software of the INCAS multicomputer testbed comprising features such as MMUs, caches and network devices. Apart from measurement and monitoring, the TMPs are also used for testing and debugging [5,6] of our distributed operating system as well as distributed applications [7].

In the following chapter, we discuss the problems of current monitoring and measuring approaches for parallel systems. After listing the major objectives of the TMP monitoring system, we detail its design. In Section 2.9, the processing and display of monitoring data are presented that demonstrate functions and applicability of the TMP. Section 2.10 describes ongoing work on user-controlled evaluation and animation of parallel programs.

2.2   Problems with Monitoring and Measuring

Monitoring means the collection of data of a system while it is in operation. By measurement we understand the evaluation of these data by relating the evaluation to other values, e.g., time. Testing a system means comparing its behavior with a (mostly informal) specification, while the locating and removal of faults is called debugging. Monitoring and measurement may serve testing and debugging needs.

Monitoring tools can be classified into pure hardware, pure software and hybrid monitors. A hardware monitor [8,9] is a device that is usually not part of the monitored system. In particular, these monitors do not meet the requirements of application programmers in parallel environments. Although such devices can be designed to have minimal or no effect on the host system, the simple observation of system buses, or probes connected to the processor, memory ports, or I/O channels provide too low-level data. Furthermore, these monitors often use sophisticated features of the hardware to get valuable data. Their installation requires great expertise and thorough knowledge of the system.

By contrast, software monitors [10-14] can present information in an application-oriented manner. These monitors are usually contained within the measured system, sharing with it the same execution environment, thus producing a significant degree of interference in both the timing and space of the monitored program. This time overhead increases if the collected data are processed and displayed on-line. Therefore, pure software monitors are not adequate for on-line monitoring and for accurate measurements during the execution time. As an example, the performance measurement tool IPS [15] allows programmers to interactively evaluate the performance history of distributed programs. The off-line tool is based on software monitoring; the raw data are collected during the first phase of IPS operation, and the second phase, the data analysis, allows users to access the measurement results.

Hybrid tools [16,17] can be designed to benefit from the advantages of both hardware and software monitors with minimal effects on the monitored system. Such monitors typically consist of an independent hardware device that receives data generated by the software running in the monitored system.

In addition to the drawbacks of traditional monitoring techniques, distributed systems set up further requirements for monitoring tools and techniques, since they feature asynchronous concurrent activities, non-deterministic and unreproducible behavior. Communications among the processes introduce unpredictable delays. To provide users a unique view of their system, monitoring and measurement activities have to be performed simultaneously at each node and the results have to be evaluated in common at a central station. Since distributed systems are characterized by a lack of global state and global time, mechanisms have to be incorporated to provide a consistent global view of system behavior and system performance.

2.3 Design Objectives of the TMP Monitoring System

The objectives that guided the design of the TMP monitoring system are aimed at assisting interactive users in gaining better insights into the run-time behavior of their applications and the operating system. The major objectives were:

Interference: To avoid functional side effects the monitor must not slow down execution speed. Especially in parallel systems, functional side effects occur when decreasing execution speed leads to a different sequence of operations and different causal relations between sequential computations.

Integration: The monitoring scheme is transparently incorporated into the hardware and programming environment resulting in a permanent benefit and in an unmodified system behavior. If the overhead is negligible, this approach is better than temporary instrumentations that change the system behavior upon removal.

Continuous Monitoring During Operation: The monitoring system can trace the host system, evaluate and supervise the execution of certain applications, and display information in real-time about their progress. We note that this service is particularly important when monitoring long-running (concurrent) processes, complex distributed programs with dynamically changing structures and when considering real-time programs that control critical systems such as a nuclear power plant or an airborne system (diagnostic measurements).

Application-oriented Presentation: To not only support experts but also 'normal' application programmers the provision of a user-friendly, graphical interface is necessary. For this reason, the large amount of monitor and performance data has to be interpreted, evaluated, and presented in an appplication-oriented manner that reflects the semantics and organization of the application programs.

2.4 TMP Principles

The above listed requirements were met by the TMP approach. The tool combines the advantages of hardware and software monitors while overcoming their deficiencies. As hardware support, a special Test and Measurement Processor (TMP) was developed that is an integral part of each node in a multicomputer system. Since such a node may consist of one or more processors, the TMP could also be used in a multiprocessor environment.

During execution the software of the monitored system indicates a significant state change by so-called events; then these events are categorized, time-stamped, processed, and displayed by the TMP hardware and software. Using semantic information about the monitored programs created by the compiler, the monitoring software is able to present performance and behavior information closely related to the source level organization of programs. To process the incoming data concurrently with the execution of the monitored system and to relieve the central station of a large amount of data, each TMP is capable of executing local software for various processing and evaluation needs for its host. In an environment consisting of several nodes, each TMP can receive data from any other TMP over a network; symmetrically, each TMP is able to send data to other TMPs. The TMP can send its results to the monitored host system, to other TMPs, to a central monitoring station as well as display local results on a locally connected terminal. In Figure 2.1, the principle operations of the TMP are illustrated.

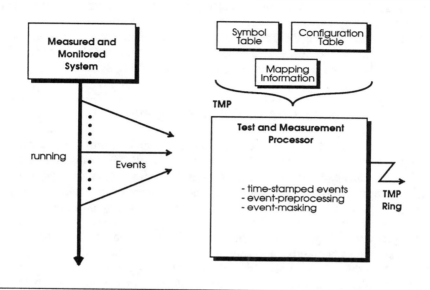

FIGURE 2.1
Principles of the TMP.

A key point of the measurement procedure is the identification of significant event types. A further problem consists in how to insert these events into the monitored software. In the current study, we are using events that represent significant trends in the behavior of the system, e.g., process creation and deletion. These events are generated by the operating system kernel, while additional events may also be inserted into the application software. First experiments with the INCAS multicomputer system showed that typically 600-800 kernel events were generated by each node per second. The only overhead of this measurement principle is caused by the event generation and is lower than 0.1% for our implementation. This was regarded as negligible and the event generating part of the software has become a permanent part of each node. In this way, we do not have corruption of system behavior by our monitoring tool at any time, and the system always behaves the same, whether the TMP is present or not.

2.5   The TMP Monitoring System

All the TMPs are connected via a separate network to a central monitoring station. The central station is used for interactive monitoring, global measurements, and distributed debugging. Ideally, the TMPs communicate via their own network, thereby avoiding disturbances to the application level. However, the communication among the TMPs can also be accomplished by the communication facility of the host system. Figure 2.2 depicts the INCAS experimental system with the transparently integrated TMP monitoring system.

2.6   Instrumentation of the Host System

An event is defined as a special condition that occurs during normal system activity, such that it can be made visible to the TMP. There are two kinds of events, optional and standard events. *Optional events* are associated with application programs. They are generated by the compilers or are placed manually into program code. Optional events mainly serve debugging purposes.

Standard events are a permanent and integral part of a system. They are intended to support monitoring and measuring during normal system operation. In this case, dispatcher, kernel and communication sub-system activities are monitored. *Dispatcher events* trace the operations of the operating system dispatcher including events that reflect the well-known states of processes: ready, blocked, running, killed. *Communication events* indicate inter-process communications including sending and receiving of messages. *Kernel events* describe low-level activities of the operating system such as initialization of queues for I/O devices, synchronization mechanisms etc.

As far as standard events are concerned, the monitored software does not need to be recompiled or relinked.

2.7   Event Generation

Events are generated by a single store instruction that is inserted at specific, well-chosen places in the software. The store instruction must write through the local processor cache so that the event is immediately visible on the system bus. The address part of the instruction represents one event class. In the current implementation, only the lowest byte of the address is exploited and therefore 256 event classes can be supported. The data part carries parameters for the event class; here all 32 bits are used by the TMP. For example, the event generated by the instruction *store 10,34* might encompass the information that process No. 34 was blocked (assume that the address 10 was assigned to the event class 'process blocked.'

For applications in a multiprocessor environment, each processor within one node is assigned a different, non-overlapping address range of 256 addresses. This way the processor can be identified by the mapping of events to the addresses that is explained in the next chapter.

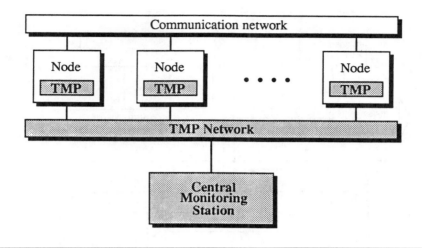

FIGURE 2.2
Integration of the TMP monitoring system.

2.8   Hardware Implementation

The TMP hardware was designed to be applicable in many different environments. It only needs to be connected to a bus where the events can be caught. Apart from the bus interface, the TMP concept is completely independent of the target system. Figure 2.3 shows the TMP hardware and its integration into a node of the INCAS system.

The main part of the TMP is the Event Processing Unit (EPU). It consists of a local event buffer, a comparator, a clock and an overflow counter. The local event buffer of the EPU is used as a FIFO for collecting sequences of events. The depth of the FIFO is 16 entries. This depth was tuned to cope with a high arrival rate of events, and is based on experiences gained with an earlier prototype. Each entry in the event buffer consists of 80 bits: 8 for the event class; 32 for the event parameter; 36 for the time stamp (ms); and 4 bits for control (CPU mode, overflow marker). Four additional bits for the processor identifier are planned for a next version of the TMP but have not been implemented yet. Since we used only 60 event classes, up to four processors could be supported by encoding the processor id in the event class. The accuracy of the timer can be interactively programmed. The timer quantum in no way affects the host system's timer.

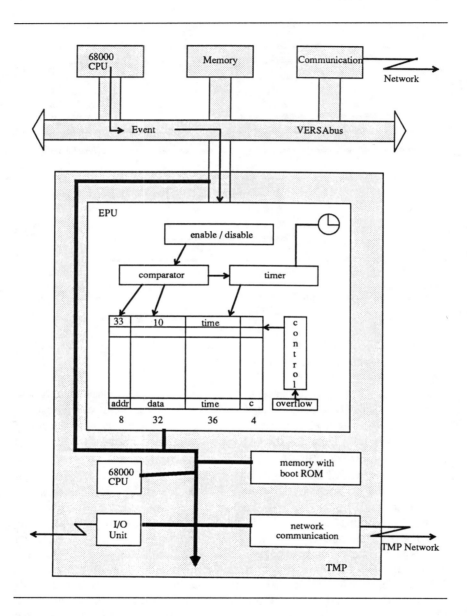

FIGURE 2.3
The TMP hardware.

The comparator checks the addresses on the host bus. If an address falls within the range that represents event classes, the matched address and the next data on the bus are stored in the event buffer, along with the local time. The location of the address range can be adapted to the actual hardware environment by a switch. The last byte of the address determines the event class; thus it is the only byte that is stored by the EPU. Since each processor within one node uses a different address range for triggering its events, the comparator can distinguish between the different sources and can write the corresponding identifier into the FIFO together with the event. The low level implementation of the TMP ensures that the address range representing events does not interfere with the main memory. This is supported by several hardware features (switches, bus acknowledge signals, etc.). Another function that is stored by the EPU is the processing mode (supervisor or user) of the host system. This information can be used to approximate the time spent in user or kernel modes.

The overflow counter of the EPU is used to count the number of events lost due to a buffer overflow. Although the specific type of each event is lost, the TMP software is aware of this inconsistency. In order to detect the occurrence of an overflow, the first event placed in the buffer after such an overflow is marked in its control field.

The EPU can be controlled by a set of commands including enable/disable EPU, reset EPU, set/ reset timer, mask events etc. The command mask event is used to disregard events that are not relevant for a given application.

The remaining components of the TMP consist of a M68000-based processor with 1 MByte of local memory, a dual RS232 port for local interactions and a network interface to other TMPs. The processor executes the monitoring software. The bus interface is a separate module that does not affect the other parts of the TMP.

More than one TMP can be inserted into one node without disturbing any other node. Thus, each TMP may run different event processing software concurrently with different analysis tasks. The TMPs may also run the same event processing software, but each TMP might look at different event classes. In each case, the monitoring instrumentation and the application processes need no further preparation. Using several TMPs, larger numbers of events can be processed or the preprocessing capacity can be increased.

2.9 Evaluation and Display of Measurement Data

The main goal of the TMP approach consists in providing application programmers with valuable information about the run-time behavior of distributed programs to improve the understanding of these programs and to assess their performance. In this paper, we focus on the presentation of measurement data

at the central station, while referring to [18-20] for more details on event collection, exploitation of the compiler-generated type and structure database, and
system management applications of the TMP.

Typical performance indices of sequential systems are CPU utilization,
throughput, paging rate, memory references, utilization of I/O-channels, response
times, interrupt rates etc. It is common to all these measures that they provide
information that is of little value for application programmers. Mostly they are
not familiar with nor interested in system details that are machine-dependent. In
sequential systems, execution profilers have proven to be worthy tools for the
analysis of programs. Such profilers monitor the number of executions of certain
program parts, references to variables, stack and heap usage etc. To obtain these
data, extra instructions are optionally generated by the compilers causing the
execution to be slowed down significantly. Generally this does not affect the
results of the computation of real-time systems.

In distributed systems, due to the lack of global time and state, all concurrent activities cannot be globally controlled. Interference with the observed
system leads to different executions as well as to a different degree of parallelism and thus to the above-mentioned functional side effects. However, if
global control without any interference was available, users would not be interested in the same information as for sequential programs. Assume that several
hundred processes are executing in parallel; variable references or heap usage of
all processes would not contribute very much to the understanding of the whole
program. Therefore, a more abstract view of the run-time behavior is required.

Considering a distributed application, all operations of a system involved
in parallel activities are of interest, such as exchange of messages, synchronization, logical interconnection structure and communication overhead, to name
just a few. (Before analyzing the complete distributed program, the existing
tools ought to be applied to the sequential parts.) Thinking again of several
hundred processes executing concurrently, users will not be able to cope with
the vast amount of data; further structuring means are needed also. In the exchange of information between persons, abstraction mechanisms play a crucial
role. Depending on the degree of detail, an appropriate level of abstraction
can be selected, e.g. the population of the world, a country or a town . These
abstraction mechanisms are also used to master the complexity of large programs; a distributed file system might consist of subsystems which themselves
are composed of many processes. The key idea of the TMP visualization concept consists in exploiting these hierarchies and making them available to users.
In the course of the INCAS Project we have developed a distributed language
called LADY, which supports recursive structuring capabilities at the language
level (see [21]). We used the INCAS system and distributed programs written in
LADY as a test environment to implement and investigate the general concepts
of the TMP tools.

Figure 2.4 depicts the hierarchical structure of a distributed system including the view of the physical distribution of programs. Different measures and displays are used on different levels. At the highest level, the program level, the parallelism is displayed indicating the exploitation of the machine by a given program. The parallelism is computed periodically as the relation of the total execution time to the sum of the CPU-times of all machines. After selectable time intervals, the graph is updated.

On the machine level, CPU, ready, block and idle times are presented as load graphs, that have been derived from Kiviat graphs [22] (Figure 2.5). These two levels consider the physical view of the system rather than the logical. Here a flat structure of the multicomputer was assumed. If a hierarchy of nodes existed, it would not cause any problems for the evaluation and display software, e.g., to allow selection of a subset of machines.

The remaining display features follow the logical structure of the software and present the measurement data at selectable levels of abstraction; the logical interconnection of program units, its dynamic modifications and the number of messages exchanged are depicted on the screen at the central station (Figure 2.6).

The internal structure of a distribution unit cluster can be shown, or several units or clusters can be combined to form a new cluster; the clustering mechanism is recursive. If the hierarchical facilities are supported by a language as in the INCAS environment, the logical structure is therefore derived by the display software. Since the central station is "instructed" which cluster a program unit belongs, it is ensured that the dynamic creation and deletion of processes and program units is related to the appropriate clusters on the screen. For example, if the internal structure of a cluster is displayed and processes are created within the cluster, they are also displayed. If the next higher cluster level is chosen for display, the creation of lower level processes is not visible anymore. This property is not available if the language does not contain any clustering means. Nevertheless, a hierarchy can be defined by the user at the central station by clicking at several program units, which are to be combined in a new cluster.

Bar graphs show CPU, blocked, ready and communication times of each unit. These data can be displayed for the last measurement interval, for the complete measurement period, or for both.

A further display format was introduced the focuses on the message exchange between program units without following the hierarchy imposed by the programmer. This was particularly useful when observing a part of a computation in which processes that participated belonged to different clusters. Without having the display available as shown in Figure 2.7, the internal structure of all clusters would have to be selected to display all processes. This usually leads to too many processes, which cannot be depicted on the screen.

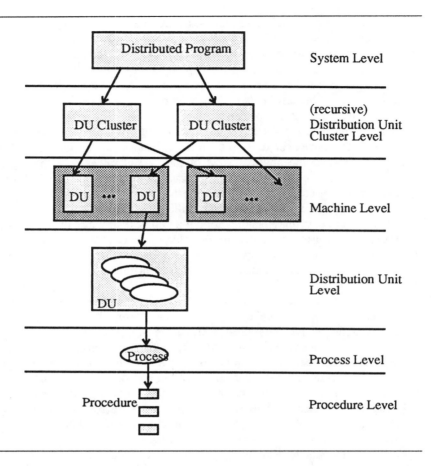

FIGURE 2.4
Hierarchies of computation.

2.10 Current Work: User-controlled Evaluation and Display

The first experiences with the TMP revealed that users wanted to control the presentation and evaluation of data. Furthermore, they inserted optional events into the application code. Since the TMP software described so far only supports standard events, users had to download their own evaluation software to the TMPs and also to write their own display software. In order to overcome these

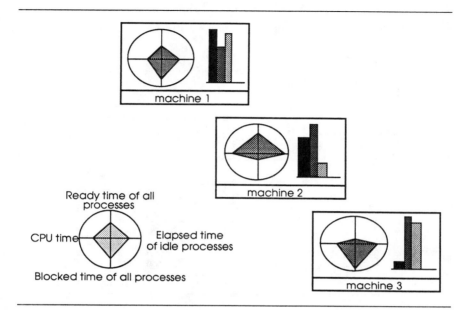

FIGURE 2.5
Display for the machine level.

deficiencies—at least up to a certain extent—users were able to define rules that determined the evaluation and display of events. The new features were meant as additions to the existing software and are described in [23].The primary goal was to offer more flexibility and to direct the user's attention to special measurement results specified by the predefined rules.

Having these intentions in mind, concurrently a completely new concept for the evaluation and display was developed as part of the INCAS Project. Based on the experiences gained, the INCAS Project now aims at the development of a fully integrated and graphics-oriented environment that supports the design, implementation, testing, monitoring, and measuring of distributed applications. Tool integration is the most important goal, which means that all the tools needed during the life cycle of distributed programs are incorporated into a single programming environment and are accessible by a homogeneous user interface (Figure 2.8). This integration aspect is also reflected by the usage of graphical display tools and strategies within all the components of the environment. The user interface allows the graphical description of the structure of distributed programs as well as the applications-oriented display of informations that occur during testing, monitoring and measuring these programs. During execution, monitors collect and preprocess behavior and measurement information of the

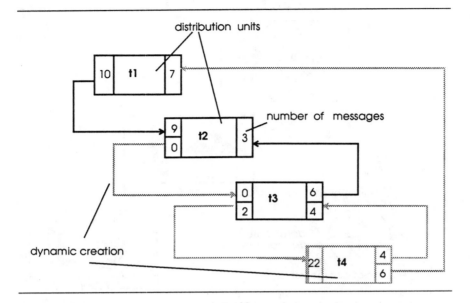

FIGURE 2.6
Animated program execution.

system that are sent to a central evaluation station. At the graphical interface, the user can select the amount and type of information he wants and the way how it is presented.

Internally, events are evaluated by "methods." A method is triggered by an event and generates a set of output events depending on the state of the method. Methods can be combined by connecting their input and output interfaces, thus forming a method net, which is computed according to the data flow principle. Each event is distributed to all methods to which it is connected. As soon as a method receives an event, it performs its computations and generates output events. Methods can be dynamically created and deleted, the method net can be interactively defined and modified by users. To cope with the problem of overloading the monitoring system, a priority-controlled execution scheme is applied, that allows the reduction of events displayed, while keeping the internal state consistent.

The method-based evaluation software was completed in January 1990 [4]; work on a user-interface for the definition and maintenance of methods is proceeding. We will report on experiences with this flexible tool in a future paper.

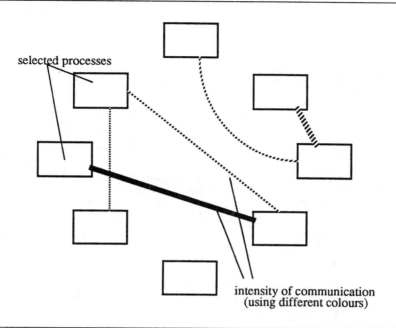

selected processes

intensity of communication
(using different colours)

FIGURE 2.7
Display of inter-process communications.

2.11 Conclusions

Now, after years of research and experimental evaluation, first commercial parallel and distributed systems have become available in the market; the wide-spread use of these machines will heavily depend on the tool support for programming, testing, debugging, measuring and maintenance. The primary goal consists in the integration of such tools. In this paper, we concentrated on on-line monitoring and measurements. The TMP approach fulfills important requirements such as application-oriented presentation of the collected data and negligible interference with the target system thus avoiding functional side effects. To cope with the additional complexities of concurrent programs, various levels of abstraction mechanisms and visualization techniques are desirable to simplify the problem and to isolate its origin and cause.

For debugging purposes, the TMPs were primarily used to store event traces. We would have appreciated being able to reproduce the events slowly

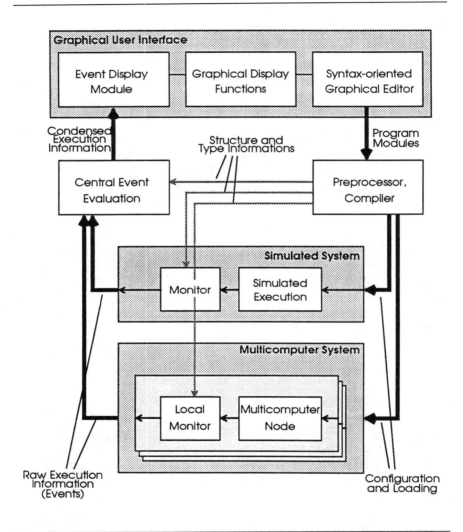

FIGURE 2.8
The architecture of the integrated programming environment.

and to observe the effects. This was only possible when the events were generated by our simulator [7,25], where the simulation speed could be controlled interactively. The reproducibility of program executions as described in [26] would have been even more helpful. The TMPs could be used to store the traces and to speed up debugging. In [6] the application of TMPs for the implementation of global breakpoints was described using a pragmatic approach. The trace facility is also necessary for short computations where the relevant events occur so fast that they cannot be observed anymore.

In the INCAS Project, it turned out that the flexibility of monitoring tools and their adaptability to user requirements is very important. More generally, the standardization of interfaces for monitoring and measurements would be very desirable. This includes hardware (where and how to collect the events without interference), the operating system (which events, which semantics) and the event format. As already indicated in the previous section, a repository of display formats could be created enabling users to configure their application-specific program or algorithm animation. As the integration density increases and more and more functions and components such as MMU, caches, memory, and I/O-support are incorporated into a single chip, this also will include the hardware support for measurements and debugging. Internal interfaces will be made available at the output pins of a chip to provide access to internal components. For example, the Motorola 68332 microcontroller is an interface to the chip-internal bus. Chip designers already consider the integration of parts of an emulator on the chip to allow in-circuit emulations. In this context, it is not unrealistic to think of parts of the TMP or a similar device being put on a chip, e.g., the EPU. By selecting an appropriate processor, users can decide which preprocessing capacity they need.

Acknowledgments

The authors wish to thank the contributions of many members of the INCAS Project, especially M. Abel, P. Buhler, T. Gauweiler, J. Lichtermann, F.Mattern, J. Nehmer, R. Reske, K. Rohleffs, R. Schwarz, P. Sturm, and W. Weigel. Also thanks to members of the FGAN/FFM research institute for interesting discussions.

References

1. C.L. Seitz, "The Cosmic Cube," Commun. ACM, vol. 28, no. 1, pp. 22-33, 1985.

2. C. Brown et al., "Research with the Butterfly Multicomputer," Computer Science and Computer Engineering Research Review 1984-1985, University of Rochester, 1985.

3. K.A. Frenkel, "Evaluating Two Massively Parallel Machines," Commun. ACM, vol. 29, no. 8, pp. 752-758, Aug. 1986.

4. J. Nehmer, D. Haban, F. Mattern, D. Wybranietz and D. Rombach, "Key Concepts of the INCAS Multicomputer Project," IEEE Trans. on Software Engineering, vol. SE-13, no. 8, pp. 913-923, Aug. 1987.

5. D. Haban, "DTM - A Distributed Test Methodology," Proc. 6th Symposium on Reliability in Distributed Software and Database Systems, pp. 66-73, March 1987.

6. D. Haban and W. Weigel, "Global Events and Global Breakpoints in Distributed Systems," Proc. 21st Hawaii Int. Conf. on System Sciences, vol. 2, pp. 166-175, Jan. 1988.

7. D. Wybranietz and D. Haban, "Monitoring and Performance Measuring Distributed Systems," Proc. ACM SIGMETRICS, Santa Fe, in: ACM Performance Evaluation Review, vol. 16, no. 1, pp. 197-206, May 1988.

8. W.A. Wulf et al., "Hydra/C.mmp: An Experimental Computer System," McGraw-Hill, 1981.

9. H. Fromm et al., "Experiences with Performance Measurements and Modeling of a Processor Array, " IEEE Trans. on Computers, vol. C-32, no. 1, pp. 15-31, Jan. 1983.

10. R. Snodgras, "A Relational Approach to Monitoring Complex Systems," ACM Trans. on Computer Systems, vol. 6, no. 2, pp. 157-196, May 1988.

11. B. Bates, J.C. Wileden, "High-level Debugging of Distributed Systems: The Behavioral Abstraction Approach," The Journal of Systems and Software, pp. 225-264; March 1983.

12. H. Garcia-Molina et al., "Debugging a Distributed System,"IEEE Trans. on Software Eng., vol. SE-10, no. 2, pp. 210-219, March 1984.

13. P.K. Harter, D.M. Heimbigner, R. King, "IDD: An Interactive Distributed Debugger," Proc. 5th Int. Conf. on Distributed Computing Systems, pp. 498-506, May 1985.

14. J. Joyce et al., "Monitoring Distributed Systems," ACM Trans. on Computer Systems, vol. 5, no. 2, pp. 121-150, May 1987.

15. B.P. Miller, C.-Q. Yang, "IPS: An Interactive and Automatic Performance Measurement Tool for Parallel and Distributed Programs," Proc 7th Int. Conf. on Distributed Computing Systems, pp. 482-489, Sept. 1987.

16. D. Ferrari and V. Minetti, "A Hybrid Measurement Tool for Minicomputers," Experimental Computer Performance and Evaluation, D.Ferrari and M. Spadoni (eds), North-Holland Publishing Company, 1981.

17. L.Svobodova, "Online System Performance Measurements with Software and Hybrid Monitors," Operating Systems Rev, vol. 7, no. 4, pp. 45-53, Oct. 1973.

18. D. Haban, D. Wybranietz, "A Hybrid Monitor for Behaviour and Performance Analysis of Distributed Systems," IEEE Trans. on Software Eng., Vol. 16, No. 2, February 1990.

19. D. Haban, D. Wybranietz, A. Barak, "Monitoring and Management Support of Distributed Systems," to appear in Springer LNCS, also available as ICSI TR-88-007, International Computer Science Institute, Berkeley, Nov. 1988

20. D. Haban, K. G. Shin, "Monitoring Distributed Systems and Their Applications," Proc. 10th Real-Time Systems Symp., Santa Monica, pp. 172-181, Dec. 1989

21. D. Wybranietz and P. Buhler, "The LADY Programming Environment for Distributed Operating Systems," Proc. Parallel Architectures and Languages Europe, PARLE '89; Eindhoven, June 1989; a revised version to appear in Future Generation Computing Systems, May 1990.

22. K. W. Kolence, P.J. Kiviat, "Software Unit Profiles and Kiviat figures,"ACM Sigmetrics Performance & Evaluation Review, June 1976.

23. D. Habran and D. Wybranietz, "Monitoring and Measuring Parallel Systems," Proc. 3rd Annual Parallel Processing Symposium; Fullerton, CA, March 1989.

24. R. Schwarz, "Ein Systemkern fuer methodengesteuertes Monitoren und Messen verteilter Systeme," Diploma Thesis, University of Kaiserslautern, Jan. 1990.

25. D. Wybranietz, "A Simulation System for Multicast Communications with Interactive Facilities," Proc. 15th Simula Users Conf., St. Helier, Jersey, Channel Islands, Sept. 1987.

26. T. J. LeBlanc, J. M. Mellion-Crummey, "Debugging Parallel Programs with Instant Replay," IEEE Trans. on Computers, vol. C-36, no. 4, April 1987.

3

Scientific Visualization at Los Alamos

Melvin L. Prueitt

3.1 Introduction

For ages the human race tried to understand the universe in which it found itself by relying on its senses. Water was wet, the sun was warm, flowers smelled better than skunks, and stars were inscrutable lights shimmering in night's black curtain. It never occurred to those curious, but naive, people that there was more to the universe than what was immediately observable. They didn't need gravity because they knew absolutely that objects fell always in a downward direction when dropped. (Why shouldn't they fall; they were heavy). They did not need tiny invisible entities we call electrons. They did not even need body cells; bugs and people were filled with juices.

The Greeks, in all their search for knowledge, did not push for better tools for probing nature. The surprises brought by the development of the microscope and telescope shocked the philosophers into the realization that nature held hidden components that might have some bearing on reality. With this rude awakening, scientists began to search for and develop tools that could detect invisible aspects of the world.

They found out that people could see only a small span of the total electro-magnetic spectrum and could hear only a limited range of sounds. We can smell only a relatively few odors. Our sense of touch extends only as far as our reach. Even our minds, in generating internal models of the surrounding cosmos, does not stretch across some of the counter-intuitive characteristics of physical laws.

Science-developed instruments to extend our senses and mathematics to extend our minds. Computers were invented to consolidate the enormous amounts of data and shift the information into our narrow window for study and understanding. Our sense of vision is an excellent input channel with an extremely high bandwidth, and even more importantly, we have a visual system with incredibly fast interpretive powers that allows us to readily perceive subtle features in extremely complex surfaces. Indeed, our visual system forms a perfect link between the high speed computer and the human intellect when appropriate graphics are produced by the computer.

At the Los Alamos National Laboratory scientists have found that computer graphics provide the key to much faster turn around time from computer input to understanding and back to fresh computer input. Discoveries have been made that would not have been possible without the graphics.

This paper is a quick tour of some of the images produced in research projects at Los Alamos. It is not intended to be an in-depth study of any one research project. By presenting a number of varied images, perhaps the reader will see some ways in which visualization of data can be used in current research.

3.2   Molecular Structures

By using spheres to represent atoms and letting colors designate the different elements, it is simple to create graphics of crystal lattices or molecular structures. Such images are valuable for visually studying the structure and for planning alterations in the structure and can serve pedagogical purposes.

Plate 1 shows the crystal structure of a high-temperature superconductor. The key on the right gives the colors of the elements. Black spheres represent vacancies where atoms could be inserted to alter the properties of the crystal. Electron paths are shown in transparent blue.

Plate 2 shows the structure of a 60 carbon atom molecule which consists of nothing but carbon. The green rods represent double bonds, while the white rods represent single bonds. We can see the large void in the interior where one might consider "isolating" various atoms or molecules.

Zeolites are minerals which have a large capacity for absorption of water vapor. Plate 3 represents the structure of a zeolite. Water molecules can enter the hole in the middle of the structure and attach to the walls inside.

3.3   Three-Dimensional Contour Surfaces

Most people are familiar with contour plots in which two-dimensional curves represent constant values of some characteristic of the subjects. But we live in a three-dimensional world and most variables in real physical phenomena vary in three-dimensions. A program, called CON3D, plots surfaces in three-dimensions to represent constant values of some function of a set of experimental data. Mark Ekerhart calculated the probability density of electrons throughout the volume of a high-temperature superconductor crystal unit cell. We used CON3D to draw the contour surfaces of the electron densities (Plate 4). Pictures like these answer the question: "Where do the electrons spend most of their time?" This program can plot contour surfaces for any variable for which data exist on a three-dimensional grid throughout a volume. Colors can be defined to represent various aspects of the problem.

Even mathematical functions can be represented by contour plots. First we calculate the values of the function on a three-dimensional grid and then let CON3D plot the contours at a specified value. Plate 5 is the result. The color bands represent constant distances from the origin, so we have contour curves plotted on contour surfaces.

3.4   Chemistry

The popular stereotype image of a chemist is that of a person in a white robe pouring a liquid from one vial into another. We could make a computer graphic depicting that activity, but it would be of little value to the chemist. We might wonder how chemists can effectively use computer graphics.

A good example of chemistry in action at Los Alamos is the salvaging of plutonium from wastes. A very efficient system is needed so that no expensive plutonium is lost and so that the radioactivity of the waste is reduced. Edward Cokal studied the process of plutonium reclamation using anion exchange resins. In Plate 6 we see the representation of a plutonium atom (green central sphere) surrounded by eight water molecules. (The atoms in these images are not to exact scale). In Plate 7, when a water molecule happens to break its bond with the plutonium atom, a nitrate ion quickly takes its place. Soon the plutonium atom is surrounded by nitrate ions. The resulting molecule approaches a long chain exchange resin with a nitrate ion attached in Plate 8. Plate 9 shows the final docking. The resin may then be chemically treated to remove the plutonium. The importance of the graphics in this case is that the sequence of events can be clearly shown at a technical conference or to a non-technical audience.

Rick Day wanted to be able to compare the spectra of plutonium nitrate solutions as he varied the nitric acid concentration. Plate 10 is one of the many plots that covers part of the wide range of variables. From these pictures, he could study the relative changes in the spectra as the chemicals were varied.

In physical chemistry, the spectra of molecules was so complex that scientists began to despair of gaining an understanding of the source of some' of the spectral lines. But when William Harter spent a sabbatical year at Los Alamos (now at the University of Arkansas), we looked at the possibility of plotting the rotational energy surfaces of molecules by computer (Plate 11). The surface represents the possible locations of the end of a vector that defines the spin of the molecule. In the presence of external forces, the vector precesses. For different starting conditions, the paths of the vector end point are different. Pictures like these opened up a totally new way of analyzing the spectra of molecules [1]. In Professor Harter's words, "Discoveries are being made that would be impossible without this technique" [2].

When Art Winfree, of the University of Arizona, was at Los Alamos we helped him produce computer pictures that modeled the structure of chemical reaction waves that occur in certain chemicals. Plate 12 shows a cutaway view of one such calculation [2-4]. Of these images, Dr. Winfree said, "Within a few months it became possible to visualize the essence of a difficult physics problem which had defied both analysis and intuition for a decade" [5].

3.5 Earth Sciences

Geology is the study of extremely complex structures involving many variables. Although geologists can readily see the landscape without artificial aids, many aspects of a problem cannot be seen. Methods have been derived to determine the location of underground formations, and computer graphics can provide pictures of the formations.

Scott Baldridge of the Earth and Space Sciences Division at Los Alamos studied the Rio Grande Rift where the earth's crust is pulling apart. Plate 13 shows a computer representation of a portion of the Rio Grande Rift in North-Central New Mexico. The faint white lines represent the present day surface of the earth while the solid surface shows bedrock. The space between bedrock and the surface is filled with sediment. The white patches represent the locations of Albuquerque, Santa Fe and Los Alamos. Beneath Albuquerque are 15,000 feet of sediment. By studying this picture, geologists can quickly see the relationships between the surface and underground formations.

Tetsuji Yamada simulates the behavior of air pollution over mountain terrain. Scientists want to know how wind and terrain disperse the pollutants. Yamada's computer program that simulates the movement of pollution produces thousands of numbers, which are difficult to interpret. Those same numbers can give us a picture such as Plate 14 in which we can see both the terrain and the pollution. This is a single frame from a movie in which we can see not only the positions of the pollutant particles but we can also observe the dynamics of the flow.

As the earth's plates shift and slide past one another, bits and pieces are scraped off and deposited here and there. In Plate 15, we can see a number of terranes that have accumulated around the San Francisco Bay area from this process. Each color represents a different terrane with an age that is quite different than that of the neighbor.

We normally think of geological features as being very large on the human scale, but they all consist of many small particles. Bruce Trent studied the behavior and compaction of soil particles under various conditions. Plate 16 shows one instant in a sequence during a computer calculation. The shadows cast by some spheres (which represent soil particles) on others help to visualize depth relationships.

3.6 Physics

A physicist can easily pick up a manual of nuclear scattering cross sections and scan through large tables to try to find the properties he needs for a materials application, but the process is slow and laborious, and he may miss some important characteristic. It is much faster to look at a picture such as Plate 17, which shows in-scattering and down-scattering of neutrons among energy groups as given in Hansen-Roach tables [6]. Armed with a book of such images, if a reactor physicist needs a material with certain neutron scattering properties, he or she can flip through the pages until the appropriate features appear.

Computer graphics can be used in many applications in astrophysics. A simple example is a height plot of light from the Orion Nebula (Plate 18). The height of the surface represents the intensity of light that was received by a photographic plate from the nebula. Astrophysicists can look for subtle characteristics in the nebula by studying the shapes of the surface. Colors help to define constant intensity levels.

3.7 Biology

Gary Salzman of the Life Sciences Division at Los Alamos found that computer graphics provided a quick method of visualizing microscopic biota and made it easy to explain his work at technical meetings. Plate 19 is a representation of one turn of a spiral bacteria he was studying.

Dr. Salzman also provided the data for the image of Plate 20, which gives the light scattering envelope of a small particle. This information is used in the study of light scattering from biological cells.

Biology involves the geometry of living objects. We see that biologists are increasingly turning to computer graphics to visually define internal and external structures and to show the locations of cells, molecules, or atoms. The shape of cellular structures help to define their function and can also identify abnormalities.

3.8   Mathematics

The possible applications of computer images in mathematics are too numerous to mention, but we can give a couple of examples. Plate 21 shows the distortion of a cube by trigonometric functions. Varying the parameters can give radically different shapes. One can quickly see the results of parameter changes. Experimental mathematicians need computer graphics in their work as they interactively vary parameters.

Computer graphics offers a way to look at a number of variables in statistics at once. In Plate 22, we see the population statistics of the more developed (left) and less developed (right) countries from 1925 to 2025 AD [7]. The vertical projections represent the death rates. The yellow layers represent the number of women of reproductive age, while the red layers show the number of children. The orange rods show the number of people between the ages of 15 and 49, and the gray rods show the number of people older than 49.

3.9   Conclusion

There are other sciences, and each has its own set of data representing the fruits of many years of research. By translating the data into images, scientists are finding faster methods of assimilating information. Discoveries are being made by the interpretive powers of the human visual system.

One of the important jobs of the computer graphicist in the future is to convince the scientists who are not presently using computer graphics of the value of three-dimensional images. For some scientists it is necessary to develop new ways of handling data to make meaningful pictures, so that the scientist can gain a better understanding of his work. Once computer graphics becomes part of the research, the scientist will wonder how he or she ever got along without those colorful images. Perhaps one of the pictures in this paper has caused the reader to think of ways computer graphics can be used in his or her work.

References

1. Search and Discovery, Physics Today , July 1984, pp. 17-20.

2. Private communication from W. G. Harter.

3. A. T. Winfree, "Rotating Chemical Reactions," Scientific American Vol. 230, No. 6, 1974, pp. 82-95.

4. S. H. Strogatz, M. L. Prueitt, and A.T. Winfree, IEEE Computer Graphics and Applications, Vol. 4, No.1, 1984, pp. 66-69.

5. Private communications from A. T. Winfree.

6. N. Pruvost and M. L. Prueitt, "Hansen-Roach Cross Sections," Los Alamos National Laboratory Report, LALP-88-20.

7. R. Fox,"Population Images," United Nations Fund for Population Activities document.

4

Visualization Techniques for High Dimensional Data Sets

Jeffrey Saltzman

4.1 Introduction

The purpose of parallel computers is to process data at great speeds. In many instances these machines also generate a large quantity of data in proportion to their speed. In relation to this collection of papers, further data may be generated, again in large amounts, from the instrumentation of the parallel computer. What follows is a discussion of how to transform data to a state that is amenable for human beings to understand or gain insight into. This transformation is often called data visualization or just visualization. Visualization is certainly a large field of endeavor and this article is accordingly restricted in scope.

This paper limits itself to the analysis of data with dimensionality greater than two. Data sets with dimensionality greater than two are called high dimensional data sets in the rest of this paper. What makes this area challenging is the problem of mapping higher dimensional data into a two-dimensional (2-D) region. A region may be a screen on a computer or a piece of paper. The scope of this paper is further restricted to three- and four-dimensional data. However, these techniques can certainly be applied to five or more dimensions by projecting down to three or four dimensions.

What follows after this introduction, is further discussion of high dimensional data sets and some examples. Next, several visual tools are described. A description of the software that uses some of these visual tools is then given. Finally some examples of what is produced by the software are shown. This paper stems from a demonstration of visualization tools at the conference documented by these proceedings. Unfortunately the printed medium cannot reproduce all of the information given in the demonstration. As a result, the reader who attended the conference will find this paper's content altered slightly to fit the constraints of the printed page.

4.2   Higher Dimensional Data Sets

As mentioned in the introduction, higher dimensional data sets are those that cannot be mapped onto a page or screen in a one to one fashion. For the purposes of exposition, two data sets are described for use as examples in the rest of the paper. The first data set is generated from the examination of bank conflicts on a Cray Y-MP/8 supercomputer [1]. The second data set is generated from a three-dimensional hydrodynamics simulation of a jet from a stellar source into the intergalactic medium (IGM) [2]. The bank conflict data is three-dimensional (3-D) and the hydrodynamic simulation is also three-dimensional.

Examination of bank conflict data is made difficult by the number of parameters involved in the generation of this data. The first example studies the computation of the following vector construct:

```
do i=1, n
  z(i) = x(i) + y(i)
continue
```

On the surface there is only one interesting piece of information in this construct. This information is how long does it take to complete the loop. But on a supercomputer such as the Cray Y-MP, where the data are placed in memory affects the computation time. When data reside in the same section of memory, called a bank, an additional delay occurs in fetching the data. There are 64 banks of memory within a Cray and two new parameters emerge. If the z array is considered to always be starting at the first bank, then the two new parameters are the offsets of the x and y arrays, in bank coordinates, from the z array. It turns out that there actually won't be any bank conflicts unless there are two or more of the variables aligned on the same bank boundaries. This is because the memory is interleaved 64 ways and memory strides of one will always result in the same distance, in banks, between fetches and stores.

An additional factor is the number of processors available to simultaneously work on completing the loop. The processors are not tightly synchronized so the probability of bank conflicts is much larger. In generating bank conflict data, there is the dependent variable indicating how long the loop computation takes and the independent variables are the bank offsets of the x and y arrays from the z array, and the number of processors used in the calculation.

The second sample data set is generated from a hydrodynamic simulation code. The simulation is in three space dimensions and evolves in time so there are four independent variables. The number of independent variables is even larger. The variables evolved are density, three components of momentum, and energy. With some very simple postprocessing of the data, further information can be derived such as three components of velocity, temperature, pressure, entropy. Differencing the data leads to the vorticity and local compression of the flow as well.

4.3   Visual Tools

Graphical output devices are capable of displaying many types of geometrical objects. The simplest object is the line. Lines are used to construct two objects that are useful in displaying 3-D data. The most obvious application of lines is to generate meshes to represent surfaces of constant value within the data. Surfaces of constant values are called isoparametric surfaces. An example of software that produces this type of graphical display is the NCAR package [3]. The major advantage of this type of rendering is speed, but meshes lack any type of depth. Depth cuing (making the lines darker as they go further away from the viewer) can improve the situation greatly but slows down the processing.

A second example of using lines in 3-D is for displaying continuously changing vector fields. By integrating a particle path along a given vector field a stream line is created. A relatively straight path is often called laminar flow in fluid dynamics. Where the stream line is more convoluted, the flow is often called turbulent. An example of software that produces stream lines is the Plot3D package [4]. The major advantage of this type of rendering is again speed and the ability to see how the vector field is pointing in an easy way. On the down side, there is a loss of information since stream lines give no hint of the magnitude of the vector at any given point. Having many stream lines in a single picture also is confusing.

The next most complicated graphical object is the surface. Most graphical output devices today can efficiently render polygonal surfaces with a variety of lighting and texturing models. Surfaces have the advantage over line meshes in being able to exhibit depth by hiding the proper surfaces behind others. Polygons can be used in a wide variety of ways. The most common use is certainly for isoparametric surface generation. The current state of the art in surface generation is the Marching Cubes algorithm developed by Lorensen and Cline [5]. Surfaces don't have to be isoparametric but instead could be used to cut a 3-D data set. The surface could then be colored to display scalar or 2-D tangent vector information on this surface using a combination of contours, color, or arrows.

Using an algorithm like Marching Cubes for isoparametric surface generation creates a list of polygons very quickly. Often, though, a very fast rendering device must be used to display the polygons since there may be a great number of polygons generated if the data are turbulent. Unfortunately isoparametric surface generation cannot be used like contour plots in two dimensions. The reason for having only a limited number of surfaces in a given picture is most surfaces will obscure others. Transparency will help some but for most images four or fives separate surfaces already is difficult to interpret. A two-dimensional contour plot is very unsatisfactory with only four or five contours!

Another graphical concept to discuss in this paper is quite different from lines or surfaces. This graphical concept is transparency. Transparency is a useful concept in its own right. In looking into a foggy scene we often can tell how the fog itself is distributed by how objects are obscured by it. A dense fog obscures more than a light fog. If the fog is uniform, objects tend to disappear in a uniform fashion as they move further away. This concept can be incorporated into our data analysis. Software can be developed to send light through a data set and let the light be attenuated in proportion to the numerical values of the data. Data with higher numerical values will attenuate the light faster than data with lower numerical values. The flavor of this technique is much like radiation transport. This technique is often called volumetric ray tracing [6-8]. Volumetric rendering also suffers from problems similar to isoparametric surfaces in that important structures in the data may be obscured by other data.

The last concept to discuss is animation. With animation perception of another dimension can be achieved using time. Static images can be rotated over time to aquire different views, or data sets can vary over time to see evolution. In addition, different planar slices of a given set of data can be viewed to build up an impression of the entire set of data. The greatest disadvantage of animation is that it still is the burden of the user to assimilate the data well enough to get an idea of all that is appearing within the data. Although the expense (expense might be CPU, user time, or hardware) of creating animations is changing, it is still a hurdle.

From the previous discussion, it is clear no graphical method can completely convey all the information in a 3-D data set. It is really a limitation of the human visual system that 3-D data can't be seen without resorting to looking at many 2-D parts of the data. To counter this difficulty it is necessary to use tools that are interactive to allow the user to make multiple images of the 3-D data set. This way he or she can integrate the 2-D images into a single 3-D image in the mind.

4.4 Software

This paper focuses on software covering only a small subset of the visual tools described in the previous section. The software used in the demonstration at the conference is supplied in source form from Sun Microsystems. An integrated volume slicing and volumetric ray tracing code for the TAAC-1[1] accelerator board attached to a Sun workstation is called "voxvu" [9]. An animation program loosely integrated with voxvu, called "a2bitmovie," is also used. The voxvu program is modified to generate time dependent data for a2bitmovie. Further minor modifications are done to voxvu to generate figures for this paper.

The TAAC-1 accelerator board is a separate processing unit and frame buffer with a variety of hardware features. The video output of the TAAC-1 can be viewed through the host (Sun workstation) window system or in its entirety. It has four programmable 8-bit color channels allowing a variety of color display formats from true color with an overlay channel to quadruple-buffered 8-bit formats. The TAAC-1 also has a powerful Very Long Instruction Word (VLIW) processor capable of doing several operations in parallel. Further information can be found in [10].

Voxvu is an interactive tool for examining data in several ways. The simplest method allows the user to rotate and slice a cube of data. The slicing can be done along an arbitrary plane. The slice displays contouring information about the scalar data cut by the slicing plane using color. The angle of the slice as well as the location of the slice is controlled by sliders. Response time for moving the slicing plane is quick as only a small number of polygons need be rendered to display surfaces. The color tables can be shifted quickly and one can choose from two interpolation algorithms.

An alternative visual tool is offered by voxvu. Volumetric ray tracing can also be selected to display data. The user can rotate the image, change the lighting, and select an interpolation method. In addition, ranges of data can be interactively selected to indicate to the software where to draw isosurfaces along with the ray traced image. The isosurfaces are drawn at values between two adjacent data ranges. Drawing time is much slower for these images. To compensate, three passes are made. The first is a course pass that uses few rays and takes little time. The second and third passes take longer but use more rays to get a better resolved image. The third pass can easily exceed a minute in execution time. Once a good viewpoint is set, a button can be pushed to generate a sequence of raster files. The sequence can be a either a single data set seen from a continuum of different angles or multiple data sets seen from a single angle.

---

[1]TAAC-1 is a registered trademark of Sun Microsystems.

Once the images are generated, they are compressed from 24 bits per pixel to 2 bits per pixel using the Color Coded Compression (CCC) algorithm [11]. The compressed images are then read into the TAAC-1 memory and displayed with a2bitmovie. A2bitmovie uncompresses the images up to a display rate of 25 frames per second. The display stream can be reversed and slowed down. Using sliders, a smaller contiguous subset of the stream can be selected and displayed. The images can also be stepped through one at a time as well by using a button on the control panel. Because this paper cannot display animations no further mention will be made of a2bitmovie.

4.5   Examples

The first example (Plate 23) is a picture of the bank conflict data previously discussed. The data are unsliced but the surfaces of the data are interesting enough to be included.

To get oriented, the coordinate origin of the data is the lowest corner of the figure. The axis starting from this origin and extending to the right is the x axis and corresponds to the bank offset of the x array. The axis starting at the origin and extending straight up is the y axis and corresponds to the bank offset of the y array. The axis extending towards the left from the origin is the z axis and corresponds to the number of processors used in a given calculation of the z array. The colorbar on the right side of the figure corresponds to how much time was spent in calculating the array sum. The cooler the color the longer the time it took.

The face of the cube pointing out of the page (the x-y plane) is very regular and displays mostly fast times. The light blue diagonal strips indicate some conflicts do happen. This plane also corresponds to using only one processor. Looking at the sides of the cubes one sees that the bank conflicts are already slowing down the calculation when there is more than one processor. To get a picture of all the data generated in this experiment at least 8 x-y slices must be made. This can be done quickly with the software so most of the slices will persist in the user's mind.

There is no reason to stop at making slices only in one direction. Plate 24 shows a slice made at an angle to the x and z axes. With this capability one can look for different ways the data may vary. From this illustration it is clear that bank conflicts will appear even when the array offsets are not a multiple of the number of banks.

The next two figures illustrate the use of volumetric ray tracing. Both of these pictures attempt to display some of the characteristics of the density of a flow field. Plate 25 shows the density field at a late time in a calculation where fluid was injected into the corner of a box. This simulation is meant to model a jet piercing the intergalactic medium.

The static image is simply overwhelming. There are eight regions within the image and seven interfacial surfaces. Within the picture several features are noticeable. The largest surface engulfing the jet is called the bow shock. This shock separates the turbulent flow from the quiet background. The background is almost transparent as it offers no variation of density in space. Within the bow shock there are two different regions. The innermost region is the beam itself which looks rather coherent. The middle region is turbulent and is often referred to as the "cocoon" around the beam. This kind of image is far more effective when used as part of an animation as movement delineates surfaces well.

Plate 26 illustrates the same data set as Plate 25. The opacities of four of the regions in the data set were set to zero allowing light to only reflect or be absorbed by the remaining four regions. This has considerably simplified the picture allowing one to see a turbulent surface, the bow shock and the background. This type of image is more appropriate for static analysis. The software allows the user to quickly vary which ranges and surfaces can be displayed.

4.6 Conclusions

The volumetric ray tracing and slicing examples show ways of looking at data that are moderate departures from what has been done before. Slicing is based on graphical tools that are quite common and quick while the ray tracing algorithm is based on graphical tools that are relatively new and somewhat slow. These tools exemplify the two directions scientific visualization will go in the future. The first direction is the creation of simple but fast tools that allow the user to interact with tools quickly. By having tools that render graphical images quickly, the user of the tools can integrate several images in his or her head to get a richer perspective. The second direction will tend to yield more compute intensive but also more insightful tools. Volumetric ray tracing of moderately large data sets is still only within the reach of users with fast hardware. However, the dividends from investing in hardware capable of rendering ray traced images may well be worth it.

As dimensionality of data sets increases, it is clear that the difficulty in analyzing these sets also increases. Even if the trends predicted above happen, there will never be a single tool able to give a complete picture of given data set. The user will require a variety of tools that may require separate software and/or hardware. In order to accommodate the need for this flexibility there will be a need for standards for data formats so it is easy to move between different software packages and machines. As the diversity of software and hardware increases in response to the impending increase of data complexity, it will be imperative that graphical output standards be settled on. Otherwise the old problem of how to get a diverse set of graphical data to a single point of access (the user's office) will prevent any forward progress.

Acknowledgments

This work was done under the auspices of the United States Department of Energy. The author would like to thank Becky Koskela and Margaret Simmons for both organizing the workshop and for their patience and encouragement.

References

1. I. Y. Bucher, M. L. Simmons, "Memory Access Contentions in Multiple Vector Processor Systems," in *Proceedings of the International Conference on Supercomputing*, 1989.

2. J. S. Saltzman, "An Unsplit 3-D Upwind Method of Hyperbolic Conservation Laws," Los Alamos Unclassified Report (LAUR)-89-3442, October 1989 (submitted to *Jour. Comp. Phys.*).

3. G. R. McArthur, "The SCD Graphics Utilities," NCAR-TN/166+IA, May 1983.

4. P. Buning, J. Steger, "Graphics and Flow Visualization in Computational Fluid Dynamics," AIAA-85-1507-CP, *Proc. AIAA 7th Computational Fluid Dynamics Conf.*, July 15-17, 1985.

5. W. E. Lorensen, H. E. Cline, "Marching Cubes: A High Resolution 3D Surface Construction Algorithm," *ACM Computer Graphics*, 21, (4), July 1987, 163.

6. R. Drebin, L. Carpenter, P. Hanrahan, "Volume Rendering," *ACM Computer Graphics*, 22, (4), August 1988, 65.

7. P. A. Sabella, "Rendering Algorithm for Visualizing 3D Scalar Fields," *ACM Computer Graphics* 22, (4), August 1988 51.

8. C. Upson, M. Keeler, "V-BUFFER: Visible Volume Rendering," *ACM Computer Graphics*, 22, (4), August 1988, 59.

9. Sun Microsystems, "TAAC-1 Applications Accelerator: Software Reference Manual version 2.3", Sun Microsystems, 800-3203-11

10. Sun Microsystems, "TAAC-1 Applications Accelerator: User Guide version 2.3", Sun Microsystems, 800-2177-11

11. G. Campbell, T. DeFanti, J. Frederiksen, S. A. Joyce, L. A. Leske, J. A. Lindberg, and D. J. Sandin, "Two Bit/Pixel Full Color Encoding," SIG-GRAPH'86, 215-223.

5

Performance Instrumentation and Visualization Using AXE

Jerry C. Yan

5.1 Research Background

While multiprocessors promise to deliver orders of magnitude speed-up, the effective use of such computers critically depends on the ability of their resource management systems to properly trade off communication loss and concurrency gain, exploit behavioral characteristics of the application programs, and take advantage of specific architectural features of the hardware. Unfortunately, the performance of many proposed resource management strategies can only be evaluated indirectly by simple objective functions (such as execution cost or mapping cardinality) [1,2].

Research has been conducted to determine how concurrent computations can be mapped onto multiprocessors to minimize execution time. The approach being studied, known as post-game analysis (PGA), offers an unconventional alternative to reduce program execution time [3]. As shown in Figure 5.1, program-machine mapping is improved in-between program executions. Instead of using simple abstract models, PGA utilizes actual timing data gathered during program execution. Program execution time is reduced based on many optimization sub-goals. Because heuristics are applied to improve the current mapping

1.	start with some initial configuration
2.	execute the program on the target machine
3.	gather data during program execution
4.	analyze the data and propose a new mapping (configuration)
5.	go to step 2

FIGURE 5.1
Post-game analysis — an iterative refinement framework.

and resolve conflicting sub-goals, PGA can be incrementally refined and tailored to specific applications and architectures.

PGA's performance has been compared against other strategies using various program structures and multiprocessor models. Results obtained from simulations show that it out-performs random placement and load-balancing as well as clustering algorithms by 15%. Because intermediate program/machine models are not used, PGA is very promising for immediate application on today's programs with today's machines.

5.2   AXE — An Experimentation Environment

Realistic evaluation of resource management strategies should be based on the study of real applications on real machines. However, the development of complete language and compiler tools, together with run-time environments is currently prohibitive for short term use in research. Therefore, a software test-bed, AXE, was designed to facilitate such investigations at the process level using discrete-time simulation — without the need to resort to lengthy instruction-set level simulations or general stochastic models. AXE enables the following activities to be carried out smoothly and quickly:

□ COMPUTATION MODEL SPECIFICATION — By analyzing program text, the researcher constructs a program model using BDL, a Behavior Description Language for parallel object-oriented computations [4]. This model, as opposed to actual program text, is simulated. BDL can be used to describe computations based on various programming paradigms such as communicating sequential processes, remote procedures, macro-dataflow, and actors. As shown in Figure 5.2, the BDL compiler is implemented as a separate front-end to AXE. It converts application program models

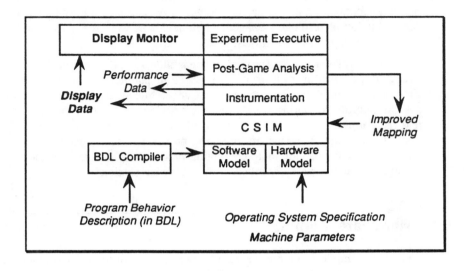

FIGURE 5.2
Components of the AXE experimentation environment.

written in BDL into forms understood by other modules of the simulation environment.

□ MULTIPROCESSOR ARCHITECTURE SPECIFICATION — The particular class of multiprocessors considered here is known as MultiComputers. It consists of a collection of homogeneous processing sites, each of which is connected to its nearest neighbors in a regular fashion. Each site is autonomous; it contains its own storage, processor(s) and an operating system kernel governing local activities such as message forwarding, process scheduling, and memory management. By changing certain simple parameters, the architecture of the hardware may be modified. These include:

— the number of processing sites,
— interconnection topology, network speed, routing algorithm, and
— operating system scheduling algorithm.

□ SIMULATION — A discrete-time event-driven simulator based on CSIM [5] is responsible for predicting the execution time of BDL program models on various multiprocessor models.

□ DATA COLLECTION — Data that indicate program behavior and resource utilization/contention are gathered automatically. These data may be used for evaluation of resource management strategies as well as software and hardware architecture alternatives.

□ EXPERIMENTATION — The researcher is able to study resource management strategies as well as various issues in parallel processing such as problem formulation, alternate hardware architectures, and operating system algorithms. During simulation, the activities of the multiprocessor and the parallel software can be displayed dynamically via a color monitor. These include message transmission, processing load at each site as well as the status of individual computing processes. The details of these monitoring facilities are described in the following sections.

5.3 Hardware Monitor

The use of color graphics to represent parallel program execution on multicomputers has been researched elsewhere to help interpret parallel system performance [6] as well as alternative architectures for executing parallel knowledge-based systems [7]. The monitoring facilities described in this section were designed primarily to help evaluate/understand resource management strategies for multicomputers. In particular, the researcher is able to observe the improvements made as the program-machine mapping is incrementally modified by post-game analysis. As shown in Figure 5.3, the basic layout of the display consists of three panels:

a. The MULTIPROCESSOR ACTIVITY PANEL illustrates CPU bottlenecks and message routing.

b. The SYSTEM LOAD PANEL demonstrates the overall effectiveness of utilizing available processing sites in the system.

c. The GLOBAL TRAFFIC PANEL monitors the amount of inter-site communication.

Figure 5.3 illustrates the hardware monitor when a multicomputer that consists' of 16 processing sites connected as a 2-dimensional grid is simulated. A line joining sites $< s_{x1,y1} >$ and $< s_{x2,y2} >$ indicates that a message is being transmitted between the two sites. A color column (known as the load-indicator) inside each site indicates how busy the CPU at that processing site is by both changes in its height and color. A vertical color bar on the right-hand side of the panel indicates the color scheme used — light blue represents the lowest load, through green, yellow and red, to magenta as the highest. Instead of using the instantaneous ready-queue length directly as a load- measure, a moving-average

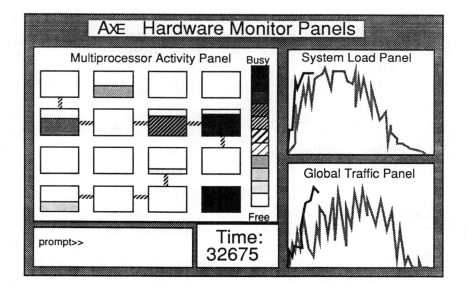

FIGURE 5.3
The hardware monitor for AXE.

function is chosen. Suppose that at site $< s_{x,y} >$, the length of the queue at time τ is λ_τ. At time τ_1, the load at $< s_{x,y} >$ is $a\lambda_{\tau 1} + b\lambda_\tau$ where a and b are non-negative constants and $a + b = 1$. A moving-average function is used to filter out rapidly varying load values so that the researcher can observe general trends in load variation easily. As illustrated in Figure 5.4, higher values should be chosen for a in order to track the actual load more closely.

Because AXE is an event-driven simulator, the panel is only updated (by default) every time a process is added or removed from the ready-queue. Unfortunately, when a process is scheduled and executes for a long time, the load value at that site will never reach the actual value because of the effect of the moving-average function. Figure 5.5 illustrates this situation when the load of a site is changed from 0 to 1. Therefore, the MULTIPROCESSOR ACTIVITY PANEL is designed so that each site updates its load value every now and then (ΔT).

The two panels on the right-hand side of Figure 5.3 give a system-wide summary during the course of the computation:

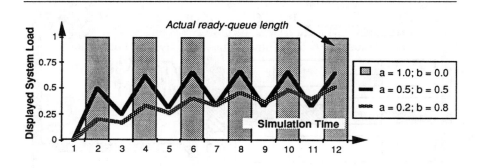

FIGURE 5.4
Effect of displayed load values using various values of a and b.

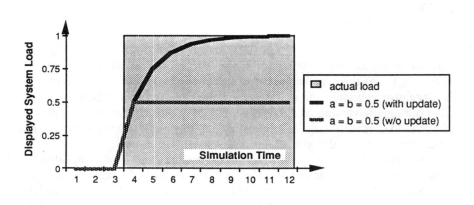

FIGURE 5.5
Effect of a "self-updating" panel.

On the SYSTEM LOAD PANEL, the number of active processors is plotted against simulation time every ΔT time units. On the GLOBAL TRAFFIC PANEL, the number of messages sent across sites between each sampling interval (ΔT) is plotted against simulation time.

Both panels are not erased between applications of post-game analysis for comparison purposes (see Section 6).

5.4 Software Monitors

In addition to monitoring how hardware resources are used in response to the demands placed on the system by the computation, AXE also monitors and presents the status of the software. The SOFTWARE MONITOR PANEL shown in Figure 5.6 is similar to the multiprocessor activity panel shown earlier in Figure 5.3. An array of rectangles is used to represent a 2-dimensional grid of sites. A link connecting two adjacent sites lights up if a message is in transit. On the left-hand side of each site is a load indicator. On the right-hand side of each site-box are a number of smaller rectangles (called process status indicators). These boxes represent the status of each process:

Empty (☐): no computational process is instantiated;

Yellow (▨): process is scheduled, ready to use (but has not got hold of) the processor;

Red (▰): process gets hold of the CPU and is executing;

Blue (▦): process is blocked, waiting for the arrival of a specific message from another process (e.g. the reply to a message it sent earlier, the evaluation of a future [9] or a the return of a remote procedure call);

Grey (▨): otherwise, the process is in a dormant or idle state, waiting to be activated by the arrival of a message.

Figure 5.7 illustrates the events that causes state transition for processes.

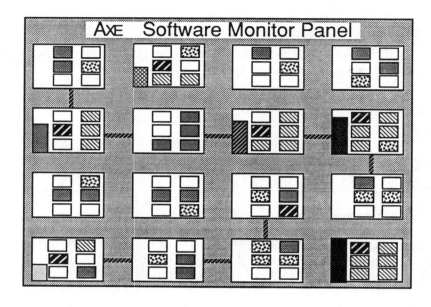

FIGURE 5.6
The software monitor for AXE.

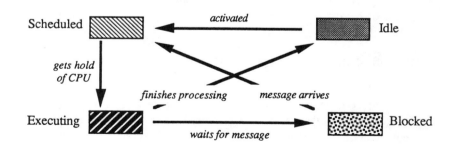

FIGURE 5.7
State transition for a computing process.

5.5 Experimental Usage

AXE was built to develop resource management strategies for multiprocessors. A good strategy produces good mappings consistently for various program-machine pairs. The optimality of such mappings can be evaluated as follows:

1. Resources are not optimally allocated if some sites are overloaded while others are idle. This is indicated by the presence of both red (or magenta) boxes and black boxes on the MULTIPROCESSOR ACTIVITY PANEL (see Plate 27). After 5 applications of post-game analysis (Plate 28), all such imbalances are eliminated for this example —a parallel tree-search algorithm that consists of over 200 processes.

2. An ideal program-machine mapping would produce a rectangular curve on the SYSTEM LOAD PANEL — *all* sites start work simultaneously, remain busy throughout the entire time and terminate simultaneously.[1] Although the curves in this panel have different shapes, the area underneath remains constant because it represents the amount of computation performed on the same application. Therefore, execution time will shorten if we can force the curves to rise quickly and remain high for longer duration. Observe the improvements made by post-game analysis (PGA):

   – green curve: initial random mapping,
   – magenta curve: 1st application of PGA,
   – blue curve: 2nd application,
   – red curve: 3rd application, and
   – yellow curve: 4th application in progress.

5.6 Conclusions and Future Research

The AXE experimentation environment was designed to facilitate research in resource management strategies for concurrent systems using discrete-time simulation. The hardware and software monitoring facilities in AXE enable the performance of the simulated multi-processor to be observed dynamically. The hardware monitor displays (i) the instantaneous load of each processing site and inter-site message transmission, (ii) overall system load and (iii) overall utilization of communication channels. The software monitor captures the state of

---

[1]This requires an ideal parallel program as well as a parallel machine!

individual computing processes (whether it is computing, idle or blocked). The researcher can visually evaluate the performance of the resource management strategy currently studied.

Acknowledgments

The author wishes to acknowledge Roger Bartlett of Digital Equipment Corporation for doing most of the programming for the visualization package based on a prototype developed by Sonie Lau of NASA Ames Research Center. John West of STX also made constructive suggestions that led to the current configuration of the display. I would also like to thank MCC for permitting the use of CSIM simulation package.

References

1. Craig Steele. Placement of Communicating Processes on Multiprocessor Networks. Technical Report 5184:TR:85, MS Thesis, Department of Computer Science, California Institute of Technology, CA, 1985.

2. S. H. Bokhari, "On the Mapping Problem," *IEEE Transactions on Computers*, C-30(3):207-214, March 1981.

3. J. C. Yan, *Post-game Analysis — A Heuristic Resource Management Framework for Concurrent Systems*, PhD Thesis, Department of Electrical Engineering, Stanford University, December 1988.

4. J. C. Yan, "Parallel Program Behavior Specification and Abstraction using BDL," CSL-TR-86-298, Computer System Laboratory, Stanford University, August 1986.

5. H. Schwetman, "CSIM: A C-Based, Process-Oriented Simulation Language," in Proceedings of the Winter Simulation Conference '86, Washington, DC, 1986.

6. Allen Malony and Daniel Reed, "Visualizing Parallel Computer System Performance," Report UIUCDCS-R-88-1465, Department of Computer Science, University of Illinois at Urbana-Champaign, September 1988.

7. Bruck Delagi, Nakul Saraiya, Sayuri Nishimura, and Greg Byrd,"Instrumented Architectural Simulation," Report KSL-87-65, Knowledge Systems Laboratory, Department of Computer Science, Stanford University, November 1987.

COLOR PLATES

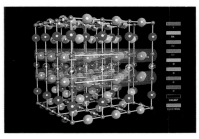

1

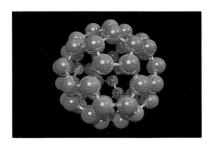

2

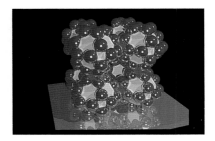

3

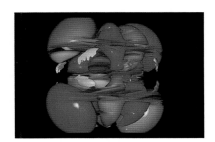

4

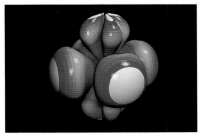

5

6

7

8

9

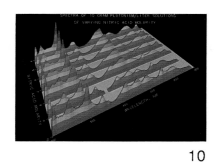

10

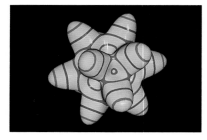

11

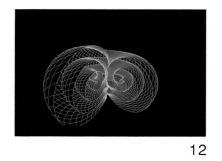

12

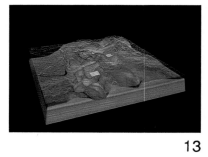

13

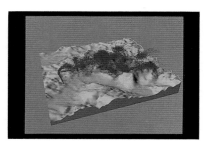

14

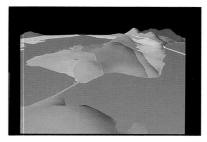

15

16

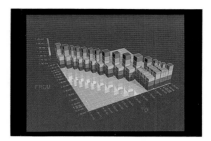

17

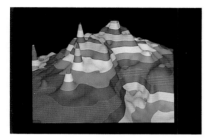

18

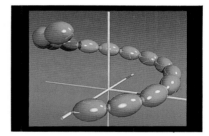

19

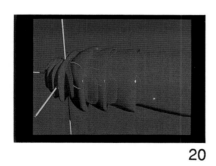

20

21

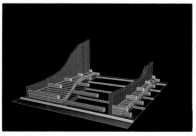

22

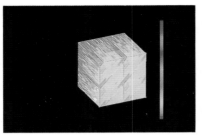

23

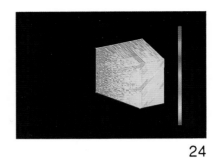

24

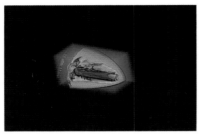

25

26

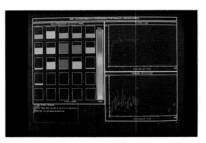

27

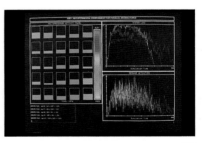

28

29

CAPTIONS

PRUEITT

1. High-temperature superconductor. Electron paths are shown in transparent blue. Atoms are represented by spheres and are 1/2 scale. Data from Fred Mueller, Los Alamos National Laboratory.

2. Sixty carbon atom molecule. Green rods represent double bonds, while white rods represent single bonds. Data from William Harter, University of Arkansas.

3. A zeolite crystal structure.

4. Three-dimensional contour surfaces of electron density in a high-temperature superconductor. Data from Mark Eberhart, Los Alamos.

5. Contour surface plot of a mathematical function.

6. Octa aqua Pu IV. The central green sphere represents a plutonium atom. It is surrounded by eight water molecules. This and the following three plates show some of the stages in a sequence of events in the reclamation of plutonium from wastes. (Atoms are not drawn to scale). Data from Edward Cokal, Los Alamos.

7. Replacement of a water molecule by a nitrate ion.

8. Molecule containing plutonium approaching anion exchange resin.

9. Molecule containing plutonium docked to exchange resin.

10. Spectra of plutonium nitrate solutions with variation of nitric acid concentration. Data from Rick Day, Los Alamos.

11. Rotational energy surface of a molecule. The surface represents the possible location of end points of the rotation vector. Data from William Harter, University of Arkansas.

12. Cutaway view of chemical wave fronts. Data from Art Winfree, University of Arizona.

13. Rio Grande Rift in north-central New Mexico. Faint white lines represent present-day surface of the earth. Solid surface represents bedrock. Data provided by Scott Baldridge, Los Alamos.

14. Air pollution from an oil shale plant in Colorado. Calculation by Tetsuji Yamada, Los Alamos.

15. Terranes around San Francisco Bay. Data supplied by M. Clark Blake Jr., U.S. Geological Survey.

16. Bruce Trent's (Los Alamos) study of soil compaction. Spheres represent soil particles.

17. Neutron scattering cross sections. Data supplied by Norman Pruvost, Los Alamos.

18. Light intensity from the Orion Nebula. Data from Martin Burkhead, University of Indiana.

19. Part of spiral bacteria. Data from Gary Salzman, Los Alamos National Laboratory.

20. Light scattering envelope from a small particle. Data from Gary Salzman, Los Alamos.

21. A cube distorted by trigonometric functions.

22. Population statistics of more developed (left) and less developed (right) countries. Data from Robert Fox.

SALTZMAN

23. Unsliced bank conflict data. The outer surface corresponds to the outer lattices of the 3-D data set.

24. Sliced bank conflict data using a slice not aligned with any coordinate axis.

25. Volumetrically ray traced image of an intergalactic jet using eight regions and seven interface surfaces.

26. Volumetrically ray traced image of an intergalactic jet using four regions and three interface surfaces.

YAN

27. Imbalanced initial loading.

28. Final loading after 4 applications of post-game analysis.

29. AXE software monitor in action.

6

Integrating Performance Data Collection, Analysis, and Visualization[1]

Allen D. Malony[2]
Daniel A. Reed[3]
David C. Rudolph

6.1 Introduction

Despite continued technical advances, parallel system design remains *ad hoc*, an art form practiced by a small cadre of experienced, highly valued designers. No known, general purpose methods can predict the performance of a proposed system design. Moreover, seemingly minor perturbations of parallel architecture, system software, or application algorithms can induce large changes in observed

[1] An abridged version of this paper appeared in the Proceedings of the *Fourth Conference on Hypercubes, Concurrent Computers, and Applications*, March 1989, Monterey, CA.

[2] Supported in part by NSF Grants NSF MIP-8410110 and NSF DCR 84-06916, DOE Grant DOE DE-FG02-85ER25001, Air Force Office of Scientific Research Grant AFOSR-F496200, and a donation from IBM.

[3] Supported in part by the National Science Foundation under grants NSF CCR86-57696, NSF CCR87-06653 and NSF CDA87-22836, by the National Aeronautics and Space Administration under NASA Contract Number NAG-1-613, and by grants from AT&T, Intel Scientific Computers and the Digital Equipment Corporation External Research Program.

performance. In numerical analysis, such problems are called ill-conditioned — small changes in the input x of a function $f(x)$ yield large changes in $f(x)$ (i.e., $f(x + \epsilon) \not\approx f(x)$). Clearly, approximating $f(x)$ by $f(\overline{x})$, by $\overline{f(x)}$, or by $\max_x f(x)$, is dangerous, if not wrong. Yet, peak performance ratings in MIPS (millions of instructions per second) or MFLOPS (millions of floating point operations per second) are precisely such an approximation.

In reality, the performance of a parallel computing system is the complex product of its component interactions. A complete performance analysis requires both *static* and *dynamic* characterizations. Static or average behavior analysis may mask transients that dramatically alter system performance. Simply put, the performance of parallel system components depends on the frequency and types of their interactions; these interactions often cannot be predicted, but they can be measured.

Despite the manifest need for dynamic performance instrumentation and data capture, their efficient implementation is non-trivial. Instrumentation, no matter how unobtrusive, introduces performance perturbations, and the degree of perturbation is proportional to the fraction of the system state that is captured — volume and accuracy are antithetical. The degree of uncertainty manifested depends on the programming paradigm, the system software, and the underlying hardware. As a consequence, performance instrumentation mandates a delicate balance between volume and accuracy. Excessive instrumentation perturbs the measured system; limited instrumentation reduces measurement detail — system behavior must be inferred from insufficient data. From a performance evaluation perspective, instrumentation perturbations must be balanced against the need for detailed performance data.[4]

Even when the perturbations of a performance instrumentation environment are reduced to acceptable levels, a parallel system can quickly generate vast quantities of performance data. These data must be presented in ways that emphasize important events while eliding irrelevant details. Just as visual presentation of scientific data can provide new insights, a performance visualization environment would permit the performance analyst to browse and explore interesting data components by dynamically interconnecting new performance displays and data analysis tools.

To provide insight into dynamic system performance, we are developing an integrated data collection, analysis, and data visualization environment for a specific parallel system — the Intel iPSC/2 hypercube. In §6.2, we begin with a description of the Intel iPSC/2, followed by an overview of the performance environment in §6.3. The data collection components of the environment, discussed in §6.4 and §6.5, include software event tracing at the operating system

---

[4] See [1] for a formal model of performance perturbation that permits quantitative evaluation of perturbations given instrumentation costs, measured event frequency, and desired instrumentation detail.

and program level plus a hardware-based performance monitoring system used to unobtrusively capture software events. In §6.6, we describe a visualization system, based on the X window environment, that permits dynamic display and reduction of performance data. Finally, §6.7 summarizes our experience and development plans.

6.2 Intel iPSC/2 Description

Given the nascent state of parallel computer systems, an efficient implementation of an instrumentation environment necessarily reflects the characteristics, and often the idiosyncrasies, of the associated parallel architecture. Thus, an instrumentation environment must be understood in the context of the intended architecture — the Intel iPSC/2, a second generation, distributed memory parallel system.

A generic distributed memory system, or multicomputer, contains a processor with some locally addressable memory, a communication controller capable of routing messages without delaying the processor, and a small number of connections to other nodes. Because multicomputer networks contain no shared memory, the cooperating tasks of a parallel algorithm must execute asynchronously on different nodes and communicate solely via message passing. Although a large number of possible interconnection network topologies exist, the binary N-cube (or *hypercube*) [2] has, to date, been most common. A binary N-cube contains 2^N nodes numbered from 0 to $2^N - 1$, and the labels for a pair of physically connected nodes differ by a single digit in their binary representation.

As an exemplar of this approach to parallel processing, the second generation Intel iPSC/2 hypercube [3,4] incorporates evolutionary advances in technology, including an Intel 80386/80387 microprocessor pair, a 64K byte cache, and up to 16 megabytes of memory on each node. The iPSC/2 includes an autonomous routing controller to support fixed path, circuit-switched communication between nodes. This communication system eliminates most of the store-and-forward latency that existed in earlier distributed memory systems. The software development interface for the iPSC/2 is a standard UNIX[5] system that transmits executable programs to the nodes, accepts results from the nodes, and can, if desired, participate in the computation. Finally, the UNIX host supports node file I/O to its local disk and to remote disks via a network file system protocol.

To reduce dependence on the UNIX host and to provide input/output performance commensurate with computing power, the Intel iPSC/2 nodes also

---

[5]Unix is a trademark of AT&T Bell Lab oratories.

support parallel I/O link connections to I/O nodes.[6] Each I/O node is identical to a standard compute node, with the exception of an additional daughter card that provides a SCSI bus interface. The SCSI bus supports up to seven peripherals and has a peak transfer rate of 4 megabytes/second.

Because the I/O nodes provide a superset of the compute node functionality, software support for disk and file access is realized by augmenting the functionality of the NX/2 operating system on both the compute and I/O nodes. This Concurrent File System (CFS) provides a UNIX System V file interface that allows the user or any iPSC/2 compute node to create, access, or delete files either on the hypercube host (i.e., the host's disks) or on the disks attached to the I/O nodes. File accesses by node application programs are translated into file request messages and are sent via the hypercube communication network to the appropriate I/O nodes. CFS supports a single file directory hierarchy that spans all I/O node disks; to the user, the I/O node disks appear as a single large disk.

The ability to expand a distributed memory parallel system's total processing power and memory size by adding nodes is both an advantage and a limitation. The total memory, although potentially large, is distributed, and data must be partitioned across the nodes. The degree of internode data sharing is limited by the latency and bandwidth of the communication network. On the Intel iPSC/2, the latency to initiate a message transmission is approximately 270 microseconds with a bandwidth of 2.8 megabytes/second [5]; such a system favors a small number of large messages over a large number of small messages. Thus, the performance of different application algorithms is sensitive to the distribution of data, computation, and volume of interprocessor communication. Quantifying this performance is the motivation for performance instrumentation.

Message passing systems, including the Intel iPSC/2, pose particularly acute instrumentation problems. First, detectable events occur locally at each processor. Identifying global events requires associating two or more events from different processors. The obvious approach imposes a total order on events, based on event timestamps, and identifies global events from temporally proximate event groups. Unfortunately, the second problem complicates solutions to the first: most message passing systems, including the Intel iPSC/2, lack a globally synchronized clock to create event timestamps — this clock is needed to maintain event causality. With a global time reference, the distributed event data still must be collected for analysis and presentation. Our solution to these problems is the subject of the remainder of the paper.

---

[6] The importance of a parallel I/O system for performance trace data will become clear in §6.5.

6.3 Environment Organization

In [6], we argued that integration and flexibility are the twin keys to an effective performance analysis environment. If the interactions among environment components are awkward or inefficient, the performance analyst will seek simpler tools. Similarly, if the environment does not permit diverse approaches to performance data reduction and analysis, including addition of new environment components (e.g., data filters and displays), its functional lifetime will be limited. Given the implications of integration and flexibility and our experience with an earlier environment design [6], we established several specific environment design goals. Not all of these goals are simultaneously realizable, nor were they all met in our prototype. However, they provided a framework for system design.

- The individual analysis and visualization components should be **easy to build** for many different application types and system software environments.

- An **extension language** should permit addition of new components or modification of existing components without intimate knowledge of environment infrastructure.

- The environment should be **fast**, preferably fast enough to process bursts of real-time data.

- It should be possible to **dynamically configure** data analysis and visualization components, allowing the performance analyst to change data perspectives during execution.

- The environment should support **multiple analysis levels**, including hardware, system software, and application.

- Finally, the environment should be **portable** to different systems. Although the mechanisms for performance data capture are inherently system dependent, performance data reduction (e.g., computation of sliding window averages) and visualization are largely system independent.

Given these design goals, Figure 6.1 shows the organization of our performance environment. The environment's fundamental performance measure is an *event*. Given a "complete set" of event types, a timestamped event trace suffices to construct general performance measures. As the figure suggests, our performance instrumentation includes event tracing at both the program and operating system levels.

At the program level, the performance analyst can direct a modified version of the GNU C compiler to automatically generate code to create a timestamped log of procedure entries and exits; this requires no modification to the applica-

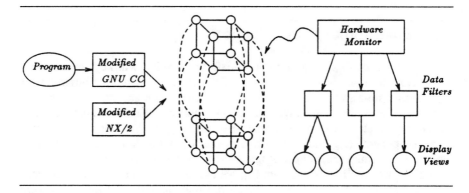

FIGURE 6.1
Environment organization.

tion source code. Additional program performance events can be generated by inserting calls to event tracing routines; these include marking the entry and exit of code sections and marking the occurrence of a user specified event [7,8]. In our current implementation on the Intel iPSC/2, all application program events are passed to the hypercube operating system NX/2. NX/2 has been modified to record both these application events and operating system events corresponding to message transmissions, process state changes, and system calls.

The events produced as a result of this instrumentation are transmitted from each node to the hardware monitor via additional signal lines on the iPSC/2 backplane.[7] Because the hardware monitor generates event timestamps and can accept simultaneous events from all nodes, causality is assured. The resulting event stream can be either stored in an event trace file or, if the event frequency is low enough to permit real-time processing, sent to a set of data filters and displays.

Clearly, the number of generated events is potentially enormous; the event data must be presented in ways that emphasize important primitive events (i.e., those generated during execution) and that reflect aggregate system behavior (i.e., by synthesizing compound events). The environment includes a set of data filters that process the event data, either by eliding irrelevant events or by computing dynamic statistics (e.g., sliding window averages).

Given the diversity of performance data and possible statistics, a variety of performance displays (including meters, plots, histograms, event graphs, dynamic call graphs, and topological views) are needed to display the dynamics of

---

[7] Until the hardware monitor is complete, these events are timestamped and recorded in the memories of individual nodes [8].

system performance. These displays are implemented as X window widgets [9], providing display portability across a variety of vendor workstations. Because the display filters limit the propagation of performance data semantics, the same data can be displayed in multiple ways (e.g., histograms and meters) without embedding the data semantics in each display. Via an environment control, the binding of data filter and display can be changed dynamically, allowing the user to select the filters and display formats best suited to the data. Finally, if the performance analyst wished to view the raw event trace, a X windows timeline permits event trace browsing and correlation of events across nodes. The remainder of this paper discusses the hardware and software implementation of this environment, including examples of its use.

6.4   Software Instrumentation

There are many levels in the hierarchy of performance instrumentation, including hardware, system software, and application program. The answer to the oft-asked question, "How fast is it?" depends on the intended use of the performance data. Operating system instrumentation can capture the interplay of hardware and system software, but it cannot identify the performance bottlenecks in an application program. Consequently, our instrumentation system provides both, allowing the performance analyst to correlate system and application performance.

6.4.1   Application Instrumentation

If extensive source code modifications are required to capture application performance data, analysis of many competing application algorithms is impractical — the manpower is prohibitive. Thus, the great appeal of compile time instrumentation is its flexibility and ease of use; no source code modifications are required, yet execution traces or profiles can be generated.

To capture application performance data, we have modified the Free Software Foundation's GNU C compiler [10] to emit instrumented code for the Intel iPSC/2. Not only is the source to the GNU C compiler readily available, it generates code whose quality is competitive with many commercial compilers.[8]

Compiler command line options enable generation of instrumented code. If only selective instrumentation is desired, the user can specify either the list of procedures to be instrumented or, equivalently, those not to be instrumented. As each procedure is compiled, calls to monitoring functions are inserted in the procedure's prologue and epilogue. These calls are inserted in the intermediate

---

[8]Our benchmarks show little difference between GNU C and the Greenhills C provided with the Intel iPSC/2.

RTL representation used internally by the compiler, not the generated assembly code. Thus, the instrumentation is instruction set independent, and given the requisite system software support, would allow instrumentation of other machine architectures. At execution time, the monitoring functions invoked by each procedure's prologue and epilogue pass the procedure's name and entry or exit events to NX/2, the iPSC/2 node operating system. This creates a timestamped trace of procedure entry and exit events for each hypercube node.

If additional application trace events are needed the user can manually insert calls to monitoring functions that mark the occurrence of an event, measure the execution time of a particular code section or record a string of text. Like the automatic instrumentation, these calls generate events that are passed to NX/2 and embedded in the event trace. From this trace, the visualization subsystem can construct program execution profiles and dynamic displays of program activity.

6.4.2   Operating System Instrumentation

As just noted, application performance events are passed to NX/2. These application events are merged with three classes of operating system events: message, process, and system call. These operating system events are captured by an instrumentation of the NX/2 operating system source code [8]. For message transmissions, NX/2 captures the parameters of the application program's csend or isend call and the time that physical transmission of the message began and completed. NX/2 captures corresponding events for message receipt, permitting correlation of message sends and receives on different nodes. In addition, the NX/2 instrumentation captures context switches, including the identity of the processes, and all system calls.

Because the hardware monitor is not yet operational, NX/2 currently records both application and operating system events in a portion of each node's memory. After the application program completes, the individual node traces are transmitted to the iPSC/2 host for post-processing and display.

Software capture and recording of performance trace events is not without price; data capture perturbs system behavior. The primary source of instrumentation perturbations is execution of additional instructions by both the application code and the operating system. Table 6.1 shows the trace statistics for four application programs and associated input data when executed on eight nodes of the Intel iPSC/2.[9] The application programs include, *Life*, a parallel implementation of Conway's famous cellular automaton [11], a standard cell placement algorithm based on simulated annealing [12], and two variants of a parallel linear optimization program based on the Simplex algorithm [13,14].

---

[9]In Table 6.1, the column labeled "simple trace" denotes instrumentation without the recording of procedure entry and exit. The "complete trace" column includes both operating system and procedure tracing.

TABLE 6.1
Event Trace Statistics

Program	Messages per Second	Procedure Calls per Second	Simple Trace Size (bytes)	Complete Trace Size (bytes)
Life	20	11	209,035	225,055
Cell Placement	193	1004	1,026,818	2,037,357
Row Simplex	35	64	237,733	280,708
Column Simplex	18	14	388,343	398,857

The magnitude of performance perturbations and the size of the associated event trace depend on the frequency of event logging (i.e., the number of system and application events). As Table 6.1 suggests, the cell placement algorithm is procedure call intensive; the frequency of these procedure calls increases total execution time by nearly forty percent. If procedure call tracing is disabled, the perturbation of the cell placement program drops to less than ten percent. For the other three applications, total perturbation, even with procedure call tracing, is less than five percent. Additional data suggest that perturbations of less than ten percent are typical for most applications; to further reduce perturbations, hardware trace support is needed.

6.5 Hardware Monitoring

The absence of a global, accurate, and consistent time [15] exacerbates the already difficult measurement of distributed events. Unfortunately, the Intel iPSC/2 lacks a global clock, requiring complex software solutions to synchronize individual node clocks and to re-order events generated asynchronously on different nodes. The constraints on measurement resolution created by distributed clock synchronization, coupled with the overheads of software tracing, limit the range of performance behavior that can be accurately observed. To circumvent these problems we are developing HYPERMON, a hardware-assisted monitoring system for the Intel iPSC/2. Below, we describe the components of the HYPERMON and HYPERMON's relationship to the remainder of the analysis and visualization system.

6.5.1 Hypermon Architecture

Figure 6.2 shows the primary components of the HYPERMON architecture and their physical relation to the Intel iPSC/2. Physically, HYPERMON is partitioned

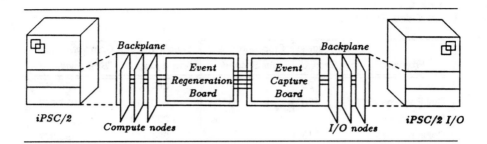

FIGURE 6.2
Hypermon architecture.

between the cabinet that contains the iPSC/2 compute nodes and the one containing the I/O nodes and disks. Each iPSC/2 node independently sends event data to HYPERMON via backplane connections distinct from the node's communication links. HYPERMON regenerates event signals at the event regeneration board (ERB) before transfer to the event capture board (ECB) residing in the I/O cabinet. The ECB captures the events, generates global timestamps, and stores the resulting event data in internal memory buffers for access by I/O nodes. Because the I/O nodes each contain a processor and local memory, preliminary analysis of the event data (e.g., format conversion) can occur at the point of data capture, albeit with a consequent decrease in the maximum recording rate. The resulting performance data can then be stored on disk or transferred through the hypercube host to a workstation for further analysis and presentation.

There are two major requirements for the HYPERMON hardware. First, HYPERMON must accept events from the hypercube nodes at their nominal rate. The design guideline allows each node to generate events at a sustained rate of one every 100 microseconds, with bursts of up to 256 events with inter-event times as small as 10 microseconds. Second, HYPERMON must support the transfer and storage of event data. Assuming the representation of each event requires at most 10 bytes, approximately 1.5 MBytes/second of event data must be transferred to disk or to remote workstations.

6.5.2   iPSC/2 Event Visibility

An Intel modification of the iPSC/2 hypercube makes possible external access to software events generated by each node. Five "performance" bits from a port in the I/O address space on each hypercube node board are routed via the system backplane to an empty slot in the system cabinet. The ERB sits in this slot and converts the performance bits to differential signals for transfer to the

ECB, where the bits are interpreted. Up to 16 iPSC/2 nodes can be supported by one ERB-ECB pair; an additional ERB-ECB pair is needed for each group of 16 nodes.

Because the NX/2 operating system generates event data by writing to an I/O port, one bit must be reserved as a strobe to signal the ECB that the remaining four event data bits are valid. Thus, a software event is generated by the following two operations:

1. WRITE: Event.strobe = 0, Event.data = *undefined*

2. WRITE: Event.strobe = 1, Event.data = *new event data*

The 80386 microprocessor in the Intel iPSC/2 requires approximately six cycles to complete an I/O write operation, versus two for a standard memory access. Thus, a minimum of twelve cycles are needed to write a software event. Up to sixteen events can be represented uniquely by four bits of data. If additional events are needed, or if data are associated with an event, multiple I/O write operations are required. Software events can be reconstructed from this data during event analysis.

Clearly, a larger event field is desirable to increase event bandwidth — trace analysis suggests that an average event requires ten hardware event frames. However, hardware constraints limit the number of available backplane signals. The three-fold difference in machine cycle count for I/O writes, plus the need for duplicate writes to assert the data strobe, further limit event bandwidth. Despite these limitations, the potential software event bandwidth remains substantial. Moreover, hardware support permits real-time extraction of performance data and, consequently, capture of larger traces than otherwise possible with node memory trace buffering.[10]

6.5.3 Event Capture

Figure 6.3 shows the functional design of the event capture hardware, the primary hardware component of HYPERMON. The event data for each hypercube node is placed in a separate FIFO buffer that is clocked by the corresponding event strobe signal. All events occurring within a given *event time window*, defined by the rate of the *timestamp* clock (approximately 4 MHz), are combined to form an *event frame*.[11] Each event frame is then placed in the event frame FIFO for transfer to an I/O node processor.

All events present within a time window are given the same timestamp. Because the event signals are generated from processors with asynchronous

---

[10] System perturbations are too great to permit real-time trace extraction via the hypercube communication network.

[11] The event data FIFO's provide data buffering during this process.

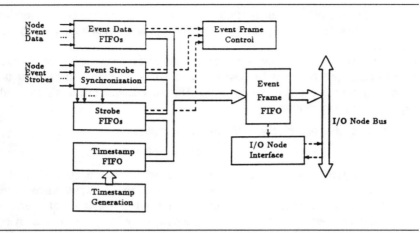

FIGURE 6.3
Hypermon event capture.

clocks, the event strobes for each node must be synchronized with respect to the window to determine event presence. An event frame is constructed for a time window only if one of the nodes produces an event during the window. The strobe signals are captured as part of the frame to indicate which nodes generated events.

Each event frame consists of four 32-bit words; see Figure 6.4. Four event data bits from each node FIFO are always placed in the frame. However, only those FIFO's with valid data for this time window will be shifted into the event frame; the other event data fields in the frame are undefined. As mentioned above, the strobe vector identifies which of the event data in the frame are valid for the time window. Finally, a 32-bit timestamp is saved with each frame. Once an event frame is constructed, it is saved in the ECB's frame FIFO.

6.5.4 Event Processing

The ECB supports a parallel bus interface to an I/O node. Via this bus, event frames can be transferred to the I/O node's memory from (potentially) several ECB's; the prototype system has only on ECB. The event frame FIFO is directly accessible through this interface.

Event frames are transferred to the I/O node's memory where event initial preprocessing decomposes the frame into separate event streams for each instrumented node. Additionally, the I/O node's processor can be used to compress the event trace by computing statistics directly from the event data. Finally, the

Event 15	Event 14	Event 13	Event 12
Event 11	Event 10	Event 9	Event 8
Event 7	Event 6	Event 5	Event 4
Event 3	Event 2	Event 1	Event 0
Unused		Strobe Vector	
Timestamp			

FIGURE 6.4
Hypermon event frame.

event trace data can be stored on the I/O node CFS disks for post-mortem analysis or transferred to the iPSC/2 host and associated workstations for analysis and presentation.

The ability to record trace data on local CFS disks or on remote disks attached to either the iPSC/2 host or a workstation, coupled with real-time or deferred trace analysis, provide a wide variety of analysis configurations with distinct costs; see Figure 6.5. Selection of a trace processing mode depends on event frequency, density, and complexity. If the mean time interval between valid event frames is small, real-time event processing (e.g., statistical analysis) may not be possible — the I/O node minimally must record event data without loss. Event frames that contain large numbers of valid events and complex events that require a sequence of event frames further increase the I/O node load.

The site of trace data storage also depends on aggregate event data rates. The highest performance option, storage on CFS disks, does not permit real-time visualization. However, transmission to either the iPSC/2 system host or a remote workstation holds hypercube communication links and may further perturb the system. The best choice for the event data processing mode and the site of trace storage depends on application program characteristics and the acceptable perturbation level.

6.6 Data Analysis and Visualization

As discussed in §6.3 and [6], flexibility and dynamic reconfigurability were primary design goals for the data analysis and visualization environment. Thus, the environment infrastructure permits addition of new data analysis functions and data views.

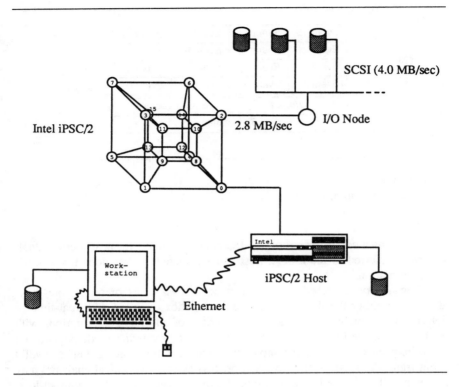

FIGURE 6.5
Event trace processing options.

6.6.1 Infrastructure Design

The data analysis and visualization system contains a *user interface*, an *event preprocessor*, a set of generic data analysis *filters*, a set of filter-display interfaces called *strainers*, and a set of display *views*. The event preprocessor converts the event stream produced by software instrumentation into a standard format for use by the event filters.[12]

The event filters accept the trace events and maintain an internal event summary for each node. At present, these include

□ message counts and message volume, ordered by message type, message size, and source and destination node,

---

[12]This isolates idiosyncrasies of the trace event format and permits compact data representations for network transfer and disk storage.

□ processor state, including utilization and context switches, and

□ program state, including current procedure and execution profile.

Although the semantics of each filter's internal state differ, these semantics need not be known by the display tools. By isolating semantic issues, different filter data can be displayed in multiple ways using standard views (e.g., bar charts and meters). Thus, each filter has an associated set of event strainers that, via access to the internal filter state, create a view specific data representation.

The user interface allows the performance analyst to configure and manage the filters, strainers and views. Via this interface, the user can change the attributes of performance views or open new views.

The environment defines several interface standards, allowing addition of new filters, strainers and views. These include standards for module initialization, termination and user customization. The builder of a standard module (i.e., filter, strainer, or view) need only meet these interface standards. The environment infrastructure then provides intermodule communication. Early experience suggests that this design promotes extensibility and design flexibility.

6.6.2 Performance Displays

Understanding dynamic system behavior requires the performance analyst to assimilate potentially vast amounts of performance data; even at a modest 500K byte/second event generation rate, an application that executes for one minute will generate 30 megabytes of trace data. Although performance data filters reduce the total data volume by creating dynamic statistics from the raw event trace, understanding these statistics remains a substantial intellectual burden. Fortunately, the information density of graphical displays greatly exceeds that of printed text, and the human visual system is remarkably adept at interpreting and identifying anomalies in false color data. This permits the "visual abstraction" of dynamic performance data in easily interpretable graphic forms. The resulting insights often would be difficult or impossible to obtain from from textual representations alone,

The diversity of the performance data demands an equally rich set of performance displays. Because a display might be used for data from a variety of sources, embedding data semantics in the display would restrict its domain of applicability. Rather, a set of *resources* and *methods* should be provided by each display. Display resources are the configuration parameters used to define a display instance; the display methods control the display's operation. Further, each display should support standard interface conventions; this promotes ease of use and rapid construction of new displays.

Although the most useful set of displays can be determined only from experience, we have constructed a prototype set of displays using the widgets of the X window system [13]. The displays include

□ dials

□ bar charts

□ LEDs

□ Kiviat diagrams

□ matrix views

□ X-Y plots

□ contour plots

□ strip charts, and a

□ general purpose graph display.

Each display is configurable, via the environment control and the X window manager, and is capable of displaying data of various types. In addition, the portability provided by X permits the display environment to execute on a wide variety of vendor workstations.

Although space precludes a detailed discussion of each display, three examples illustrate our approach to display development. First, we consider an *LED* display that can represent a scalar with a finite range of assumable values; see Figure 6.6a.[13] The display includes an single method, used to set the scalar value, and four display resources, *range*, *levels*, *markers*, and *interval*. The *range* resource defines the range of displayable values. Within this range, the *levels* resource controls the number of display levels and the mapping to a level (i.e., what values within the display range are mapped to each level). For the current display value, the display will enable the level indicators, either with bitmaps or colors, from the minimum value up to, and including, the level for current display value. The *markers* resource defines the bitmaps or colors associated with each display level. Finally, the *interval* resources specifies the number of display updates over which a maximum value, a "high water mark," should be shown. Figure 6.6 shows ten LED displays, each with twenty levels.

Our second example is a general matrix display that can be used to show one- and two-dimensional array data. Widget resources specify the number of matrix rows and columns, the range of expected values expected, and the mapping of values to bitmaps or colors. The single display update method accepts a pointer to an array of display values. In the display, each matrix cell corresponds to a particular value in the array. Its representation depends on the value's position within the range of values and the bitmap or color corresponding to that position. Figure 6.6b shows a ten row matrix with ten columns; see Figure 6.9 for matrix displays of actual performance data.

---

[13] Conceptually, an LED widget provides a bar chart with user definable discretization of display values.

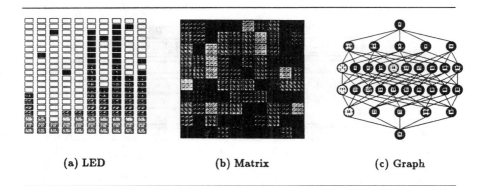

(a) LED	(b) Matrix	(c) Graph

FIGURE 6.6
Performance data displays.

Finally, the graph display can draw an input graph (representing nodes and arcs in a virtual coordinate space) within the dimensions of the display window. Resources specify node shapes, labels, and connectivity. Via the graph display methods, nodes can be bitmap or color filled, and links can be flashed or color coded. Finally, mouse clicks on nodes or links are reported to the application using the widget.[14] The generality of the graph display permits many uses, including display of procedure call graphs and communication traffic. Figure 6.6c shows a Pascal triangle representation of a 32-node hypercube topology. The colors of nodes and links might be used to display node and link utilization.

6.6.3 Environment Examples

Because our performance visualization environment and its display widgets are designed to show dynamic performance, much is lost in the description of static, monochrome images. Despite these limitations, we discuss the environment as a performance analyst might encounter it, beginning with the top-level user interface, the *Visual* window, shown in Figure 6.7. All displays, both below and in §6.6.4, are based on performance trace data from a parallel implementation of the simplex linear optimization algorithm [13,14].

The command buttons in the *Visual* window permit the performance analyst to control the environment and create new display views. The trace description and control windows shown in Figure 6.7 are created via a pulldown menu from the **Trace** button.   In the *Description* window, a performance analyst can

---

[14] Most displays provide some form of *callback* functionality.

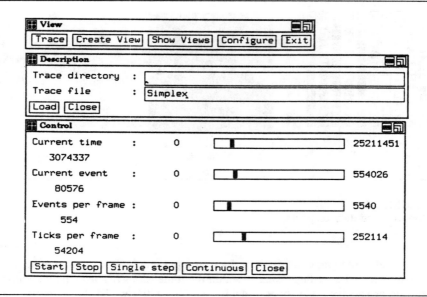

FIGURE 6.7
Visualization environment control.

select a trace file that contains the event information captured by the compiler
and operating system instrumentation.

As the name suggests, the *Control* window allows the performance analyst
to control the updates to the display views. The current time and current event
displays show the current trace location and are updated automatically. In the
display environment, a *Frame* corresponds to a displayed system state. The
user can change two aspects of a frame display — mode and state differential.
Frames can be displayed either in single-step mode or continuous mode. If
the mouse is clicked on the **Single step** button, the user must explicitly request
display of the next frame. Conversely, *Continuous* mode automatically advances
to the next frame specified by the frame rate and differential controls. The
second aspect of frame control is the change in system state, in events or time,
between successively displayed frames. This state difference is the minimum of
the specified number of *Events per frame* and the number of *Ticks per frame*.
By adjusting the mode and state differential, the performance analyst can study
gross behavior, examining a small subset of all system states, or examine the
trace event by event.

As discussed in §6.6.1 and §6.6.2, the visualization environment includes
a set of data analysis filters and a set of display views. Figure 6.8 shows the

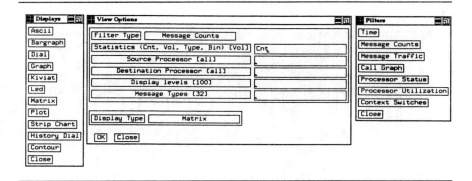

FIGURE 6.8
Visualization environment configuration.

configuration interface for connecting filters and views. The *View Options* window is created via the **Create View** button in Figure 6.7. In turn, the *Display table* and *Filter table* windows are created via the **Filter Type** and **Display Type** buttons. In Figure 6.8, the user has previously selected a filter that counts the volume and number of messages transmitted among processors, and has opted to view message counts as a source-destination processor matrix. Finally, the options particular to this display choice are shown in the *View Options* window, including the defaults. Because display views are dynamically bound to data filters, the user can add new display views at any time and in arbitrary combinations.

Finally, Figure 6.9 shows the currently operational display views. As noted earlier, the event trace file used to generate these views was obtained via compiler and operating system instrumentation on an eight node Intel iPSC/2, and reflects the computation and communication behavior of a simplex linear optimization code [13].

The displays in the upper left of Figure 6.9 show communication traffic. The message count and volume bar charts show the fraction of message counts and volume sent by each processor. The two-dimensional message count and volume views reflect the total number of messages and volume of data, respectively, sent between each source (row) and destination (column) processor; the ninth row and column denote communication traffic to and from the host processor. Notice that the distribution of message sizes is bimodal; the diagonal pattern in message counts display is much less pronounced in the message volume display. Why? In each cycle of the simplex algorithm, the processor collectively determine a global minimum via logarithmic condensation [15], this generates many small messages — the diagonal pattern seen in the message counts matrix display. This

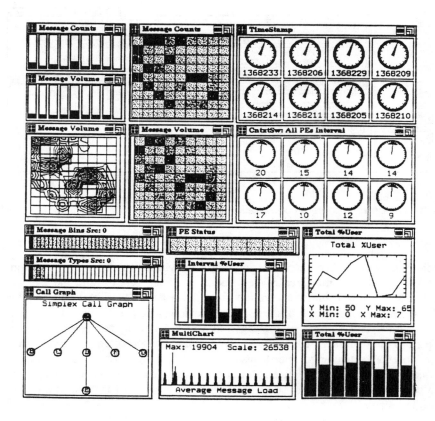

FIGURE 6.9
Visualization environment displays (simplex trace).

minimization is followed by the broadcast of a row or column of the optimization constraint matrix. These row broadcasts constitute most of the communication data volume but only a small fraction of the total message count. The message bins and message types views are histograms of message sizes and message types, respectively; as just noted, most messages are small, and there are only a few message types. Finally, the average message load display at the bottom of Figure 6.9 shows the sliding window average of the network communication traffic; in the display, the repeated cycles of communication traffic caused by minimization and broadcast are evident.

The call graph window in the lower left shows dynamic procedure activation for a single process; colors denote the currently active procedure. Computation asynchrony can be observed by displaying the procedure activation states of multiple processes.

The processor status (PE) view in the center of Figure 6.9 shows the current state of each processor (idle, user computation, system state, or message transmission). The *percent user* bar charts and X-Y plot in the lower left corner show both the processor utilization since the beginning of the computation and during a sliding window interval. Although the computation is well balanced, the disparity in processor computation times for a single cycle is evident in the interval display.

The context switches view shows the number of state changes by each processor in a sliding window of time. Although not clearly shown in Figure 6.9, the *history dial* view leaves shadows of the dial pointer, showing the rate of change in the displayed variable. Finally, the *timestamp* display in the upper right corner of Figure 6.9 shows the effects of local processor clocks.

The views and options of Figure 6.9 are but a subset of those possible. Each view has many options and can be bound to many data filters; this permits diverse display idioms.

6.6.4 Timeline Examples

Although reconfigurable data filters and displays permit analysis of dynamic performance statistics, there are times when detailed analysis of raw trace data is required. Performance statistics may reveal that processes often are blocked awaiting message receipt. By examining the temporal pattern of individual message transmissions and matching message transmission with receipt, unnecessary software message latencies can be identified and corrected.

To complement the dynamic statistics displays, we developed an X windows event trace timeline capable of displaying and correlating individual trace events across processors. Figure 6.10 shows the highest level view of the same simplex trace data as Figure 6.9. The display view is a window on the two-dimensional space of processors and time. The *Up* and *Down* bottons control scrolling across processors. Similarly, the *Left* and *Right* buttons control scrolling forward and backward in time. In the timeline display, colors represent processor states (e.g., user computation, system, software message preparation, hardware message transmission, and idle). In the monochrome image of Figure 6.10, black represents user computation. As this scale, many small intervals of processor idle time are visible — the gray lines in the figure.

The *Expand* and *Zoom* menus at the upper left of the display window control the fraction of the trace that will fill the display. Figure 6.11, the result of a display expansion, shows the the first 0.7 seconds of the event trace. In this figure, the dark bands of processor activity are clearly delimited by intervals of

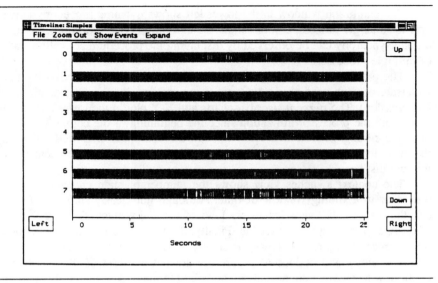

FIGURE 6.10
Simplex event trace timeline (entire trace).

communication, the dotted regions, and idle time, the white regions. Expanding the trace display further shows the true power of this display medium.

In Figure 6.12, we have expanded the display to show only ten milliseconds of the simplex program's total execution. In addition, we have chosen *All Events* from the *Show Events* menu. With this option, each user-visible event (i.e., message transmissions and user defined trace events), is marked on the timeline. In Figure 6.12 message transmissions are marked by s and r for message send and receive, respectively. Clicking the mouse on an event marker displays additional event data. For a message, this includes source and destination nodes, time of message transmission and receipt, message size in bytes, and user defined message type.[15] Finally, the parallel bars drawn through each node's timeline delimit intervals when the iPSC/2's autonomous routing hardware was transmitting a message.

By combining the macroscopic performance views of the visualization environment with the microscopic views of the visual timeline, one can quickly identify performance bottlenecks and load imbalances.

---

[15] The destination of -1 in Figure 6.12 denotes a message broadcast to all other nodes.

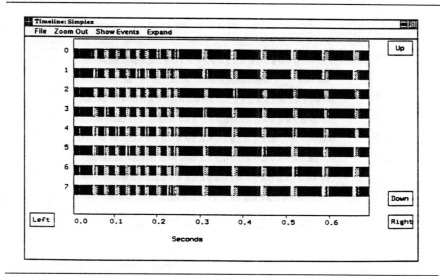

FIGURE 6.11
Simplex event trace timeline (detail).

6.7 Summary

The complexity of parallel systems makes *a priori* performance prediction difficult and experimental performance analysis crucial. A performance data collection, analysis, and visualization environment is needed to access the effects of architectural and system software variations. The environment described here is an ongoing effort. Completion of the hardware monitor should permit performance data capture with minimal performance perturbations. Similarly, an expanded set of data analysis filters and displays would permit exploration of additional performance questions, including memory access patterns, input-output behavior, and task scheduling.

Acknowledgments

Justin Rattner (Intel Scientific Computers) first suggested implementing a performance monitor via signals from the iPSC/2 backplane. Since that time, Paul Close (Intel Scientific Computers), has provided technical information and

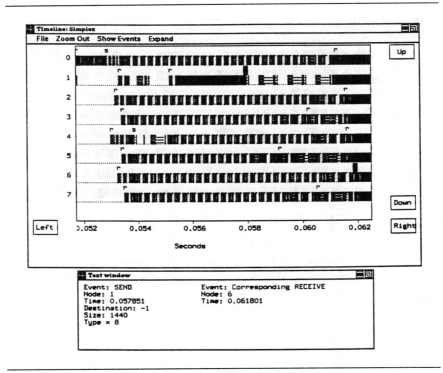

FIGURE 6.12
Simplex event trace timeline (fine detail).

support. Without their help, the design of the iPSC/2 hardware monitor would not have been possible.

Finally, Ruth Aydt, James Arendt, Dominique Grabas, and Brian Totty contributed to the design and implementation of the software instrumentation and visualization environment. Their enthusiasm was infectious and their assistance invaluable.

References

1. A. D. Malony, D. A. Reed, and H. Wijshoff, "Performance Measurement Intrusion and Perturbation Analysis," Tech. Rep. CSRD No. 923, University of Illinois at Urbana-Champaign, 1989.

2. Y. Saad and M. H. Schultz, "Topological Properties of Hypercubes," *IEEE Transactions on Computers C-37*, **7** 1988, pp. 867-872.

3. R. Arlauskas, "iPSC/2 System: A Second Generation Hypercube," in *Proceedings of the Third Conference on Hypercube Concurrent Computers and Applications, Volume I*, (Pasadena, CA, 1988), Association for Computing Machinery, pp. 38-42.

4. P. Close, "The iPSC/2 Node Architecture," in *Proceedings of the Third Confeence on Hypercube Concurrent Computers and Applications, Volume I*, (Pasadena, CA 1988), Association for Computing Machinery, pp. 43-50.

5. D. K. Bradley, "First and Second Generation Hypercube Performance," Master's thesis, University of Illinois at Urbana-Champaign, Department of Computer Science, 1988.

6. A. D. Malony and D. A. Reed, "Visualizing Parallel Computer System Performance," in Instrumentation for Future Parallel Computing Systems, M. Simmons, R. Koskela, and I. Bucher, Eds. (Addison-Wesley Publishing Company, 1989).

7. D. C. Rudolph, "Performance Instrumentation for the Intel iPSC/2," Master's thesis, University of Illinois at Urbana-Champaign, 1989.

8. D. C. Rudolph and D. A. Reed, "CRYSTAL: Operating System Instrumentation for the Intel iPSC/2," in Proceedings of the Fourth Conference on Hypercube Concurrent Computers and Applications (Monterey, CA 1989).

9. R. W. Scheifler and J. Gettys, "The X Window System," *ACM Transactions on Graphics 5*, **2** (1986), pp. 79-109.

10. R. M. Stallman, "Using and Porting GNU CC," Technical report, Free Software Foundation, Inc., Cambridge, MA, 1988.

11. M. Gardner, "Mathematical Games," *Scientific American* (1970), pp. 120-123.

12. R. J. Brouwer and P. Banerjee, "A Parallel Simulated Annealing Algorithm for Channel Routing on a Hypercube Multiprocessor," in *Proceedings of the International Conference on Computer Design* (Rye Brook, NY, 1988), pp. 4-7.

13. C. B. Stunkel and D. A. Reed, "Hypercube Implementation of the Simplex Algorithm," in *Proceedings of the Third Conference on Hypercube Computers and Concurrent Applications* (Pasadena, CA 1988), Association for Computing Machinery, pp. 1473-1482.

14. L. R. Foulds, *Optimization Techniques: An Introduction*, Springer-Verlag, New York, NY 1981.

15. L. Lamport, "Time, Clocks, and the Ordering of Events in a Distributed System," *Communications of the ACM 21*, **7** (1978), pp. 558-565.

7

JED: Just An Event Display

Allen D. Malony[1]

7.1 Introduction

Event tracing has become a popular form of gathering performance data on multiprocessor computer systems. Indeed, a performance measurement facility has been developed for the Cedar multiprocessor that uses tracing as a back-end mechanism for collecting several run-time measurements including count, time, virtual memory, and event data [1,2]. Tools to study an event trace, however, are typically specialized according to the type of data collected. Usually various trace analyses and displays are developed based on some event interpretation model. Whereas this approach will give specific information about particular events and their occurrence in a trace, it is not particularly easy to extend; new events often require new analysis and display techniques.

One approach to developing a more flexible performance analysis and visualization system is that proposed in Hyperview [3]. The Hyperview architecture supports the easy addition of new event filter and display modules into the

[1] Supported in part by NSF Grants NSF MIP-8410110 and NSF DCR 84-06916, DOE Grant DOE DE-FG02-85ER25001, Air Force Office of Scientific Research Grant AFOSR-F496200, and a donation from IBM.

system and provides a patch-cord style of interconnection of filter/display combinations. This approach is the desired one for developing high-end performance environments where there are a variety of analyses and displays that must be integrated in a single system.

In the first phases of performance measurement, a user is often interested in such data as the relative sequence of events on different execution threads, the time a certain event occurs in the computation, or the state of each task as execution proceeds. High-end environments such as Hyperview, although powerful, can be overkill in situations where the user only desires to observe the sequence of events present in the trace together with information about each event's type, its time of occurrence, its place of occurrence, and any other information associated with the events as recorded in the trace. Simple analysis and presentation of individual events might be all that is required for these situations.

The goal of the project reported in this paper was to design a simple event display tool that provided basic trace management support, user-definable event specification, user-customizable graphical presentation based on a standard Gantt chart (timeline) display, and a user-extensible analysis and display architecture. The project was not without an example. In fact, the BBN GIST tool supports some of these features for the Butterfly multiprocessor [4]. We enhanced GIST's functionality in the context of the Cedar multiprocessor system to allow events to be displayed relative to "logical" tasks instead of physical processors only, to provide multiple viewports into the trace, and to run under X Windows. We also provide the user with more flexibility in display customization.

The tool we developed is named JED for (J)ust an (E)vent (D)isplay tool. It uses event traces produced by the Cedar performance measurement system referred to above. The following sections discuss the organization and operation of JED. The mechanisms to extend the standard event analysis and display features of JED are also described.

7.2   Target Environment

The current implementation of JED is targeted at parallel, multitask programs running on the Cedar multiprocessor system. In this environment, parallel programs use the multitasking capabilities of the Xylem operating system to partition themselves into individual tasks for execution on the Cedar clusters. A task can further take advantage of hardware concurrency support on each cluster, an Alliant FX/8, to execute loops in parallel across up to eight processors.

The Cedar performance measurement facility allows the collection of trace data from multiple program tasks. The facility is implemented as a library of counting, timing, and tracing routines that use a trace buffering run-time system for storing performance data. Currently, trace buffers are implemented in software. Every task is assigned eight trace buffers, one for each potentially concurrent execution thread, to be used for tracing during execution.

The measurement facility produces a trace file for each task at program completion that is a time-ordered merge of a task's eight processor trace streams. The file contains a header portion that gives information about the task and about the file such as the number of events generated. The format of an event appearing in a trace file is shown below:

event id
processor id
cluster state
event data size (*dsize*)
timestanp
dsize bytes of event data

All performance measurements made using the library routines are represented as events in the trace. The event data portion is used to store information associated with a particular event. This allows measurements such as task execution times, although not specifically an event, to be recorded as such using a special event id and using the event data field to store the timing data.

7.3 Organization

JED is an X Windows [5] (Version X11.R3) application organized into four separate components; see Figure 7.1. The Trace Control component is responsible for reading the trace, positioning within the trace, and searching for particular events. It provides these functions for each viewport open on the trace. The Event Control component provides event definition services. It allows the user to associate names and graphic icons to events. The event to graphic icon mapping can be controlled interactively as can the visibility of events in a task trace display. The Task Display component opens viewports onto the trace and allows events for tasks assigned to the viewports to be displayed in a Gantt chart-style form. Finally, the Event Display component controls how events are shown when "clicked" on in the task display. A standard event display is provided but the user can override this default by specifying event display modules that will be dynamically linked with JED at run-time; see Event Display section.

The implementation of JED is roughly 6000 lines of C code. It uses the Xt toolkit [6], the Athena widget set [7], and the HP widget set [8]. The current version works both in black and white and in color. The dynamic linking of event display modules is currently being implemented.

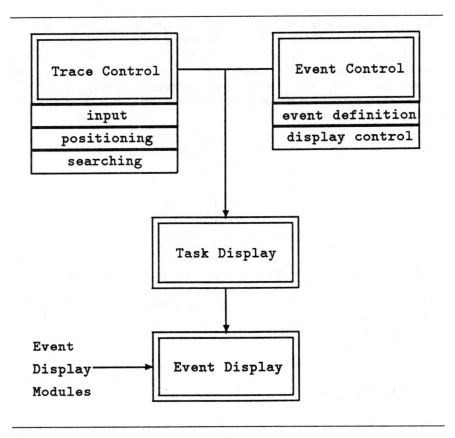

FIGURE 7.1
JED organization.

7.4   Top-Level Interface

The top-level interface to JED is shown in Figure 7.2. It allows the user to input
information as to where the trace files are located and where to find information
about the events that appear in the task traces. The LOAD, NEW TASK
GROUP, and EVENT CONTROL command buttons provide access to the
the trace control, event control, and task display components, respectively. These
are discussed in the following sections. The QUIT button exits JED.

```
┌──────────────────────────────────────────────────────────────┐
│ ⊞ jed ▓▓▓▓▓▓▓▓▓▓▓▓▓▓▓▓▓▓▓▓▓▓▓▓▓▓▓▓▓▓▓▓▓▓▓▓▓▓▓▓▓▓▓▓▓  ▭ ▯│
│                  JED - Just an Event Display                   │
│  Trace Directory:    ┌─────────────────────────────┐          │
│                      │ tests⌄                      │          │
│  Trace File List:    ┌─────────────────────────────┐          │
│                      │ tasks⌄                      │          │
│  Event Directory:    ┌─────────────────────────────┐          │
│                      │ tests⌄                      │          │
│  Event Definition:   ┌─────────────────────────────┐          │
│                      │ events⌄                     │          │
│  Images Directory:   ┌─────────────────────────────┐          │
│                      │ tests⌄                      │          │
│  Image Map:          ┌─────────────────────────────┐          │
│                      │ map⌄                        │          │
│  Event Types:    ┌─────────┐   Total Events:  ┌──────────┐    │
│                  │   40    │                  │   5000   │    │
│  Start Time:     ┌─────────┐   End Time:      ┌──────────┐    │
│                  │    0    │                  │  10000   │    │
│  Total Tasks:    ┌─────────┐                                  │
│                  │    5    │                                  │
│ ┌──────────┬──────────────────┬──────────────────┬──────────┐│
│ │   LOAD   │  NEW TASK GROUP  │  EVENT CONTROL   │   QUIT   ││
│ └──────────┴──────────────────┴──────────────────┴──────────┘│
└──────────────────────────────────────────────────────────────┘
```

FIGURE 7.2
JED top-level interface.

7.5   Trace Control

The trace control portion of JED implements various trace management functions. In particular, it reads task trace files according to the event trace format specification. All trace management functions operate on a per task basis. That is, trace control information is maintained for each task separately allowing operations such as trace positioning to occur on each task independently. The trace control component uses this technique to improve the efficiency of trace handling.

7.5.1   Trace Loading

Clicking the LOAD button in the main panel activates the trace control component. The Trace Directory input string is used as the directory path to find the Trace File List file. The *trace file list* contains a list of task trace files produced by a parallel program execution. In the example in Figure 7.2, the file *tasks* looks like:

```
task.0
task.1
task.2
task.3
task.4
```

The total number of tasks for which trace files are present is reported in the Total Tasks field.

7.5.2 Trace Statistics

JED opens each task trace file and reads its header. From the header, the number of events generated for this task, the time of the START_TASK_TRACE event, and the time of the END_TASK_TRACE event can be determined; START_TASK_TRACE and END_TASK_TRACE are special events inserted by the performance measurement facility . The sum of all task events is reported in the Total Events field. The earliest event time and latest event time across all tasks are shown in the Start Time and End Time fields, respectively.

7.5.3 Task Trace Control

As mentioned earlier, JED maintains separate trace control information for each task. It does so to increase the efficiency of updating the task displays that have different viewports opened on the trace; this will become apparent later. Since the main display items are events from a task trace, JED must be able to quickly interrogate events of a particular task. Maintaining separate task trace files and control information allows this to occur.

The C structure for task trace control information is shown below:

```
typedef struct task
int     tid;                          /* task id for this trace */
int     tracesize;                    /* task trace size        */
int     indexsize;                    /* trace index size       */
int     indexfactor;                  /* trace index factor     */
int     eventcachesize;               /* number in event cache  */
Hrc     begin, end;                   /* beginning, ending time */
Event   event;                        /* current event          */
Event   eventbegin;                   /* beginning event        */
Event   eventend;                     /* ending event           */
Event   eventsearch;                  /* search event           */
Event   eventcache[MAX_EVENT_CACHE];  /* task event cache       */
Index   index[MAX_TRACE_INDEX];       /* trace index array      */
FILE    *file;                        /* task trace file        */
  Task;
```

Because trace files can be large, JED maintains an index of each task trace file for rapid event searching. The *indexfactor* gives the number of events between each event index as determine by *tracesize* and the maximum size of

the index array. Since the index factor is an integer, index array sizes less than
the maximum may result; *indexsize* is the actual size. JED also stores in memory
the beginning and ending event for each task trace. Storage for a search event
is also provided.

Although indexed trace files improves the speed of positioning within a file,
we would like to avoid constantly returning to a task trace file to find events.
This is especially true when studying events local to each other in a trace. The
solution is to cache events for each task. If when looking for an event it is
not found in the cache, it is located in the task trace file and a new block of
events from that event forward *MAX_EVENT_CACHE* events is read into the
event cache. It is hoped that further accessing of events local to this one will
already be present in the cache and will not have to be searched for on disk.

It was found that after implementing the event caching scheme, the speed
of certain operations reflecting local movement within a trace file was significantly improved. These operations include scrolling forward, scrolling backing,
zooming in, and zooming out. Of course, the maximum event cache size determines the locality of event reference that can be supported. This has to be traded
off against the space required to hold the events in memory which additionally
depends on the number of tasks.

7.6 Event Control

The event control component of JED maintains information about the events
appearing in the traces and how they are to be shown in the displays. A definition file is provided at start-up for labeling events and indicating how data for
events should be displayed. Additionally, a user-supplied image map for showing events in task displays is used at start-up to assign default graphic event
icons. Interactive control over how events are displayed is also provided.

7.6.1 Event Definition

The Event Directory and Event Definition input strings together indicate where
the *event definition file* is found. The format on an entry in the file is:

```
event id      event name      "event data format"
```

The *event id* is the integer number of an event as it appears in the trace file. The
event name is character string naming an event. The *event data format* is used
to format data associated with an event in the default event display; see Event
Display section. A few entries from the sample *events* file are shown below:

```
0     Routine_A_entry
1     Routine_B_entry
2     Routine_C_entry
6     Routine_A_exit
7     Routine_B_exit
8     Routine_C_exit
```

In this case, no event data format has been specified.

7.6.2 Event Image Map

The Images Directory and Image Map input strings together indicate where the
event image map file is found. This file contains file names of bitmap images
created by the X Windows application bitmap that will be assigned to events.
The default event icon mapping is to assign successive images to successive
events in a round-robin fashion until all events have been assigned images.
   Some entries from the file *images* are shown below:

```
black
square
boxes
diamond
arrow_down
arrow_left
arrow_right
arrow_up
circle
dot
```

All the images in this example are shown in the *Image Map Window* in
Figure 7.3. Naturally, the user can create her own set of images using the bitmap
program. All images are assumed to be 16×16 pixels. Currently, only black and
white images are accepted. We will be adding the ability to specify foreground
and background colors for images in the future.

7.6.3 Event Control Window

The *Event Control Window* shows the user the current event display control
for each event; see Figure 7.4. The name of the event is given together with
the current icon assignment and a visibility control. The window is scrollable
allowing the user to see all events.
   Clicking on an event's icon opens the image map window. A new icon for
this event can then be selected. This has the immediate effect of replacing the

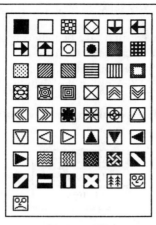

FIGURE 7.3
Event image map.

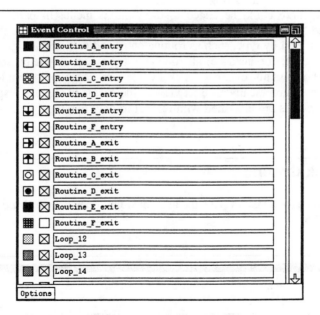

FIGURE 7.4
Event control.

event's old icon with the newly selected on in all task displays; see Task Display section.

The visibility of an event in a task display can be controlled. An event is visible if the *visibility box* is crossed out. This is true of the Routine_A_entry event in Figure 7.4. An empty visibility box indicates the event is invisible as in the case of Routine_F_exit. Clicking on the visibility box toggles the visibility setting.

The items in the Options pop-up menu allow further event display control. They are:

All Visible
All Invisible
All Image
Reset

The All Visible and All Invisible items set all the events to be visible and invisible, respectively. All Image sets all the events to the same graphic image; the image map window is popped-up and the user selects an icon. Reset returns all event image assignments to their original defaults.

Clearly, more could be added to the Options menu. In particular, more sophisticated "event coloring" choices would be useful. The idea is that events could be classified by type, such as routine entry and exit, and assigned an icon based on its type; for instance, all routine entry events might be shown as a black-filled box and all routine exits as a white box. This would enable the user to obtain a more graphically abstract view of the events in the task display. As it is currently, events are classified with respect to only one type, i.e., "an event".

7.7   Task Groups

To see the trace for a task in JED, the user must first open a *Task Group Window*; see Figure 7.5.

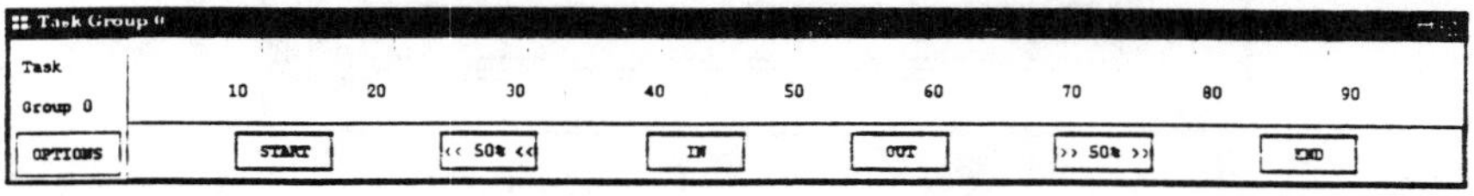

FIGURE 7.5
Task group.

A *task group* is essentially a viewport (time window) into the trace files for all tasks assigned to the task group. A viewport is defined by beginning and ending execution times. The task group window implements operations allowing the attributes of the time window to be changed by scrolling forwards or backwards in time, or by zooming in or zooming out in time. Multiple task groups can be created allowing task events from different times for different tasks to be viewed simultaneously.

7.7.1 Time Ruler

The *time ruler* shown in a task group window shows divisions of the current task group time interval in units of clock ticks. JED makes no assumptions about the resolution of a clock tick.[1] The time values shown are global times across the entire program execution. The difference between the beginning and ending times for a time window defines the current time window *resolution*.

7.7.2 Time Commands

At the bottom of a task group window are commands buttons for changing the attributes of the time window. The START button sets the beginning time to be that of the first event generated across ALL task traces. The time window resolution is maintained so the ending time value is set to be the beginning time plus the resolution; for instance, if the first event occurred at time 100 and the current time window resolution is 1000, clicking START would set the beginning time to 100 and the ending time to 1100. The END button is defined similarly except the ending time is set to the time of the last event generated across ALL task traces.

The ≪ 50% ≪ button scrolls the time window to the left by 50% of the current resolution with the resolution maintained. The ≫ 50% ≫ button scrolls the time window to the right by 50% of the current resolution with the resolution maintained. The IN button zooms in on the current time window by dividing the time interval in half and maintaining the beginning time. The OUT button zooms out (grows) the current time window by twice its size while maintaining the beginning time.

7.7.3 Options

The Options pop-up menu provides functions for adding tasks to a task group, marking interesting points in time, and iconifying or closing the task group window. The menu items are:

---

[1] For the Cedar machine, a clock tick is 10 μseconds.

New Task
Set Mark
Delete Mark
Delete All Marks
Go To Mark
Rotate Marks
Iconify
Close

The New Task item lets the user assign a task to a task group. A list of tasks are shown from which the desired one is selected. A new task display is then created; see Figure 7.6 and the Task Display section. Any or all tasks can be assigned to a task group; notice, it does not make sense to assign the same task to a task group more than once.

JED lets the user to "mark" interesting points in time for a task group. The intent is to let the user return to these interesting points in the future. Setting a mark is done by selecting the Set Mark menu item and then clicking at a point on the current time ruler. When a mark is set it becomes the *current mark*. JED maintains a queue of marks for each task group. A mark icon (a triangle) is shown on the ruler at the time where the mouse click occurred; a black triangle indicates the current mark. Marks can be seen in Figure 7.6.

A variety of things can be done with marks. Delete Mark deletes the current mark. Delete All Marks does what it says for a task group. Go To Mark goes to the current mark. The time window is moved such that the beginning time is that of the mark and the resolution stays the same. Rotate Marks places the current mark at the tail of the mark queue, makes the next mark in the queue the current mark, and goes to that mark.

The Iconify menu item unmaps a task group window and shows it iconified in the top-level window. This feature is currently not implemented although it would be easy to add. Close closes the task group window and all assigned task displays.

7.8 Task Display

A *task display* is a region of the task group window that gets created when a task is assigned to a task group; Figure 7.6 shows a task group window with one task display and Figure 7.7 shows one with two task displays.

The graphics part of the region displays events for the particular task occurring in the time window as defined by the task group. Events are shown by their graphic icons. In the case of our Cedar implementation, task-level concur-

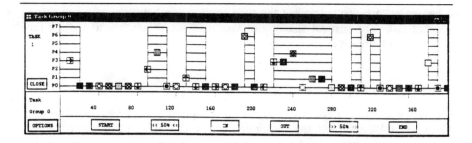

FIGURE 7.6
Task display—one task.

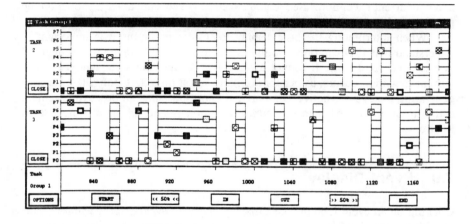

FIGURE 7.7
Task display—two tasks.

rency is also shown in the form of lines of sequential and concurrent activity. The CLOSE button de-assigns a task from a task group.

7.8.1 Gantt Chart Display

The type of display chosen to show task events is a Gantt chart. The intent was to have a simple display that would show event history. The task display does this by showing events for each task assigned to a task group occurring within the task group time window. The horizontal placement of event icons for a particular task display reflect the time relationship between events occurring for that task. The vertical stacking of task displays allows one to see the time relationship between events occurring on different tasks.

7.8.2 Cedar Implementation

The task display for Cedar tasks needs some explaining. Because each task executes on an Alliant FX/8, the cluster component of Cedar, it can take advantage of special concurrency hardware to have up to eight processors working concurrently. Each processor can be generating events. Therefore, there are eight possible event streams for each task.

The events for each processor are shown separately in the task display. Further, concurrency lines are shown to distinguish between periods of sequential and concurrent execution.[2] Sequential execution events are always shown on the processor 1's event line.

When interpreting the task display for Cedar programs it is important to understand that JED can only use the event information to determine sequential versus concurrent state. It cannot assume that at the time a sequential to concurrent transition occurs, as occurs in Figure 7.6 at time 220, only the processor generating the event is active. Similarly, JED must assume all processors remain active until a concurrent to sequential transition is noticed, as at time 280 in Figure 7.6.

7.9   Event Display

Clicking on an event icon in a task display opens an *event display window*. This provides detailed information about that particular event: the event name, the time the event occurred, and some representation of the data field, if any. JED provides a standard textual event display. Additions are being implemented that will allow a user to link to JED his own special displays for certain events.

7.9.1 Standard Event Display

An example of the standard event display is shown in Figure 7.8. It simply gives the event name, the time of the event, and the event data textually formatted using the format string specification from the event definition file.[3] In this example there are no data associated with the event. The CLOSE button closes the

---

[2] Notice, by setting all events to be invisible, only the concurrency lines will be shown allowing the user to observe sequential/concurrent transitions.

[3] At this time, textual event data formatting is not implemented.

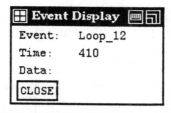

FIGURE 7.8
Event display.

event display window. An event display window can also be closed by again clicking on the event icon.

The BBN GIST tool also has this capability of popping-up a textual event display window. In fact, the idea of using a format specification string to format the event data was borrowed from GIST.

7.9.2 Custom Event Displays

Often the event data can be represented in ways other than textually. Also, a large amount of event data can pose problems with textual event layout. For instance, an event trace may contain events recording the number of entries in a work queue. It might be desired to show these data in the form of a bargraph with the amount the bargraph is filled relative to the number of queue entries.

To provide the capability for extending the standard set of event displays, we are taking the following approach in JED; see Figure 7.9. An interface is specified in JED that allows user-defined event displays to be linked with the JED program. Essentially this interface passes an event structure from JED to a user's event display through a special *create event display* routine specific for that display. The event display interprets the event information and presents the data accordingly. JED also requires the event display modules to support a *close event display* routine to be used for closing event display windows from JED.

User-defined event display modules will be specified as part of the event definition file. For each event, there will be an indication as to what event display to use—standard or user-defined—and if user-defined, where the event display object code module resides. JED will make use of an object code instrumentation tool developed for Cedar to perform the module linking.

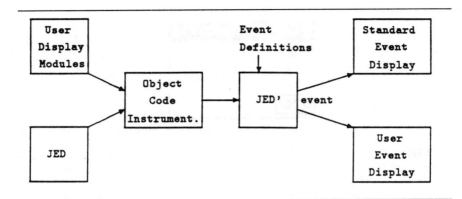

FIGURE 7.9
User-defined event displays.

7.10 Conclusion

The JED tool attempts to fill a gap between rudimentary performance reporting tools and sophisticated performance analysis and visualization systems. JED concentrates on managing and displaying event traces produced from parallel, multitasked programs running on multiprocessor systems. Currently, JED is working for traces from programs running on the Cedar machine.

Schemes have been implemented in JED to improve the efficiency of browsing multiple, potentially large, task event traces. These include per task trace control, indexing of task trace files, and event caching

Certain decisions about task trace displays and event displays have been made in JED. A Gantt chart-style display was selected because it shows event history and the time relationship between events. Events are represented in this display as graphic icons. JED support multiple viewing ports onto the traces allowing events from multiple tasks to be seen from different time periods simultaneously. Details of an event can be shown using the standard textual event display.

JED can be customized in several ways. First, there are no assumptions about events except for the event format. All event information is provided by the event definition file set up by the user. This includes the event id, event name, textual format specification, and special event displays. Second, the user can control how events are shown in the task displays using special image maps. Finally, the user can replace the standard textual event display with a custom

display. For the Cedar implementation, we are building event display modules
to show counting, timing, and virtual memory statistics.

References

1. Allen D. Malony, *Program Tracing in Cedar*, CSRD Report No. 660, University of Illinois at Urbana-hampaign, April 1987.

2. K. Gallivan, W. Jalby, A. Malony, and P.-C. Yew, *Performance Analysis on the Cedar System*, CSRD Report No. 680, University of Illinois at Urbana-Champaign, June 1988.

3. A. Malony, D. Reed, R. Aydt, B. Totty, J. Arendt, and D. Grabas, *An Integrated Performance Data Collection, Analysis, and Visualization System*, 4th Conf. on Hypercubes, Concurrent Computers, and Applications, March 1988.

4. *GIST User's Manual*, Bolt, Beranek and Newman, 1988.

5. R. Scheifler and J. Gettys, *The X Window System*, ACM Trans. on Graphics, Vol. 5, No. 2, April 1986, pp. 79–109.

6. J. McCormak, P. Asente, R. Swick, *X Toolkit Intrinsics – C Language Interface*, MIT, 1988.

7. Ralph R. Swick and Terry Weissman, *X Toolkit Athena Widgets – C Language Interface*, MIT, 1988.

8. *Programming With the HP X Widgets*, Hewlett-Packard, Nov. 1988.

8

Support Environment for RP3 Performance Monitor

William C. Brantley
Henry Y. Chang

8.1 Introduction

The performance of a parallel application on a multiprocessor is affected by a plethora of factors which include algorithm design, program construct, operating system, and hardware architecture. Due to the complex interplay between these factors, it is necessary to take a holistic approach to collect and interpret performance data. To find out how each factor contributes to the overall performance, one must collect performance data from each component and analyze the data as a whole. To help users achieve this goal, one needs a set of integrated tools for data collection, data visualization, and data analysis. Because that data visualization and analysis rely on a large quantity of high quality data, data collection is the first and most important step of performance analysis.

Data collection in general faces a dilemma of quantity and quality. The amount of data collected is proportional to the perturbation to the system, which is translated into worse quality data. On the other hand, minimal instrumentation with minimal perturbation to the system generates higher quality data, but the data often tell little about interesting dynamic behavior of the system.

The performance monitoring hardware for existing systems fall into two camps, the full service camp and the self-service camp. In the full service camp, each processor is shadowed by another monitoring processor which is powerful enough to do complicated event detection, data reduction, or even real-time visualization. These shadow processors form a separate distributed network side by side with the existing network of processors. For example, Sequent [1] has a resource monitoring system that is capable of catching user-defined events and returning resource usage among events to a data analysis computer.

In the self-service camp, the performance monitoring hardware is an I/O device. The device is controlled by the processor, thus demands a certain portion of processor capacity. The device is often limited by resource. In order to collect information from more than one group of counters, a performance experiment may need to be repeated multiple times. For example, Cray offers a performance monitoring hardware for each processor, which contains eight multiplexed counters among four group of events. In order to get a complete set of data, one either alternates the counters among event groups or repeats the same experiment four times [2].

In this paper, we present the instrumentation of a self-service performance monitor for RP3, a 64-way prototype shared-memory parallel processor. We will briefly discuss our hardware performance monitoring facility and then focus on the operating system (OS) instrumentation. We then examine trade-offs of function, perturbation, and timeliness of data collection.

8.2   Overview of RP3 Performance Monitor

The IBM Research Parallel Processor [3,4] is a prototype highly parallel processor intended to be used to gain insight into closely-coupled shared-memory machine organizations. The RP3 has a rich memory hierarchy including cache, local and global addressing, with interleaving and address hashing available for global memory references. The ratio of access times for global memory references to local to cache references is 16:10:1 on a moderately loaded interconnection network. Partitioning of the memory hierarchy into its various levels is under dynamic software control. The RP3 also has built in Performance Measuring Circuitry (PMC) [5] capable of nearly unobtrusive measurement of many system activities.

There is one PMC for each processor shown in Figure 8.1. The PMC is connected to components of a Processor Memory Element (PME) that transmit events and samples to the PMC without interfering with PME operation. The PMC counts the occurrences of specific events in the PME and also collects sample information from both the PME network interface (NI) and the processor bus.

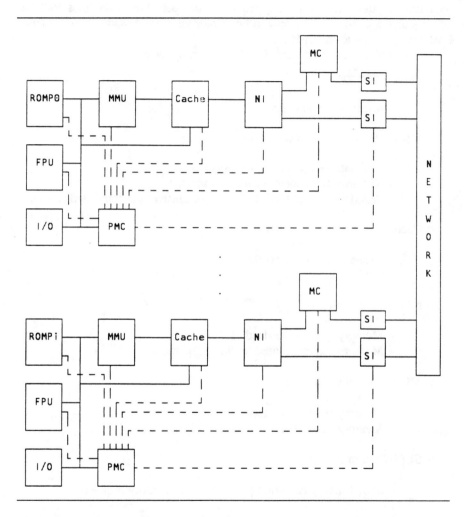

FIGURE 8.1
RP3 data flow showing PMCs with each processor.

The PMC can be accessed by both processor and I/O processor. The PMC's internal registers, counters, and sample memory are accessible via processor I/O reads and writes that can be initiated by both processor and I/O processor. The data flow of the PME node is given in Figure 8.1. The solid lines indicate address and data busses. The broken lines indicate event or sample busses from PME components to the PMC.

The PMC contains counters for the following events:

□ PME processor

  – Instruction completed

□ MMU (Memory management unit)

  – Translated memory request serviced
  – Non-translated memory request serviced
  – Translation Lookaside Buffer miss caused by a translated request

□ Cache

  – Cacheable request serviced
  – Cache miss

□ NI (Network Interface)

  – Memory request serviced
  – Memory request routed to "local" memory

□ MC (Memory controller)

  – Memory request serviced
  – Memory subsystem busy

□ SI (Switch interface)

  – Switch interface waiting to transmit a memory request

The PMC also provides a 16 sample circular buffer. One can sample at rates of one sample per 2K, 8K, 32K, or 128K cycles. There are two kinds of sampled data: absolute address samples from NI and virtual address samples as they appear on the processor bus.

The PMC counters are consistent with each other in values. When any PMC counter overflows, the PMC stops all counters and interrupts the kernel. This lock-step feature guarantees counter values to be mutually consistent.

8.3 User Mode Access to PMC

A processor can start or stop acquisition by its PMC or read/write its PMC's registers in both supervisor and user modes. The advantage of using the PMC directly in user mode is its low overhead and the precision with which it can be started. With the cost of one I/O instruction, a user can stop or start the PMC at a precise location in the program. In addition, it takes only 50 instructions for the user to read out the PMC contents – an order of magnitude faster than a system call. The disadvantage is the small time for which a program can be measured; a program segment longer than a second can not be measured because of PMC counter overflow.

Furthermore, the program may be context-switched while using the PMC. The program may resume in a processor different from the original one, losing track of PMC data. Even if the program stays on the same processor, the PMC may have been polluted by other programs and system activities. To maintain PMC data integrity, one needs a scheme to detect context switches and to throw away bad data. We use a scheme based on the fact that the operating system clears the PMC annotation registers as part of the context switch operation. To detect bad data, the program writes to the PMC annotation register a unique number at the beginning of measurement and then compares the annotation register with the written value at the end of the measurement. If the unique number matches the value read, the PMC data is good; otherwise, the data are thrown away. The percentage of bad data may be high depending on the system load and the frequency of user system calls. A user system call, if it requires a serial OS service, switches the user program to the master processor for service.

8.4 Virtual PMC

Virtualization of the PMC helps protect the integrity of PMC data. First of all, the kernel extends the PMC counters by accumulating the PMC data over a long period into the large virtual PMC counters. Secondly, the kernel saves and restores virtual counters at context-switch time. The virtual counters are updated both when the PMC overflows and when the monitored program is preempted by the OS. When the monitored program resumes, the PMC is also restarted.

The Virtual PMC (VPMC) is the kernel data structure that accumulates the PMC data and the basis of the user interface. The VPMC contains the following data from the PMC and the operating system:

- 64-bit virtual counters
- system event counters
- histogram for network delay sample data

The 64-bit virtual counters are large enough for a month long computation. The system events include data such as the number of context switches. The histogram, which requires on-line data reduction, is necessitated by the amount of data produced by the PMC sampling mechanism.

The target of the VPMC is either a processor or a thread. A processor is a particular hardware processor, while a thread is a schedulable unit of flow of control to the MACH operating system. A UNIX[1] process is split into the passive task resource, and the active thread in MACH. A task may have several threads sharing the same virtual address space. The processor-based VPMC tracks the performance of each processor, while the thread-based VPMC tracks the performance of a specific thread. By tracking the performance, we mean recording PMC and system events as they occur, while the thread is running.

The processor-based VPMC and the thread-based VPMC may run concurrently. The kernel supports both VPMCs by sharing the same PMC information. Since the PMC counters are selectable, conflict in selection may happen. Priority is given to processor-based VPMC selection. The user of a thread-based VPMC may detect that its mode selection has been overwritten by comparing its original setting with current status.

The VPMC monitors processor activity at all times other than when the VPMC is being updated with the current PMC value. During update time, the PMC is stopped to allow consistent information be read out of the PMC. In other words, the VPMC service itself is excluded from the VPMC monitoring. Our measurement indicates that VPMC update adds less than 0.2% of overhead to the system.

8.5   VPMC System Interface

A system call interface provides users access to VPMC data. The interface is built on the MACH [6] operating system, which is a Carnegie Mellon University dialect of Unix. The VPMC system interface allows a user

   □ to activate a VPMC,

   □ to read VPMC (via either MACH IPC or UNIX call)

   □ to map the VPMC data area into user's address space.

   □ to close a VPMC

Details of system calls are in the appendix.

This interface provides several VPMC access methods to the user. Multiple access methods provide trade-offs in overhead and flexibility of the service.

---

[1] UNIX is a trademark of AT&T.

8.5.1 Reading the VPMC via Mapped Memory

The VPMC can be mapped into a user address space to facilitate access. Changes to the VPMC are thus immediately available to the user. A concurrent reader/writer algorithm needs to be incorporated to avoid reading inconsistent data due to concurrent kernel updating activities. The mapping reduces the cost of accessing the VPMC to that of examining a data structure in memory. The disadvantage is that the user must synchronize its VPMC access with the asynchronous update of the kernel.

8.5.2 Reading the VPMC via UNIX Call

A new UNIX system call is added for VPMC read, which lacks the generality of MACH IPC yet runs four times faster.

8.5.3 Reading the VPMC via MACH IPC

MACH IPC (InterProcess Communication) port allows a user to send/receive messages to/from the kernel or to/from another user. The mechanism hides the identity and the location of the user through communication ports. Based on this mechanism, a user may read the VPMC data from a remote workstation with the help of TCP/IP server. The costs of the access methods are tabulated in Table 8.1.

In our experience, direct access to PMC and memory mapped VPMC access are the preferred methods. The behavior of parallel programs is often nondeterministic and thus strongly correlated to how multiple threads synchronize with each other. Since synchronization order may be sensitive to perturbation, low perturbation monitoring is crucial to keeping the program behavior unaffected.

8.6 Example Uses

This section demonstrates two uses of the monitoring mechanisms. The first uses the processor-based VPMC to display system level performance. The second uses the PMC directly to estimate a histogram of memory access times during an application.

8.6.1 Workload Example

Figure 8.2 shows the performance of the workload of two applications during a 1250 second period on processor 48. The processor instructions executed and

TABLE 8.1
Overhead of VPMC Access Methods

| | Number of | |
Access Method	Instructions	Cost
Direct Access to PMC hardware	50	Fast but short coverage
Memory mapped VPMC access	500	Fast and long coverage
UNIX system call VPMC access	3000	Synchronous access
MACH IPC VPMC access	14000	Network transparent access

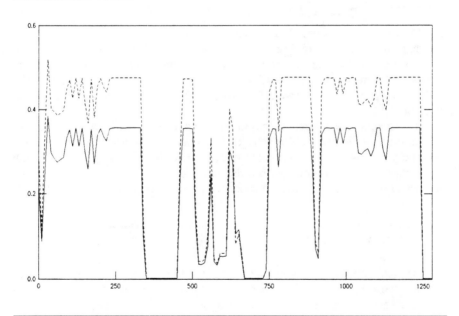

FIGURE 8.2
Workload for 1200 seconds on PME 48. Top line shows memory references made and the bottom shows instructions executed by processor 48. Both are normalized to the number of processor cycles.

the number of cache references made per processor cycle are shown. These data were acquired using the processor-based VPMC. A single processor was dedicated to acquiring the activity on the other 63 processors' processor-based VPMC. This sampling was done every ten seconds.

At the left of Figure 8.2 is the end of the execution of a hydrodynamics code. In the middle is the execution of a prime sieve. At the right, is another hydrodynamics execution. The activity of processor 0 is shown on Figure 8.3. Note that when processor 48 is active, processor 0 is not and vice versa. This is due to the version of the MACH operating system which is asymmetric. Many kernel services, including I/O, must be done by processor 0 *only*. A future version will remedy the asymmetry for most services.

8.6.2 Latency Example

Figure 8.4 and Figure 8.5 are histograms of memory references sampled during the execution of a prime sieve application. Since the VPMC does not yet acquire the sampled data from the PMC hardware, the histograms were acquired by self monitoring; that is, the application itself controlled the PMCs. Memory latency is based on samples of memory references acquired by each PMC every 2k processor cycles.

Note that both latency histograms are bimodal. One peak is centered around 12 cycles and goes to zero before the second peak. The first peak represents the requests to local memory. The other peak is due to the nonlocal references. From the figure one can see that most nonlocal references take an average of five cycles longer on the 8-way than on the 64-way machine. This is due to the additional latency of the CMOS switch. The CMOS switch components have twelve times the latency of the 64-way's bipolar switch. These measurements have confirmed our knowledge.

The measurement also uncovers a surprise that occurred on the 64-way. In Figure 8.4 the tail of the distribution, though small, extends beyond 900 cycles! Studying the information in the reference samples shows that the majority of these long references were memory swaps, an instruction used in the MACH kernel busy-wait routine. These data suggest that a "hotspot" occurred during one of the kernel busy-wait routines.

8.7 Discussion

The experience using the RP3 PMC hardware directly from an application suggests two areas of improvements for a hardware PMC. The major area is in adding support for monitoring a single user process. The second area is in help-

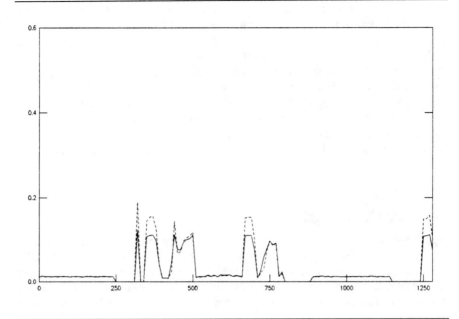

FIGURE 8.3
Workload for 1200 seconds on PME 00. Top line shows memory references
made and the bottom shows instructions executed by processor 0. Both are
normalized to the number of processor cycles.

ing correlate PMC data from multiple processors. A PMC needs the following
extensions to monitor an individual process.

☐ **Allow state to be restored by OS.**

Currently, an OS can write little of the PMC state; the remainder of the state
can only be cleared. Thus, once a thread is migrated from one machine to
another, its PMC state is lost since the state from the previous processor's
PMC cannot be written into the new processor's PMC. For this reason,
a thread needs the thread-based VPMC just to get consistent PMC data.
If the OS could restore the PMC state, the need for thread-based VPMC
might be eliminated. Furthermore, the ability to restore counters could
itself be part of a performance debugging tool by making use of the fact
that the PMC generates an interrupt whenever any counter overflows. For
example, a processor could initialize the PMC to interrupt the processor on
its hundredth remote memory reference by preloading the remote memory
reference counter with its overflow value less 100.

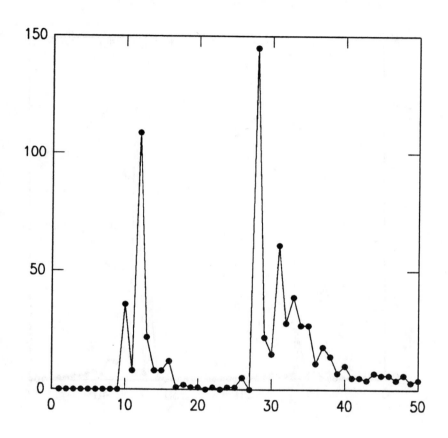

FIGURE 8.4
Histogram of memory latency during prime sieve application on 64-way RP3
(uses fast ECL switch). Abscissa is memory latency from the NI chip.
Ordinate is the number of references sampled having the memory latency
shown on the abscissa.

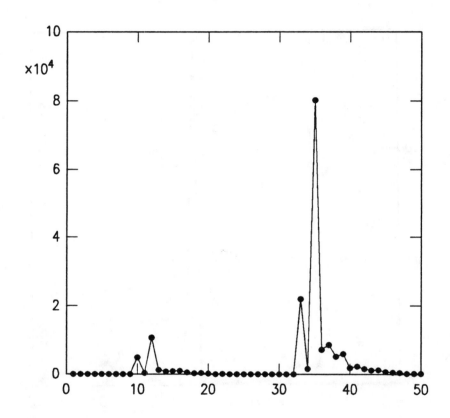

FIGURE 8.5
Histogram of memory latency during prime sieve application on 8-way
processor (uses slower CMOS switch). Abscissa is memory latency from the
NI chip. Ordinate is the number of references sampled having the memory
latency shown on the abscissa.

□ **Longer counters.**

Longer counters would reduce the frequency of PMC overflow, and afford the kernel the option to reflect an overflow interrupt to the user directly. This would not only help reduce the overhead of PMC management, but might also eliminate the need for the thread-based VPMC.

□ **User mode enable/disable by the OS.**

Currently, PMC is readable/writable by both the OS and user programs. While OS is managing the PMC and maintains a virtual image of PMC, the user can mess up the PMC contents and thus destroy the integrity of VPMC data. The integrity of VPMC data can only be guaranteed if user's access to PMC is controlled by the OS.

We have also found it difficult to correlate data from different PMCs. The problem with reconstructing a total picture of the system from individual PMCs is the lack of a high resolution clock. Although the low resolution clock in each ROMP processor is adequate for user timeout service, high precision clocks are needed for PMC performance work. Note that PMC counters are updated every machine cycle (several times per microsecond), while the ROMP clock advances every millisecond. Not only must the clock have high resolution, accesses to it must not interfere with one another. If there were only a single clock, then switch congestion in reading the clock could substantially reduce the precision of clock readings. Alternatively, a high precision clock could be a part of each processor. These independent clocks could be synchronized by software, if necessary.

8.8 Summary

We have described how the RP3 PMCs may be used directly and the limitations thereof. In addition, we have described the Virtual PMC implemented within the MACH operating system. The VPMC overcomes the shortcomings of direct use of the PMC. We have demonstrated that the overhead in using and maintaining the VPMCs is minimal. We showed one example of using the processor-based VPMC for system level monitoring. Another example showed the PMC being used directly to estimate the memory latency distribution.

Future measurement tools [7] will be constructed to allow interactive monitoring.

Acknowledgments

Kevin McAuliffe and Ton Ngo made major contributions to the RP3 performance monitor chip design and its first use. Ray Bryant suggested virtualizing the PMC.

Tony Bolmarcich incorporated PMC and VPMC drivers into EPEX. This work was sponsored in part by Defense Advanced Research Projects Agency under contract # N00039-87-C-0122.

References

1. S. S. Thakkar, "Parallel Programming: A Performance Perspective" in Parallel Computing Systems: Performance Instrumentation and Visualization, R. Koskela and M. Simmons, Addison-Wesley, 1990.

2. E. Williams, T. Myers, and R. Koskela, "The Characterization of Two Scientific Workloads Using the Cray X-MP Performance Monitor", Supercomputing Research Center SYS-89-012, 1989.

3. W. C. Brantley, K. P. McAuliffe, and J. Weiss, "RP3 Processor-Memory Element", Proceedings of the 1985 International Conference on Parallel Processing, 782-789, 1985.

4. G. F. Pfister, W. C. Brantley, D. A. George, S. L. Harvey, W. J. Kleinfelder, K. P. McAuliffe, E. A. Melton, V. A. Norton, and J. Weiss, "The IBM Research Parallel Processor Prototype (RP3): Introduction and Architecture" in Proceedings of the 1985 International Conference on Parallel Processing, 764-771, 1985.

5. W. C. Brantley, K. P. McAuliffe, and T. A. Ngo, "RP3 Performance Monitoring Hardware" in Instrumentation for Parallel Computer Systems, M. Simmons, R. Koskela, and I. Bucher, Addison-Wesley,35-47, 1989.

6. M. Accetta, R. Baron, W. Bolosky, D. Golub, R. Rashid, A. Tevanian, and M. Young, "Mach: A New Kernel Foundation for UNIX Development", Proceedings of Summer Usenix, 1986.

7. D. N. Kimelman, "Environments for Visualization of Program Execution", in Parallel Computing Systems: Performance Instrumentation and Visualization, R. Koskela and M. Simmons, Addison-Wesley, 1990.

Appendix A

The kernel extends the useability of the PMC by accumulating the counter information upon PMC counter overflow in a kernel data structure called the Virtual PMC, VPMC. With the VPMC, a user can get the performance data of the whole system, or that of a particular thread in a program. A VPMC contains 13 64-bit virtual counters as well as values of the PMC status register and cache control register.

VPMC support comes in two flavors: processor-based VPMC and thread-based VPMC. The processor-based VPMC supports one VPMC structure for each processor in the system. The thread-based VPMC supports a VPMC structure for a thread, which accumulates PMC data while the thread is running, independent of the PME on which the thread is running.

8.8.1   sysmon_setup (MACH IPC)

sysmon_setup – sets up system wide performance monitoring

sysmon_setup enables processor-based RP3 performance monitoring. One virtual PMC area is allocated for each processor. The *mode* controls the operating modes of the PMC. The following modes are supported:

```
V_CACHE_ALL           /* count all cacheable reference */
V_CACHE_INST          /* count only cacheable instruction reference */
V_CACHE_DATA          /* count only cacheable data reference */
V_CACHE_DATA_READ     /* count only cacheable data read reference */
V_USER_MODE           /* count user mode instructions */
V_SYS_MODE            /* count system mode instructions */
```

The user may change the mode setting of current PMC measurement by calling sysmon_setup again. Once processor-based VPMCs are activated, any thread can read from it, but only the originating thread may change its operating mode.

If there are active thread-based VPMCs, the mode selection of thread-based VPMC will be overwritten by this processor-based VPMC setup request. The thread-based VPMC user may detect being overruled by comparing its current VPMC status with its original setting.

8.8.2   sysmon_off (MACH IPC)

sysmon_off – turns off system-wide performance monitoring

sysmon_off – stops processor-based performance monitoring and deallocates kernel data structure. Subsequent reading of VPMC data will fail.

8.8.3   sysmon_read (UNIX syscall)

sysmon_read – reads the VPMC data of the target processor

sysmon_read reads the VPMC data structure of processor *cpu* and returns the data in buffer *vpmcd*.

8.8.4   perfmon_setup (MACH IPC)

perfmon_setup – sets up performance monitoring

perfmon_setup enables thread-based RP3 performance monitoring of thread *th*. A VPMC area is allocated in the kernel for the thread. The *mode* controls the operating modes of the PMC when the thread is running, which has the following options.

V_CACHE_ALL	/* count all cacheable references */
V_CACHE_INST	/* count only cacheable instruction references */
V_CACHE_DATA	/* count only cacheable data references */
V_CACHE_DATA_READ	/* count only cacheable data read references */
V_USER_MODE	/* count user mode instructions */
V_SYS_MODE	/* count system mode instructions */

Subsequent calls by the same thread change the mode setting of current PMC measurement to the newest setting. The mode selection of a thread-based VPMC is over-ruled whenever the processor-based VPMC is activated.

8.8.5   perfmon_off (MACH IPC)

perfmon_off – turns off performance monitoring

perfmon_off stops performance monitoring of thread *th* and deallocates the kernel data structure. Subsequent reading of VPMC data will fail.

8.8.6   perfmon_read (UNIX syscall)

perfmon_read – reads the VPMC data of the target thread

perfmon_read updates then reads the VPMC data structure of thread *th* and puts it into buffer *vpmcd*. Note: the VPMC is not updated before reading unless the *th* thread is the current thread.

8.8.7   perfmon_map

perfmon_map – maps the kernel VPMC area of the thread into user virtual address space

perfmon_map maps the kernel VPMC area of thread *th* into the caller's virtual address space, and return the created address to vpmcd_addr. User's maximal access right to the area is read only.

Since the VPMC is updated only at overflow or context switch time, the VPMC data is likely to be stale. Thread *th* may obtain up-to-date data for itself by summing values in hardware PMC counters and virtual VPMC counters. A library routine *readpmc(mapped_vpmc, result_vpmc)* has been provided to do just that.

After the performance monitor is turned off, the values in this mapped area become undefined, since subsequent thread-based VPMC setup recycles the area.

8.8.8   getvpmcdiff (memory map)

getvpmcdiff – returns the change of the thread-based VPMC of the calling thread since last call. (Note: This is a library routine.)

getvpmcdiff returns changes of the VPMC since the last call to *vp*. A null argument establishes a new base of comparison for the next call. This routine automatically initializes the thread-based VPMC and the PMC with a default mode of V_USER_MODE|V_SYS_MODE. The user can change the default mode by changing the value of an external global variable *default_vpmc_mode* before the routine is ever called.

The first time the routine is called, it allocates a unique data area and initializes thread-based VPMC for the calling thread. Subsequent calls of the thread will operate in its unique data area. To gain efficiency, the routine accesses VPMC via memory-mapped method.

The routine supports multiple threads concurrently sharing the same address space. Data corruption will not occur because calls made by different threads utilize different data areas.

8.8.9   readpmc (memory map)

readpmc – returns up-to-date VPMC data by accessing and summing up both hardware PMC and mapped VPMC (Note: This is a library routine.).

Combines values in the mapped VPMC *vp_mapped* with values in hardware PMC registers to return up-to-date VPMC data in structure it vp_user.

8.8.10   diffvpmc

diffvpmc – gets the difference of two VPMC data structures (Note: This is a library routine.).

Subtract values in VPMC *vp2* from values in VPMC *vp1* and returns results in VPMC *vp_result*. All subtraction is done in double precision integer arithmetic. Values of status, cache control, annotation registers are copied from *vp1* to *vp_result*.

9

Environments for Visualization of Program Execution

Doug Kimelman

The speedups promised for parallel systems often prove to be somewhat elusive. This paper discusses one important aspect of performance analysis and tuning: *program visualization* — helping programmers visualize the behavior of an application or system by presenting its state and progress graphically.

A working prototype for visualizing a matrix processing application is described, and a second-generation environment for visualizing program execution is proposed.

9.1 Introduction

The speedups promised for parallel systems often prove to be somewhat elusive. It is often the case during software development for large scale, high performance, parallel systems that a programmer starts an application running and then waits... and wonders, "Is it making any progress at all?" If it is, is it operating correctly? On an absolute scale, what is its performance? Further, regardless of absolute performance, will it run faster given more processors?

Debugging and tuning have always been difficult areas. Parallel systems just compound matters. Most often, interactive debuggers are not available in such situations (although much research has recently been devoted to achieving such a capability). In cases where debuggers do exist, they typically provide only rudimentary support for parallelism. Programmers can suspend execution and examine state, but they achieve only disjoint snapshots of small subsets of the total program state. Significant events can easily be missed or overlooked. If a tracing facility exists, the programmer is quickly overwhelmed by volumes of textual output.

There is a most pressing requirement for continuous graphic presentation of a program's behavior. People deal much more effectively with large amounts of data at high rates when the data are presented in a dynamic graphic fashion. Information is more rapidly assimilated, and trends and anomalies are much more readily recognized. This has recently been reaffirmed by the success of scientific visualization in the computational sciences. There, vast amounts of data are generated by simulations or real experiments, for review by the systems' users.

Program visualization is the area of helping programmers visualize the behavior of a program in execution, as opposed to visualizing scientific data or dynamic models, by presenting the program's state and progress graphically. Program visualization is increasingly becoming recognized as an important aspect of both debugging and tuning, especially for large scale parallel systems [1-3].

9.2   One View of Program Visualization

In certain respects, it seems that tools for analysis of software behavior lag far behind those for analysis of hardware. Our general approach to program visualization arises out of a software developer's (undoubtedly naive) perspective of hardware development. From this perspective, when (at least at some level) hardware under development malfunctions or behaves unexpectedly, a developer:

- rolls up a cart loaded with diagnostic equipment;
- latches onto a board with clips, extenders, probes, indicators, meters, scopes, and analyzers; and
- rapidly achieves a good graphic characterization of the logic's behavior.

Our goal is to establish this type of facility in the software domain. For a multi-threaded application, one should be able to:

- set up a graphic representation of the program;
- run it until some condition of interest is encountered;
- stop, and run backward looking for what lead up to this situation;

□ possibly, change the view of the program based on intuition concerning the underlying cause of the situation, and then run forward again;

□ continually refining the view of the program and replaying execution, in order to gain an understanding of the program's (mis)behavior.

Thus, our overall goal is to be able to rapidly achieve good graphic characterization of a program in execution.

Providing this type of facility may seem formidable. It is encouraging however to consider that even the simplest "visualization tools" have proven to be remarkably effective. A most striking example of this is the "flashing lights" found on the console panel of some systems. By the accounts of systems programmers for machines such as the RP3 and the BBN Butterfly, these lights have been invaluable. They often are as simple as a light per processor, and a light per memory unit, glowing brighter with greater activity. To the "seasoned observer", they indicate what's running and what is not, which phase a computation is in, which memory units are taking a beating and which processors are idling and which are spinning, and, "occasionally", the lights provide an indication that the system has deadlocked. As much as anything, this is a tribute to our capacity for pattern recognition, given even just a minimum of input. Without these aids, programmers could spend a lot of time wondering what, if anything, is happening inside a system, and periodically probing system state through console terminals.

An "order of magnitude" improvement over this simple facility could be achieved by generalizing the processor busy light to indicate where in the code a processor is executing. The program counter of each processor could be sampled periodically, and a floating spot could be displayed for each processor beside a listing of the program symbol table (possibly concatenated with the runtime and kernel symbol tables). Old spots could fade slowly away as new ones are plotted to provide an approximation to the program call stacks.

9.3   The RP3 Environment

The context for this work on program visualization is the IBM Research Parallel Processor Prototype (RP3) project [4]. The RP3 is an experimental 64-way shared-memory multiprocessor. Each of the 64 Processor-Memory Elements (PMEs) consists of a processor, a floating point unit, a memory management unit, an I/O interface, a performance monitor, a cache, and 8 megabytes (MB) of memory. The PMEs are interconnected by a multi-stage packet-switched omega network. The relative access times for references by a processor to its PME's cache, to its PME's memory ("local"), and to some other PME's memory ("global"), are 1, 10, and 16.

The RP3 was designed as a flexible, dynamically reconfigurable platform
for studying and experimenting with highly parallel architectures, systems, and
applications. An important manifestation of the orientation towards experimentation and analysis is the per-processor Performance Monitor Chip (PMC) [5].
The PMC contains a set of counters for events such as instruction completions,
memory references, cache and Translation Look-aside Buffer (TLB) misses, local and global memory requests, and requests to the local memory from all
processors. The PMC also contains buffers for virtual or absolute address samples.

The MACH operating system [6] has been ported to RP3, and has been
extended to provide control over RP3's unique architectural features [7]. Support
for the PMC has been incorporated into the kernel in the form of a Virtual PMC
(VPMC) facility [8]. The VPMC facility provides an application with the illusion
of much larger event counters, which overflow much less often, and PMCs that
follow a thread across context switches and across different processors.

A MACH system running on an IBM mainframe (on a virtual 370) serves
as the RP3's path to its users. The RP3 shares disks with the MACH/370 system,
and communicates with it using TCP/IP. The MACH/370 system manages batch
job queues for the RP3, and provides a gateway onto a local area network.
Residing on the network are a number of workstations, on which visualization
software can be run, and from which applications can be prepared and run
on the RP3. Finally, there is a gateway from the local area network out onto
NYSERNet and the Internet beyond.

9.4   A Prototype Visualization System

A prototype visualization system has been developed for the RP3, as an illustration of concept. A multi-threaded matrix processing application is instrumented
using a preprocessor. This instrumentation provides information, in the form
of event records, concerning the state and progress of the application. Event
records are also produced from VPMC data obtained from the kernel. The event
stream is either saved on disk, or passed live to a visualization workstation over
UDP/IP. The workstation provides either live or post-mortem replay of the program's execution, allowing the user to browse back and forth through the event
stream graphically.

9.4.1   The Application

The application, contrived for purposes of this experiment, processes the columns
of a matrix in order, one at a time. There are two phases in the processing of a
column. In the first phase (as depicted in the display in Figure 9.1, in a manner
discussed below), each thread takes an element of the column and evaluates a
function at that element. The time required for the function evaluation varies

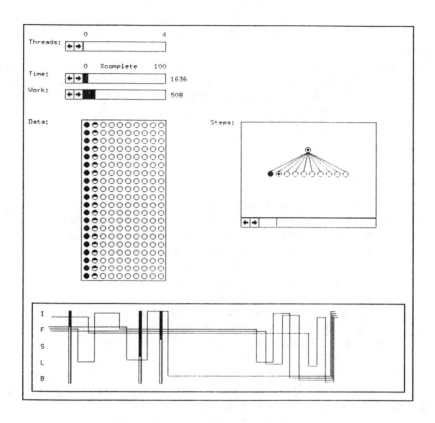

FIGURE 9.1
The main display.

widely from element to element, and is related to the value of the element.
Upon completing the function evaluation, the thread locks a per-column shared
variable and adds the result of the function evaluation to that shared variable
(the application was originally written for machines that do not provide the
fetch-and-op instruction offered by the RP3). The thread then releases the lock
on the shared variable and returns to the column to find another element that has
yet to be processed. When all the elements of a column have been processed,
a thread finds that no work remains to be done in this phase, and proceeds to
a barrier synchronization point. Once all of the threads have finished their last
element and arrived at the barrier, the barrier synchronization is complete, and
the second phase of the processing of the column begins.

In the second phase, each thread takes a number of elements at a time, and subtracts from each of them the sum accumulated in the shared variable earlier. The thread then returns to the column for another group of elements to be processed. The elements are taken a group or "chunk" at a time because the processing time for each element is small in comparison to the overhead of picking up another piece of work to perform. When no work remains to be done in the second phase, the threads proceed to a second barrier synchronization point, and then on to processing the next column.

9.4.2 The Display

Figure 9.1 is a screen dump showing the main display panel of the prototype visualization system, at the instant in time when the first phase of processing has just been completed for the second column. The display contains both data-oriented components and thread-oriented components. The display also shows statistics concerning the run. These include the number of events and the amount of time that have passed so far, and the number of threads that are actively processing an element at the present time.

The data-oriented component depicts a 20 by 10 matrix of elements. An element is shown hollow if it has yet to be processed at all, half-full if its first phase processing is complete, and completely full if its second phase processing is complete.

The thread-oriented component depicts the state history of each thread in the form of an advancing timing diagram, with one trace line for each thread. The trace lines advance to the right as time passes, and wrap from the right edge of the display back around to the left. The left edge of the timing diagram is annotated to indicate five higher level states through which a thread progresses:

'I' — getting more work;

'F' — evaluating the function at some element;

'S' — subtracting the accumulated sum from some element;

'L' — waiting for, and then holding, the lock for the shared variable; and

'B' — waiting at a barrier synchronization point.

The thick vertical bars appearing occasionally along the diagram are an elision mechanism. They indicate that time passed without any state changes. The height of the hollow bar inside the dark bar indicates the amount of time that passed — a full height hollow bar indicates time equal to the full width of the display.

It is interesting to note that one thread in Figure 9.1 seems to have arrived at the barrier a good deal before all of the others. This might indicate a load balancing problem, the need for finer grain work dispatching, unfortunate input data, or higher or lower performance of the particular processor on which the thread was running. Some of these hypotheses can be confirmed or refuted by studying the correlation of the state history diagram with other components of the display. On the other hand, considering the elision bars, the amount of time by which the one thread precedes the others to the barrier is actually quite small compared to the time required to process a single element, and may not be a cause for concern.

Figure 9.2 shows a second display panel containing an extended state history display component. On this display, the trace lines advance left to right, top to bottom, before wrapping again. Here, both the final three quarters of the first phase, and the entire second phase, can be seen for the second column. It is interesting to note that the second phase takes much less time than the first, that no locking is required in the second phase, and that there is only enough data to provide one chunk of work for each thread.

Figure 9.3 shows a third display containing a number of hardware utilization display components — one for each of PMEs 0 through 4. Processor instruction rates are shown numerically. The percentage of the processor's references which are to the cache, and the percentage of the processor's non-cache references which are to the memory on its PME, are displayed both numerically and as bar charts. Utilization of the PME's memory (from all processors) is also displayed in this fashion.

It is interesting to note that at this instant in time, processor 0 (typically reserved for system use) is making good use of the cache, while the processors running the application threads are making no use of the cache (the RP3 caches are user-controlled, and this application clearly has disabled the caches, probably for experimental purposes). The impact of cache usage on processor instruction rates is clear.

9.4.3   The User Interface

The user interface for the prototype visualization system provides comprehensive control over replay of the event stream. Through menus, or keys (for quicker reaction), the user can suspend a replay, resume it, step it one event at a time, or run it forward or backward at varying speeds. In the spirit of direct manipulation, the user can position the replay to any point in time simply by clicking on almost any part of the display. Interpretation of the click is handled differently for each component. For instance, the time display in Figure 9.1 is in fact just a conventional scrollbar; clicking on its arrows, or directly in the region of the slider, repositions the replay in time. As another example, clicking on a completely full matrix element of the display in Figure 9.1 repositions the replay to the point where the element was just about to turn from half-full to completely full.

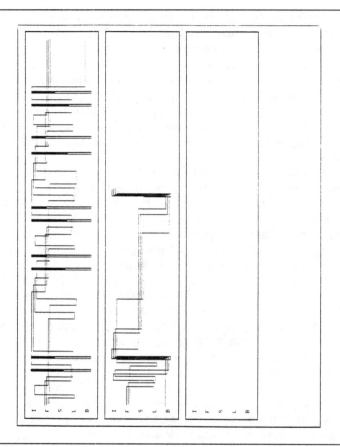

FIGURE 9.2
The extended state history display.

While this might at first seems to be just "bells and whistles", it is in fact essential for the intended mode of operation of the system. As discussed in the second section, a user is expected to run the system until a situation of interest arises, then step or run the system back and forth slowly, homing in on the precise moment of the behavior of interest. At the same time, the user looks for correlations between the various display components that might hint at the underlying cause of the given behavior. One example of such a correlation might be a dramatic decrease in processor speed when departing a particular state or accessing particular data (due, for example, to thrashing in a set associative cache as a result of unfortunate access patterns or layouts of data in memory). Note that, while temporal correlations can be transformed into spatial correlations by displays that incorporate history with a common time base, not all forms of display have an obvious or practical extension for incorporating history.

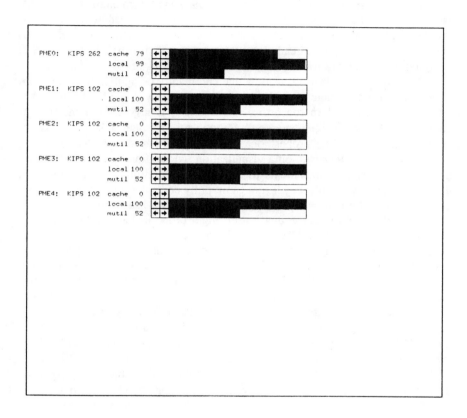

FIGURE 9.3
The hardware utilization display.

9.5   A Visualization Environment

The prototype system, and many of the visualization systems in place today, are entirely handcrafted. Code to produce the information required by the visualization system is user-provided, and this code is inserted statically at user-identified locations in the application. Further, the graphics are custom developed for each application.

The problem with this approach is that it takes far too much time, and hence is not practical for use on a day-to-day basis in developing new applications. By the time all of this scaffolding has been erected, the source of the bug or performance problem has already been uncovered, and the visualization work is being completed solely for posterity's sake or for pedagogical reasons.

What we require is a set of tools that can readily be applied to fresh problems across a broad range of applications. By analogy with the hardware realm, we propose a "toolkit" approach to visualization — a large assortment of standard, generally-applicable, "snap-on" components. At one end, on the target system, a user just clips "probes" onto a running system to extract information of interest. At the other end, on a visualization workstation, a user simply connects graphic display attachments to the information streams emanating from the various probes. In this way, users can rapidly construct an effective graphic presentation of the state and progress of an application in execution.

Examples of information that a user might probe include: at the hardware level — mips, megaflops, TLB and cache misses, memory and switch traffic, program counter samples, and instruction and data address samples; at the operating system level — page faults, binding of threads to processors, scheduling of threads, and pinning of various pieces of an address space down at various places within the memory architecture; at the runtime level — entering and exiting parallel sections, grabbing and releasing locks, arriving at and departing from barriers, dispatching loop chunks, and calling and returning from procedures; and, at the application level — high-level data operations, and algorithm state transitions. Code for capturing such information could either exist permanently within a system, and be dynamically enabled or disabled, or it could be dynamically hooked into a running system using lightweight hooks planted by an interactive debugger. Hardware assists could be applied to render the capture of this information less obtrusive.

The assortment of graphic attachments for displaying the extracted information might include: dials, meters, variable-brightness variable-color lights, scales, bar charts, plots, histograms, timing diagrams, source text, data structure diagrams, symbol tables, call graphs, control flow and dependence graphs, synchronization graphs, and architecture diagrams. These display components could be realized using any of a number of object-oriented graphics systems. All of this could be cast within the framework of a windowing system, which would provide creation of new windows, zooming and panning, and dynamic reconfiguration of windows across multi-screen displays.

An important requirement for this form of system is that it be "open" or "extensible". By clearly defining the architecture of the system, and explicitly specifying interfaces and protocols between the information generation modules on the target system, the information collection and transport mechanism on the target system, and the information display modules on the workstation, the ability to incorporate custom user-developed components into the system would be ensured.

All of this would constitute a "visualization environment" — an architecture, and a large collection of standard generally-applicable snap-on components for information capture and information display, a means of rapidly achieving an effective graphic characterization of a program's behavior, and a quick and easy way to take a first look at unexpected system behavior in order to arrive at a preliminary diagnosis.

9.6 Conclusion

Our prototype visualization system has been completed. We have demonstrated remote operation of the system over NYSERNet and CSNET, and system-independent display on MACH/RTs, SUN3s, and Ultrix VaxStations. Working at sites far removed from the RP3, we are able to start an application running, and we are able to get better feedback concerning its execution than most users get sitting right in the machine room with a parallel system.

We are highly encouraged by the effectiveness of even the simplest visualization tools, and we are optimistic about the potential of open environments for the visualization of program execution. Certainly, some problems will resist this form of attack, but even if we can resolve just the "easy" fraction of bugs and performance problems using these new methods, and then revert to older more time-consuming methods for the remainder of the problems, these environments will have been well worth the time spent on their development.

Acknowledgments

Many thanks to Ton Ngo, who is now serving as a major contributor and one-man army in the design and implementation of the next-generation visualization environment. Ton added the PMC display and the VPMC event generation to the completed prototype system. Henry Chang developed the operating system support for the PMC. In addition, the author gratefully acknowledges the assistance of Bryan Rosenburg whose constant support and good humor keeps it all in good fun.

This work was sponsored in part by The Advanced Research Project Agency under contract #N00039-87-C-0122.

References

1. T. Lehr, Z. Segall, D. F. Vrsalovic, E. Caplan, A. L. Chung, and C. E. Fineman, , Visualizing Performance Debugging. *IEEE Computer, Vol. 22 No. 10*, (October 1989), pages 38–51.

2. A. D. Malony, and D. A. Reed, Visualizing Parallel Computer System Performance. CSRD Report No. 812, Center for Supercomputing Research and Development, University of Illinois at Urbana-Champaign, May 1988.

3. A. D. Malony, D. A. Reed, Visualizing Parallel Computer System Performance. In *Instrumentation for Future Parallel Computing Systems.* Simmons, M., Koskela, R. and Bucher I., Eds. Addison-Wesley, Reading MA, 1989, pages 59–90.

4. G. F. Pfister, W. C. Brantley, D. A. George, S. L. Harvey, W. J. Kleinfelder, K. P. McAuliffe, E. A. Melton, V. A. Norton, and J. Weiss, Research Parallel Processor Prototype (RP3): Introduction and Architecture. *Proceedings of the 1985 International Conference on Parallel Processing*, pages 764–771.

5. W. C. Brantley, K. P. McAuliffe, and T. A. Ngo, RP3 Performance Monitoring Hardware. In *Instrumentation for Future Parallel Computing Systems.* Simmons, M., Koskela, R. and Bucher I., Eds. Addison-Wesley, Reading MA, 1989, pages 35–47.

6. M. Accetta, R. Baron, W. Bolosky, D. Golub, R. Rashid, A. Tevanian, and M. Young, MACH: A New Kernel Foundation for UNIX Development. *Proceedings of the USENIX 1986 Summer Conference*, 1986, pages 93–112.

7. R. M. Bryant, The RP3 Parallel Computing Environment. In *Proceedings of the USENIX 1988 Supercomputer Workshop*, pages 69–85.

8. W. C. Brantley and H. Y. Chang, Support Environment for the RP3 Performance Monitor. In *Parallel Computing Systems: Instrumentation and Visualization*, R. Koskela, and M. Simmons, Eds. (Addison-Wesley, Reading MA), 1990.

10

Software Tools for Visualization of Performance

Bill Appelbe

10.1 Introduction

Performance monitoring has been used for many years for programs that are
too complex to easily tune, either automatically or manually, for optimal performance or used often enough, in different environments, to warrant the effort
necessary to develop specialized software for monitoring and displaying performance data.

Performance monitors have been developed and used frequently for operating and networked systems, to aid users in locating systems' bottlenecks,
and improving systems' performance (response time and throughput) via tuning. However, applications programs have rarely warranted the development of
specialized performance monitoring software. Hence, application programmers
who wish to tune the performance of their applications either have to write
specialized programs or modify the applications or use general-purpose performance profilers. The performance bottlenecks of sequential programs can often
be determined by simple, non-visual tools and techniques such as execution
profiling (e.g, UNIX's[1] gprof), provided that an application is not I/O bound.

---

[1] UNIX is a trademark of AT&T Bell Laboratories.

Such tools list the percentage of time spent in each subroutine, or code segment, and can hence be used to isolate performance bottlenecks.

The development of high-performance parallel computer systems with complex memory hierarchies (cache, local, and remote memory), has meant that the performance of application programs depends upon exploiting available parallelism — restructuring and partitioning programs to maximize effective utilization of vector operations and processors. In the case of vectorization, generally the higher the percentage of instructions that have been vectorized, the faster the program executes. Hence, the percentage of loops/instructions that have been vectorized provides a simple yet generally effective performance measure for a given application/vector processor. This gives compilers and application programmers a relatively simple, although approximate, performance metric. Unfortunately, in the case of multiprocessors, increased parallelization often does not lead to faster execution and better performance, because of the high runtime overhead associated with task parallelism. Obtaining high processor utilization, and therefore high performance, often depends upon:

- The target configuration (e.g., number of physical processors).
- Runtime support (e.g., overhead of task scheduling or blocking).
- Compiler performance (e.g., optimization of runtime scheduler calls).
- Applications algorithms and data structures (algorithms that are fast sequentially often need to be modified, or different algorithms adopted).

10.1.1 Visualization

Visualization refers to the use of graphics to display complex data and their interrelationships. Often, relationships between data are entirely obscure when perusing tables of raw data can become readily apparent when the data are graphically displayed. Visualization aids users in understanding, and drawing conclusions from, the output of their application program. Some simple, general purpose visualization tools exist (e.g., UNIX's graph and plot commands), but application developers have tended to develop their own specialized visualization software.

Interactive visualization allows users to select interactively the data subset to be displayed, and the format for data display (ideally these should be decoupled, as described below). A performance visualization toolkit should thus provide:

- Tools for gathering performance data.
- Tools for interactively filtering and displaying such performance data.

Such a toolkit ideally should be usable with a range of workstations. Until recently the development of portable graphics packages was hindered by the lack of portable graphics/window management software packages. However, the recent widespread acceptance of the X-window system provides sufficient functionality for performance visualization (windows, menus, simple 2-D graphics, and event drivers).

10.1.2 Trace Data

Trace data are central to performance monitoring and postmortem debugging. They can be generated either by user calls, or by a trace package integrated with the runtime system. The latter is preferable, as a standard trace file format enables extensible tools to be developed for filtering, analyzing, and displaying trace data. For example, IBM's Parallel Fortran provides a trace facility that logs event data to a file for each selected event (call/response to/from the runtime scheduler) for the parallel constructs time, processor identity, event type, or parameters.

The fidelity of the trace data, and overhead associated with gathering such data, is critical. If the overhead is less than 10%, users are typically willing to leave tracing enabled. If timestamps are inaccurate, then debuggers and performance analyzers cannot report accurately cause or effect. However, the accuracy of timestamps is less critical than the preservation of ordering.

Filtering is critical as the volume of trace data can become immense. Filtering can be applied either at the data collection level (i.e., runtime), or at the analysis phase. Typical filters will select processes and events of interest, and incorporate a trigger mechanism to enable/disable filters. There is a close analogy between performance monitors and debugging tools. The principal difference is that debugging has the stringent requirement that it be interactive. A source debugger must be able to stop execution of a program at breakpoints (corresponding to system calls that able to be generate trace data for performance monitoring). Such breakpoints must be inserted and removed interactively, and hence a debugger must be able to modify or patch the object code. By contrast, performance monitors are generally batch oriented, and only need to modify the source code.

Ideally, a runtime trace package should provide a mechanism for user generated events, e.g., generated by explicit calls to a TRACE_EVENT runtime procedure with user definable parameters. Such user generated events should be logged with the time, processor identity, etc., as with other runtime events. The runtime package should provide the ability to enable and disable selectively event logging, as event logging potentially can generate huge volumes of trace data.

10.2 Taxonomy

Performance visualization tools can be classified according to:

□ the sophistication of their interface (i.e., graphics),

□ functionality — the range of data and statistics that can be monitored and displayed,

□ the level at which information is presented: hardware utilization and object code, source code, or high-level design.

Since a sophisticated graphics interface and functionality are highly dependent upon the environment, e.g., workstation capabilities, and system support for runtime tracing, the classification scheme we have adopted is based on the information level of the performance data. Three overlapping classes can be identified:

Trace

Simple graphical displays and listings of raw trace data (event data collected by the runtime system, and hardware support such as instruction timing and cache hit rates), e.g., GIST for the BBN Butterfly. Such tools are relatively simple to use and implement, but relating their output to the source program and its semantics is problematic. For example, if a bar chart shows that 'process p' is 'waiting on event E', it can be difficult for a user to determine the implications. For example: Are other processes also blocked? Could the event be posted earlier?

Source

Display of trace data in terms of the source program. In such systems the performance data are displayed in terms of program representations such as:

□ symbol tables,

□ call graphs,

□ flowgraphs, and

□ data dependence graphs.

These tools require access to the semantic analysis of the source program, such as that generated by optimizing compilers.

Design

Display of trace data in terms of a high-level model of program behavior. Such tools require a high-level model of the behavior of the program, (e.g., TRACE/SCHEDULE) [1] or explicit insertion of algorithm animation (e.g.,

TANGO/DANCE) [2]. Unfortunately, it is often the case that high-level design models are unavailable — the only representation of the program available is the source code.

Algorithm animation offers the highest level of representation and interaction, and has been the subject of considerable research [3]. Algorithm animation is the process of abstracting the data, operations, and semantics of computer programs, and then creating animated graphical views of those abstractions. Algorithm animations are useful for understanding programs, developing new programs, and evaluating existing programs. Hence, performance visualization at the design level can be regarded as a specialization of algorithm animation. In general, performance visualization need not be concurrent with program execution, in particular because such runtime interaction typically drastically affects fine-grained performance, and because performance visualization tools are workstation-based, whereas the trace data is often generated on a supercomputer host. Ideally, high-level performance visualization tools should also be able to display lower level machine trace data, because accurately determining the cause of performance bottlenecks may require detailed knowledge of machine and runtime support performance.

10.3 VIPER — a Source Level Performance Visualization Tool

Performance visualization at the source level offers considerable promise, provided that information gathered by the semantic analysis is available to the tool. Such a *program database* potentially is of use to a wide range of tools: version control, debuggers, compilers, preprocessors, as well as performance visualization tools. The principal challenge of developing such a program database is deciding on a standard set of interfaces, preferably object-oriented, for accessing and updating the program database, that:

□ provide both efficient low-level (e.g., deleting a compiler-generated data dependence that a user determines is spurious) and high-level interfaces (e.g., displaying the call graph); and provide both low and high bandwidth interfaces (e.g., applying a filter to all dependencies, versus interactively browsing trace events);

□ provide database wide consistency after incremental updates to interrelated information such as source code, data dependences, input and trace data. Updating, or invalidating, the entire database is obviously impractical after a single line of source code is deleted;

□ can be used by existing tools.

Currently, no complete program database exists for the scientific programming environment, although efforts are underway at several institutions to develop such a database (e.g., [4-5]). The principal interfaces needed by the proposed source Visualization Tool, VIPER, are:

1. Interactive browsing of source code, program flowgraphs, and call graphs.

2. The ability to display an animated and annotated view of these program representations (e.g., displaying statement frequencies along with source, or displaying a program flowgraph with process states superimposed).

3. The ability to modify the source code to insert/delete trace calls to generate events.

4. The ability to gather summary dependence information (e.g., the use-def graph for a given variable).

VIPER itself generates the source code for the trace calls for (3) (perhaps using an expression-tree to source code tool), based upon information returned from dependence analysis (4). An open research question is the design of a summary dependence interface to support insertion of trace probes with minimal intrusion. For example, a request to "trace the values of matrix WIND," implies:

□ Determining all statements that modify matrix elements, either directly, or via parameter aliases.

□ Inserting trace calls after these sites. A sophisticated interface might determine that all elements of WIND are being updated by a given loop, and hence hoist trace calls out of the loop for efficiency.

10.3.1   VIPER's User Interface Specification

The capabilities and interface design described below are intended as an overview of what a state of the art performance visualization tool ought to provide. These guidelines are a basis for the design and implementation of VIPER, and the interface provided by our source program analysis and transformation tool (START/PAT) [6].

VIPER's Organization.   The top-level of the tool provides three primary options:

1. **Trace**   Modify the source program to gather trace data, for either data access queries, or control queries.

2. **Run**   Execute the program, on a given data set, to gather trace data.

3. **View**   Filter and view the trace data gathered by a given trace run.

Data Access.   Data Access queries include selecting

□ A variable (scalar or array), or section of a variable in the case of an array, to monitor.

□ A region of the program over which to monitor the variable (by default the entire program).

□ A *filter* to apply. Filters include:

- Access (read/write),

- Value,

- Range (a partition of the variable's range, e.g., $> 0, = 0, < 0$), and

- Mesh (a partition of an arrays index range).

Such filters can be applied either during trace gathering or viewing. The advantage of specifying a filter before running is that by means of dependence analysis, trace calls and their associated overhead, can often be reduced. For example, a filter to "trace write access to an entire array" will cause an event trace call to be generated after a loop that updates the array, whereas a filter to "trace values of every element of an entire array" will cause trace event calls for each loop iteration.

Control Flow.   Control flow queries include selecting

□ Statement frequency and timing,

□ Processor states (blocked, running, etc.), and

□ Call frequency and timing.

Filters can also be applied to control flow tracing, e.g., monitoring only the total number of calls, versus the value of all parameters upon each call.

Viewing.   Viewing is performed by applying view filters to the trace data, and displaying it via a *view* format. View formats include:

□ bar charts and pie charts,

□ graph plots (2-D and 3-D), and

□ kiviat charts.

The associated attributes (e.g., window size, placement, scaling, labels, etc.) are also included.

In each case, dimensions can be displayed either via color or animation, although animations are generally used primarily to display the time dimension. It should also be possible to display several views concurrently, and if these are animated they need to be displayed synchronously. The X-window system will be used, as it provides the ability to manage multiple windows (one per view), and to develop widget libraries for different views. Since all trace data can be regarded as a list of tuples, and any filter as a relational operation upon that tuple (yielding a new list of tuples), each view should be able to operate upon any view filter. Thus the choice of view format should be largely independent of the choice of view filter. The view filter itself defaults to the trace filter, but may be a *subfilter* of it. An attempt to apply a viewing filter that requires more information than that gathered by the trace will cause the program to be rerun with that viewing filter applied as a trace filter.

A further refinement is the ability to view the output of several traces, on different input data sets, concurrently, or overlaid.

10.4 Implementation

The implementation of VIPER will use START/PAT's dependence analysis, and X-11 graphics-based displays of flowgraphs and dependence analysis, and sub-windowing. In addition, we have developed a prototype parser for IBM Parallel Fortran's tracefiles. PAT currently provides an interface for dependence browsing and source code modification (i.e., inserting/deleting lines of code).

START/PAT are implemented using the C language; their basic portability and adaptability derive from the modified f77 compiler front-end (which is based on the portable C compiler) on which they are built. They have been ported to a range of UNIX or UNIX-related systems, including VAX, ISI, Sun (using SunOS) and IBM (using AIX) workstations. The graphical interface relies on the X windowing system, although there is a mechanism in place to run without a graphic interface when X is not available.

START and PAT (and VIPER, in the future) use a common internal program representation that enhances the interrelationship between the tools. They share structures such as a control flow graph and a global symbol table. In addition, they rely on a generic internal representation of explicit parallelism primitives that is adaptable to numerous distinct sets of language extensions; currently, one or both have worked with Cray micro/macrotasking extensions, IBM Parallel Fortran, and Sequent Fortran multitasking extensions, as well as a more general set of extensions similar to PCF Fortran. The internal representation and I/O of multitasking primitives have been carefully designed and implemented to be easily ported to different multitasking dialects.

10.5 Conclusion

Scientific application programmers for parallel systems are currently provided with very limited support tools for exploiting potential systems' performance. Performance visualization tools are critical to the process of adapting and tuning parallel application programs. Such tools need to be interactive, portable, and integrated with compilers in order to support source level performance visualization. Although no current commercial or research software for interactive source level performance visualization is available, the tools and software technology necessary to implement source level performance visualization are currently available. We anticipate completing a prototype in the near future meeting the tool specifications outlined above.

References

1. Jack Dongarra and Danny Sorenson, "Portable Environment for Debugging Parallel Fortran Programs," *Parallel Computing*, 5 pp. 175-186, 1987.

2. John Stasko "A Practical Animation Language for Software Development," *Proceedings of the IEEE 1990 International Conference on Computer Languages*, New Orleans, LA March 1987.

3. Marc Brown *Algorithm Animation* (MIT Press, Cambridge, MA 1988).

4. Vincent A. Guarna, Jr., Dennis Gannon, Yogesh Gaur, and David Jablonowski, "FAUST: An Environment for Programming Parallel Scientific Applications," *Proceedings of Supercomputing '88* November 14-18, 1988, Orlando, Florida, pp. 3-10.

5. Alan Carle, Keith D. Cooper, Robert T. Hood, Ken Kennedy, Linda Torczon, and Scott K. Warren, "A Practical Environment for Scientific Programming," *Computer* November 1987, Vol. 20, No. 11, pp. 75-89.

6. William F. Appelbe, Kevin Smith, and Charlie McDowell, "Start/PAT: A Parallel Programming Toolkit," *IEEE Software* July 1988, Vol. 6, No. 4 pp. 29-40.

11

Parallel Program Visualization Using ParVis

Laura Bagnall Linden[1]

11.1 Introduction

Parallel computers are inherently more difficult to program than traditional von Neuman machines. In addition to worrying about program correctness within a single computation thread, the programmer must worry about communication between concurrent tasks. Even if synchronization is done correctly so that the program executes without error, the program may be written in such a way as to not fully utilize the available processors due to bottlenecks of one kind or another. Thus, it is important to provide tools to assist in parallel program understanding. Traditional program analysis tools provide only aggregate information, as in tools that plot the total number of processors in use over time. This report describes ParVis (*Par*allel *Vis*ualization), a tool that gives detailed information of individual tasks.

ParVis is designed to work with Multilisp, a parallel Lisp dialect. In order to provide the user with information regarding the behavior of a program, ParVis

[1]This research was supported in part by the Defense Advanced Research Projects Agency and was monitored by the Office of Naval Research under contract numbers N00014-83-K-0125 and N00014-84-K-0099.

records events describing state transitions within tasks and communication between tasks during a program run, and then generates a graphical display of this information. This enables the programmer to understand aspects of program execution that are impossible to learn from summary information alone. Because the additional information described by ParVis can lead to large, complex displays, a filter language is provided that allows the programmer to specify those parts of the display relevant to the analysis. Of particular interest is the interface between the filter language and the graphic display, which allows easy inclusion of display elements in filter definitions.

The larger problem of program understanding encompasses a range of tasks, of which performance tuning and debugging are two points on the spectrum. In its present incarnation, ParVis emphasizes performance analysis over correctness analysis. Another characterization of program understanding tools is the scale of program that the tool can handle. ParVis lets us examine the behavior of individual tasks. It is good for small scale programs, on the order of one to two thousand tasks, while large-scale systems remain outside of its scope. This is due both to implementation limitations and to the limitations of programmers in examining large complicated displays. At some point, automated analysis tools that recognize opportunities for increased parallelism become necessary.

Section 11.2 gives a brief overview of Multilisp. Section 11.3 describes the events that provide the interface between Multilisp and the ParVis display, and is followed by a description of the format of the display and the facilities available for moving around in the display in Section 11.4. Section 11.5 is devoted to an extended analysis of a list-processing example that demonstrates the features described in the previous sections. Section 11.6 presents the filter language used for specifying events of interest to the user, and the interface between the language and the ParVis display. The Traveling Salesman problem is then given as an example demonstrating the utility of the filter system. Finally, as a result of this example, a number of improvements are suggested. Section 11.7 discusses some of the limitations to the current ParVis system, followed by a discussion in Section 11.8 of related work in parallel program understanding. Finally, Section 11.9 envisions an integrated parallel programming environment incorporating ParVis along with other tools that address other aspects of the parallel program understanding problem.

11.2 Multilisp

Most parallel programming languages can be thought of as ways of specifying tasks (or pieces of programs) that run in parallel, and methods of communicating between tasks. Multilisp is no exception. In this section, I discuss the details of Multilisp parallel constructs. Subsequent sections describe how they interact with the ParVis display, the details of the display itself, and how the user may manipulate the display.

Although ParVis works with a variety of parallel Lisp dialects (Butterfly Lisp, Multilisp, Mul-T) running on a variety of systems (BBN Butterfly, Concert, Encore Multimax), the common element of each dialect is the `future` construct that allows a programmer to specify concurrent execution. No attempt is made by any of these systems to automatically detect opportunities for parallelism, leaving this up to the programmer. In this report I will refer to Multilisp [1], but any statements made should hold for the other dialects as well.

Another characteristic shared by the above languages is that they are designed for shared memory, tightly-coupled multiprocessors. Butterfly Lisp runs on the BBN Butterfly, consisting of between 8 and 128 Motorola 68000-based processors, interconnected with an Omega network. Multilisp runs both on Concert, 36 68000-based processors connected by a ring bus, and on the Encore Multimax, 16 National Semiconductor 32000 processors. The Multimax has fewer processors than Concert, but the processors are faster, so that on average, Multilisp programs tend to run faster on the Multimax than on Concert. Mul-T runs only on the Multimax, and, being compiled, runs quite fast. All of the examples in this report were run either on Concert or on the Multimax. Specific details of the architecture of the two systems will in general not be relevant to the discussion, with the exception of certain peculiarities of Concert, which will be discussed in Section 11.5.2.

The expression (`future`) X creates a *placeholder* for the not-yet-computed value of X, immediately making the placeholder available for use, and creates a task to concurrently evaluate X, thus allowing concurrency between the computation of a value and the use of that value. *Tasks* represent work that has been requested to be performed. *Futures* are data structures that include space for the placeholder, a reference to the associated task, and a *documentation string* describing the work that the future is performing, plus some additional system-specific items. The documentation string defaults to the printed representation of the expression X, but may be changed by the user.

During the execution of a program, a Multilisp task can be in one of several states, namely **Running**, in which the task is currently being executed by a processor, **Waiting**, in which the task is suspended waiting for a future to resolve, and **Queued**, in which the task is on a working queue waiting for an available processor. Intertask communication via futures occurs at state transition boundaries. Communication via side effects isn't recorded by ParVis.

When a task completes the evaluation of X, it *determines* the future, by storing the value of X in the placeholder. When a task requires the value of a future for some operation, it *touches* the future. If the future has already been determined, then the task uses that value and continues. If the future is undetermined, then the touching task will be suspended until the future becomes determined. Touching an undetermined future causes the task to transit from the **Running** to **Waiting** state. When the touched future is determined, the suspended task goes from the **Waiting** to **Queued** state. Multilisp also has a *delay* feature, that differs from futures only in the time of task creation. The expression (delay) X creates a placeholder for the value of X as before, but the task for evaluating X isn't created until the placeholder is touched by another task.

The scheduler is the remaining entity responsible for tasks changing state in Multilisp. When a processor becomes idle, it is the scheduler that is responsible for choosing a task from the queue of tasks waiting to be run. This causes the chosen task to go from the **Queued** state to **Running**. Similarly, when a task creates another task, the default scheduler behavior is to place the parent task on the queue, and schedule the child task to be run by the processor. This causes the parent task to change state from **Running** to **Queued**.

While the use of future implies a one-to-one correspondence between futures and tasks, there are other Multilisp constructs that result in futures without associated tasks. These forms occur relatively infrequently in Multilisp code, and will not be discussed further in this report. ParVis is capable of displaying futures both with and without associated tasks. In Multilisp, there are no tasks without associated futures.

11.3 Events: The Link Between Multilisp and the Display

One of the properties of ParVis that makes it easy to use is the simple and direct correspondence between features of the Multilisp language and the ParVis display. Events provide this link. In addition to the states **Running, Waiting,** or **Queued** described above, a future may have no associated task, or it may be determined. During the running of a Multilisp program, *events* are recorded for each transition between the above states, plus the state "not created yet". A state diagram summarizing the events is shown in Figure 11.1. A packet recording an event contains the type of the event, specifying which transition occurred, the identifier of the processor on which the event occurred, a timestamp, and a unique identifier specifying the future that is making the state transition. At the end of a program run, the collection of events, or *dataset*, is saved out to a file. The ParVis display is created from the contents of this file.

Certain events are triggered by another future. An example of this is the create event, where the triggering future is the parent of the future being created. For these events, the identifier for the triggering agent is included in the packet as well. Such events always generate an arrow in the display, in addition to a state transition.

In addition to the fields described above, create events include the documentation string associated with the future being created. Because a given piece

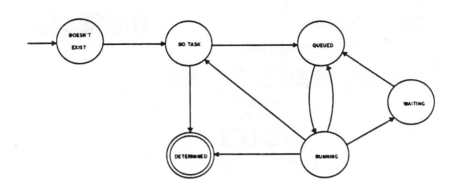

FIGURE 11.1
A state diagram of tasks.

of code containing a call to `future` is likely to be called many times, many different futures will have the same documentation string. Rather than include the entire string in each `create` packet, a table mapping integers to strings is transmitted separately, and the packets include that integer instead.

One event that is neither recorded nor displayed is that of a task touching a previously determined future. There are two problems with doing this. One is the question of how to display such an event. In the current version of ParVis, futures are no longer displayed after they have been determined, so there isn't anything to which an arrow can be drawn. The second problem lies in the implementation of Multilisp, namely that the future may no longer exist, because the garbage collector has spliced out determined futures and replaced them with their values. While it should be possible to come up with a slightly different display, and a version of Multilisp that would allow the splicing feature to be turned off, this option was not pursued.

11.4 The ParVis Display

The ParVis window is divided vertically into three panes, as shown in Figure 11.2. The topmost and largest pane is used to display information about individual tasks and the relationships between them. The pane below that contains a graph giving summary information about the tasks. The bottommost pane is for user interaction, and is used for entering commands to manipulate the display.

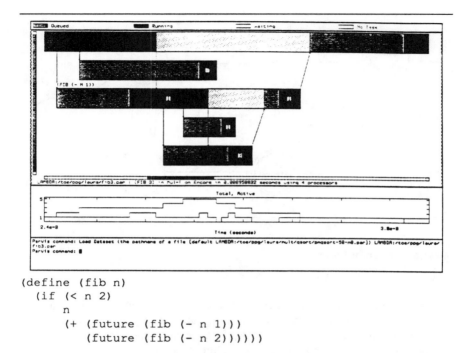

```
(define (fib n)
  (if (< n 2)
      n
      (+ (future (fib (- n 1)))
         (future (fib (- n 2))))))))
```

FIGURE 11.2
A ParVis display showing fib 3, along with the Multilisp code for Fibonacci
used to generate the display.

11.4.1 Tasks and Task States

Futures are presented by horizontal rectangular strips. In the ParVis display, the
horizontal axis represents time, increasing from left to right, and the vertical axis
represents tasks. The tasks are presented in depth-first order, according to the
spawning tree. As a future's task changes state over time, the appropriate area of
the strip is drawn with a different stipple pattern. The three possible task states
are **Running** (dark gray), in which a task is currently being run by a processor,
Queued (medium gray), in which a task is on the working queue, where it is
waiting for an available processor, and **Waiting** (light gray), in which a task
is waiting for another future to become determined. If a future doesn't have
an associated task, the rectangle depicting the future is left blank. A future's
strip starts at the time when it is created and ends when the future enters the
Determined state. See Figure 11.1 for an example showing the three states.

11.4.2 Relationships Between Tasks

Relationships between tasks are displayed with arrows. There are two types of relationships, drawn with two different types of arrows to distinguish them. The spawning, or parent-child relationship, is defined by a future creating another future, using the Multilisp forms `future` or `delay`. These arrows are drawn with thick shafts. The data-dependency relationship is defined by futures touching undetermined futures, thus becoming suspended, and by futures being determined which then wake up the suspended futures. The Fibonnaci example in Figure 11.2 shows both spawning and data-dependency arrows.

11.4.3 The Summary Graph

The display described gives information about individual events. Sometimes, however, it is useful to have information that summarizes the events, giving an overall picture of the behavior of a program. The summary graph gives such a picture. For each type of state, namely **Running, Queued, Waiting,** and **No Task**, the total number of tasks in that state is plotted at each point in time over the course of the program run. In addition, a curve is computed that is the sum of all of the above curves, and gives the total number of futures in existence over time. These graphs can be used for an overall measure of the parallelism in the program. For example, the graph of **Running** tasks shows the processor utilization. The ideal Multilisp program would minimize the queued and waiting curves, and have the total number of futures approximate the total number of available processors. The default is for the Running and Total curves to be displayed, but any combination may be chosen by the user. The summary graphs share the same horizontal (time) axis as the task plot, so that correspondences may be made between the two.

11.4.4 User Manipulation of the Display

It does not take a very big program to generate a dataset that is too large to fit on the screen all at once. When a dataset is first loaded, the initial display tries to squeeze as much as possible onto the screen. Even displaying tasks using only one vertical pixel per task limits the number of visible tasks to roughly four hundred. It is surprising how much of the overall structure of the program is understandable even at this magnification. However, the program would be very limited if we were restricted to using just the visible screen. In order to view other portions of the display, both horizontal and vertical scroll bars are provided. In order to view portions of the display at greater magnifications, there is a "zooming" facility. To zoom in, the user specifies a rectangle with the mouse, and the portion of the display within that rectangle is expanded to occupy the entire display pane. These rectangular portions of the display are known as *views*. This process can be repeated any number of times. Each view specified is remembered on a stack of views, and the user has the choice of popping back to the previous view, or going back to the outermost view.

There isn't room in the future display to show the documentation string for each future. However, one would like to access it easily. This is accomplished by making each of the future rectangles mouse sensitive, and by having the documentation string flash on the screen as the mouse moves over a task. Detailed information about that particular task can be obtained by clicking the mouse on a future.

As mentioned earlier, the future display and the summary graph share a common time axis. In order to make it easier to correlate a specific event in the future display with a point on the summary graph, or simply to find out at what time an event occurs, a *slider* is provided. This is a thin vertical line, extending the height of the future display and summary graph combined, that slides to the left or right as the mouse is moved. Attached to this line is a box containing the time corresponding to the current position of the line. This time is updated continuously as the slider is moved. Multiple copies of the slider may be dropped onto the display, and time intervals calculated by comparing the times in the various slider boxes.

11.5 A List-Processing Example

To provide an example of an application of those features of ParVis described so far, I will use ParVis to analyze one method for parallelizing `mapcar`, a Common Lisp function that maps a function over the elements of a list. I have borrowed this example from Halstead [2]. All of the examples were run using Multilisp on Concert. In his report, Halstead demonstrates that there is no one application-independent optimal way to use `future` in `mapcar` for the best tradeoff between overhead and concurrency. His analysis was done both by theorizing what the behavior of the various versions of `mapcar` should be, and by using TLINE, a tool that shows summary information similar to that shown in the ParVis summary graph. While TLINE was useful to explain much of the behavior, there were certain aspects where it was insufficient. In this section, I will use ParVis to examine the differences between Halstead's model and the actual behavior. The behavior that Halstead was unable to account for was the result of interactions between the Multilisp implementation and Concert architecture. A tool such as ParVis that shows the behavior of individual tasks was required to discover the explanation. The `mapcar` analysis demonstrates the usefulness of ParVis both in tuning the users program and in understanding and tuning the underlying Multilisp implementation.

11.5.1 Methods for Parallelizing `mapcar`

`mapcar` takes two arguments, `f` and `1`, where `f` is a procedure of one argument, and `1` is a list. It applies `f` to each element of `1`, returning the results of each call to `f` as a list. A serial implementation of `mapcar` is shown in Figure 11.3. One method for parallelizing `mapcar`, demonstrated by `pmapcar` shown in Figure 11.4, is to spawn a separate task to compute the recursive call. The " `(let ((rest (future ...`" code is necessary to ensure that the task to compute `(pmapcar f (cdr 1))` is spawned before the procedure `f` is applied to `(car 1)`, otherwise the resulting procedure will run in an entirely serial fashion. `pmapcar` returns a list whose first element is resolved but whose tail is unresolved. In the following examples, the calls to `pmapcar` are followed by a procedure that walks down the resulting list touching each of the elements, to ensure that all of the tasks are finished before terminating the recording of the dataset.

```
(defun mapcar (f 1)
  (if (null 1)
      nil
      (cons (f (car 1))
            (mapcar f (cdr 1)))))
```

FIGURE 11.3
Serial version of mapcar.

```
(defun pmapcar (f 1)
  (if (null 1)
      nil
      (let ((rest (future (pmapcar f (cdr 1)))))
        (cons (f (car 1)) rest))))
```

FIGURE 11.4
pmapcar is derived from mapcar by adding future to the recursive call
to pmapcar.

11.5.2 Limits to Concurrency

There are three different limits to the amount of concurrency that can be achieved using the parallel definition of mapcar described above. Which limits come into play for a given invocation depends on the arguments f and l used. In this analysis, l will be a list of numbers, and f a procedure that waits for a constant amount of time T_f, then adds 0 to its argument. Let L be the length of the list l, and T_{tr} be the length of the interval between spawning calls to f. In general, a ParVis plot of a single call to pmapcar in isolation has the shape of a parallelogram whose height is L, whose base is T_f, and whose slope of the spawning line is determined by T_{tr}. Two of the limits to the potential concurrency of pmapcar are the length of the list l, since only L invocations of f will be spawned, and the number of processors, since there clearly can't be more tasks running than there are processors. When $L \gg T_f/T_{tr}$ and a sufficient number of processors are available, the spawning rate is the upper limit on the number of tasks concurrently executing. In Figure 11.5, we can see that the actual behavior agrees quite closely with the predicted behavior. Note that each future is created by the previously created future, and control returns to the top-level task after time T_f, at which point the top-level task begins walking down the list, resulting in the arrows between the top-level and subsequent tasks.

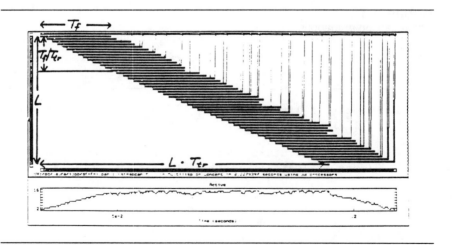

FIGURE 11.5
Behavior of (pmapcar f l) for $T_f/T_{tr} \approx 14$ and $L = 50$.

The only significant difference between the predicted and actual behavior can be seen in the ragged right edges of the parallelograms in each of the three figures discussed so far. The function f used to generate these figures simply loops a constant number of times, and should require a constant amount of time to execute. To explain the significant difference between the running times, it is necessary to explain some details of Concert's architecture.

The Concert multiprocessor consists of eight clusters of processors connected by a segmented bus in the shape of a ring, known as the *RingBus* [2]. Each cluster contains a block of globally accessible memory and a Multibus tying together a small number of processors and their private memories. A Multilisp program to be executed by Concert is first compiled into a machine-level byte-code language called MCODE. An MCODE interpreter is executed by each processor. MCODE programs reside in a garbage-collected heap distributed among the RingBus-accessible memory modules of Concert. As a result, if the MCODE instructions for a particular Multilisp program happen to reside on a certain cluster, that program will execute more quickly on the processors on that cluster than it will on other clusters, because of the increased time required to fetch MCODE instructions over the RingBus. It indeed turns out that the tasks with visibly shorter execution times were those running on processors in cluster 0.

11.5.3 Nested calls to mapcar

So far we have only analyzed the use of pmapcar in isolation. Additional interesting behavior is exhibited when two invocations are nested, as in the expression (pmapcar g (pmapcar f l)). When concurrency is limited by the length of list l, the inner nested call to pmapcar has returned before the task computing the application of f to the first element of the list has finished. As a result, the first application of g may begin as soon as the result of f is available and the amount of available concurrency is L.

When concurrency is limited by the spawning rate, the call to g on a given list element may also begin as soon as the corresponding call to f is finished, since pmapcar returns as soon as it has finished applying f to the first element of l. In this case, the concurrency of pmapcar is $(T_f + T_g)/T_{tr}$. Figure 11.6 shows our idealized model of this situation. Note that the predicted overall concurrency has the shape of a trapezoid with a flat top.

Comparing the actual plot in Figure 11.7 with the ideal plot, we see a "tail" of tasks computing g in the summary graph. This same tail was seen in Halstead's study, but his model was unable to account for it. Looking at the ParVis plot, it is immediately clear that the tail is the result of a shallower spawning slope for the g tasks than for the f tasks. What is less clear is the reason for the different slopes.

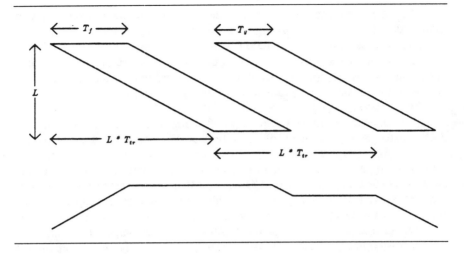

FIGURE 11.6
Idealized behavior of (pmapcar g (pmapcar f l)) when $T_f/T_{tr} \ll L$, $T_g/T_{tr} \ll L$.

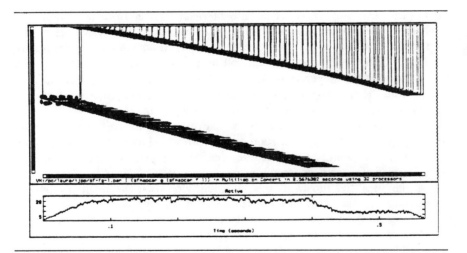

FIGURE 11.7
Actual behavior of (pmapcar g (pmapcar f l)) when $L = 50$, $T_f/T_{tr_1} \approx 15$, $T_g/T_{tr_2} \approx 7$.

To further examine this phenomenon, we start by blowing up one section of the plot, as shown in Figure 11.8. Notice that each task spawns the next while running on processor 1, and then switches to another processor. This is due to Multilisp's "depth-first" scheduling strategy, in which the parent task is suspended while the processor runs the child task instead. Since all of the f tasks were created by processor 1 in cluster 0, and all of the g tasks were created by processor 42 in cluster 4 (not shown in Figure 11.8), and since we can see that T_f is smaller for tasks running on processors in cluster 0, this helps explain why T_{tr} is smaller for f tasks than g tasks. There is an additional explanation for the observed difference in T_{tr}. The function null *touches* its argument, and the MCODE instruction TOUCH takes longer to execute when the argument is a determined future, and the value needs to be extracted from it, than it does when the argument is a cons. Thus both of these facts account for the difference in the spawning rate. It is beyond the scope of this report to determine the exact contribution of each.

11.5.4 Conclusion

This example demonstrates the usefulness of the additional information available with ParVis as opposed to traditional summary-style performance measurement tools. In particular, ParVis allowed us to compare predicted behavior of

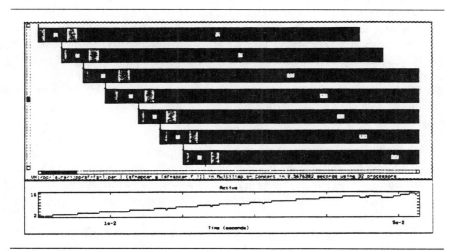

FIGURE 11.8
Enlargement of Figure 11.7, showing details of task spawning.

pmapcar with actual behavior, and explain the differences which were previously inexplicable using processor utilization information alone. In Section 11.5.3, we uncovered a hidden cause of unexpected performance characteristics when nesting calls to pmapcar due to the Multilisp implementation. Changing this behavior would require making changes to the Multilisp system. In Section 11.6.3, we will see an example where ParVis points out opportunities for modifying code to improve performance.

11.6 The Filter Facility

11.6.1 The Filter Language

All of the datasets from the mapcar example in the previous section were small enough to be displayed in a single screen, and simple enough to be easily understood. Each dataset was generated by running a single procedure with a single occurrence of future in its definition. In general, we will be interested in looking at larger, more complex datasets that aren't so easily understood. The features described in Section 11.4 aren't sufficient for this task. In this section I will describe a filter language that provides the ability to selectively examine portions of the dataset that may be of interest to the user.

A filter is a procedure that takes an event as an argument, and returns true or false indicating whether or not the event passes the filter. A filter may be thought of as a way to specify a subset of the dataset, and combining filters with AND, OR, and NOT may be thought of as set intersection, union, and complementation, respectively. In order to selectively highlight those futures of the ParVis display that are of interest, a filter is defined and applied to each event in the current dataset. Each future not containing an event that passes the filter is deemphasized by drawing a uniform gray rectangle, while futures containing events that do pass the filter are drawn in the usual manner. Filters may also be used to gather statistics by giving a count of the number of tasks and events in a given dataset that pass a filter.

The filter language is a Lisp-like typed language composed of constants, combinations, filter operators, boolean operators AND, OR, and NOT, and user-defined filters. Constants have *simple* types such as boolean, event, string, etc. A complete list of constant types, along with example constant expressions, is given in Table 11.1.

Filter operators have type (*operator* (*arg*$_1$ *arg*$_2$ ... *arg*$_n$) *value*), where *arg*$_i$ and *value* are simple types that indicate the type of the arguments passed to the operator, and the value returned by the operator, respectively. For example, the primitive is-event-type has type (operator (event event-type) boolean) and returns true if the type of its first argument

TABLE 11.1
Types of constant expressions in the filter language.

Type	Example expressions
boolean	T, NIL
event	#[CREATE 1159 NIL 1048696]
event-type	create, run, ...
level	3, ALL
string	"fib"
time	1.4
interval	.03
processor-id	11

argument. A summary of primitive operators and their types is shown in Table 11.2.

There are two kinds of event types, *basic* event types and *meta* event types. Basic event types correspond to the events of Section 11.3, with a different basic event type for each event. Meta event types correspond to task states, with each meta event type corresponding to the set of basic events that describe transitions into a given task state. For example, the enqueue meta-event refers to the two basic events, make-runnable and resume-runnable, both of which leave the task in the **Queued** state. A complete list of correspondences between meta events and basic events is given in Table 11.3. The complete definition of is-event-type is to return true if the type of event is the same as event-type, where event-type is a basic event type, or if the type of event is a member of the set of basic events referred to by event-type, where event-type is a meta event.

Combinations are of the form (*operator operand$_1$ operand$_2$ ... operand$_n$*), where the operators are primitive operators, boolean operators, or user-defined filters, and the operands are expressions (constants or other combinations). If the operator is primitive, then the types of the operands must match the types of the arguments to the operator, and the type of the combination is the value type of the operator. If the operator is a boolean operator, then the operands must be booleans and the type of the combination is also boolean. If the operator is a filter, then it must be given a single operand whose type is event, and the value of the combination is boolean.

Filters are defined using define-filter. Since a filter returns a boolean as a value, the body of a filter definition must be an expression that returns a boolean value. Within the body of the definition, the variable event is bound

TABLE 11.2
Types of primitive operators in the filter language.

Operator	Type
doc-string-search[1]	(operator (event string) boolean)
on-processor[2]	(operator (event processor-id) boolean)
is-event-type	(operator (event event-type) boolean)
is-root[3]	(operator (event) boolean)
time-later[4]	(operator (time time) boolean)
interval-longer	(operator (interval interval) boolean)
subtree	(operator (event event level) boolean)
root	(operator () event)
next-event	(operator (event) event)
event-time	(operator (event) time)
time-difference	(operator (time time) interval)
segment-duration	(operator (event) interval)

to the argument of the filter. Here is a sample filter that is true for all tasks which at some point are queued for longer than 30 milliseconds.

```
(define-filter long-queue (event)
    (and (is-event-type event 'enqueue)
         (interval-longer (segment-duration event)
                .03)))
```

In Section 11.3, we saw how events describe state transitions of futures. With respect to a given dataset, an event may be uniquely specified by giving

---

[1]Certain operators, when given an event as an argument, actually use information associated with the future in which the event occurs. As an example, doc-string-search searches for an occurrence of a string in the documentation string of the event's task.

[2]The definition of on-processor includes an implicit (is-event-type 'run), since it is only meaningful to ask on which processor an event occurred in the case of a run event.

[3]The operators root, is-root, and subtree all refer to the spawning tree. They return the create event of the future at the root of the tree, determine whether the event is the create event of the root future, and determine whether the second event is a descendent of the first event, respectively.

[4]The operators time-later, interval-longer, event-time, time-difference, and segment-duration distinguish between *times*, which are absolute quantities, and *intervals*, which are time durations. For example, time-difference takes two absolute times, and returns the interval of time between the two.

TABLE 11.3
Correspondence between meta events and basic events.

Meta Events	Basic Events
enqueue	make-runnable resume-runnable
no-task	create quit
wait	await
finish	determine terminate

the unique identifier of the future in which the event occurred and the time at which the event occurred. Clearly it is unreasonable to require the user to specify an event by typing in these two numbers, particularly since the numbers themselves aren't visible in the display. Instead, since each event is visible in the ParVis display as a vertical line separating two stipple patterns, events may be selected directly from the display using the mouse. Once selected, it is represented textually in a filter by #[*event-type time task-id other*], where the *event-type* and *other* fields are also included for descriptive purposes. (The *other* field has different uses depending on the type of the event.) Using the mouse to select an event is just one example of the user interface to the filter language, which will be discussed further in Section 11.6.2.

The example filter long-queue given above may be applied meaningfully to any dataset. In contrast, any filter whose definition includes a constant event is only meaningful when applied to the dataset containing that event. The former type of filters are known as *dataset-general* filters, and the latter as *dataset-specific*. Additionally, filters including an absolute time are also considered to be dataset-specific. It is possible to "customize" a dataset-general filter by including in its definition a reference to a dataset-specific filter that has different definitions according to which dataset the general filter is being applied.

11.6.2 The Filter Interface

Now that we've discussed the syntax of the filter language and *what* it's used for, the question arises of *how* to use it. One approach would be simply to provide a text editor and let the user just type in the definition of the filter. However, this approach is inadequate because there are some types of information that we wish to include in filter definitions that aren't conveniently able to be typed in. We saw one example of this in the previous section, where we wished to refer to a specific event from a dataset. In this case, we wish to allow the user to point at the display and say "*that* event right there". Another example where a non-textual interface would be useful would be getting a time by pointing at the display and saying, in effect, "use *that* time right there", instead of typing in a time such as "0.03 seconds".

In order to provide a structured interface to the filter language that allows us to incorporate information directly from the ParVis display into filters, there is a menu-based filter interface window. A sample window is shown in Figure 11.9. The left half of the window contains a number of menus, and the right half contains an editor pane. Below the editor pane is a type in pane. In order to create a new filter window and inserts a new filter template in the editor pane. The template looks like (define-filter filter-*n* (event) ▌), where *n* is the value of a counter that is incremented each time a new filter is defined. The filter name is mouse sensitive, and may be changed to something more mnemonic by clicking on it with the mouse. The position of the cursor within the template indicates where the next form is to be inserted. The editor pane displays the filter as it is defined. The primary function of the menu is to insert forms in the editor pane. Filter primitives are inserted via the *Filter Language* menu. The boolean combining forms are inserted with the menu items labeled with AND, OR, and NOT. Previously defined dataset-general and dataset-specific filters are listed in the *General Filters* and *Specific Filters* menu, respectively. The type in pane is used for entering those constants that are typeable, e.g. strings.

We have seen how this interface to the filter language is necessary when there are inputs to the language that cannot be typed conveniently by the user. Another place where the filter window interface is useful is enforcing the type compatibility between operators and their arguments. At any point during the definition of a filter, only expressions of a given type may be inserted legally. The interface enforces this restriction by having only those menu items that insert expressions of the correct type be mouse-sensitive.

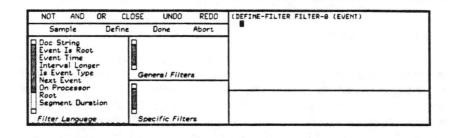

FIGURE 11.9
A sample filter window showing an initial filter template.

Many of the constants used in the filter language may be entered via selection from the ParVis display. There are three types of sensitive regions in the display, namely futures, events, and intervals. Whether any of these regions is actively sensitive at any given point depends on which type of input is being prompted for. A sensitive region is a rectangular area of the display that is highlighted by a rectangle being drawn around the area whenever the mouse is moved within that area. The sensitive area of a future is the rectangle bounding the future, that of an event is a rectangle bounding the vertical line delimiting two stipple patterns that indicate an event. An interval is a time period delimited by two consecutive events in a task, that is, a period of time in which a future is in a particular state, and the interval's sensitive area is the rectangle whose left and right edges are those events. The slider described in Section 11.4.4 may also be used to enter a specific time, or two sliders may be used to enter a time interval. A summary of the input sources for each type of filter constant is given in Table 11.4.

There are times when the user may not want the full power of the filter interface window. Searching for occurrences of a documentation string is a typical example. The Filter Dataset command can be used to define an anonymous filter by giving the command an arbitrary filter expression. In principle, any dataset-general filter may be defined this way. Thus, to search for the occurrence of the string "mapcar", the command 'Filter Dataset (doc-string-search event "mapcar")' would be used. Filter Dataset can also take the name of a previously defined filter as an argument, in which case it applies the filter to the currently displayed dataset.

TABLE 11.4
Input sources for constants in the filter language.

Type	Input Sources
boolean	*none*
event	tasks, events, or typein ("event")
event-type	typein, pop-up menu of event-types, displayed events
level	typein
string	typein, displayed tasks
time	event, slider
interval	typein, displayed interval, 2 sliders
processor-id	typein

11.6.3 Traveling Salesman

In this section, we look at an implementation of the traveling salesman problem, taken from Osborne [3]. This program differs from the previous examples in a number of respects:

1. The program is much more complex in that the source code occupies a number of pages, rather than half a page, and uses futures in a number of different places.

2. The program communicates using shared variables protected by spin-locks.

3. The program uses speculative parallelism.

This is the first example where it is not immediately obvious how the source code leads to the ParVis display, due to the complicated nature of the code. Here, the filter system is quite useful in analyzing program structure. I will not present a complete analysis of the program, since we are more interested in ParVis than in the traveling salesman problem itself, but I will show an example of filters aiding in program understanding and speedup.

The traveling salesman program takes a list of two-dimensional coordinates of cities and returns the cost of the shortest traveling salesman route covering all of the cities, along with the itinerary that achieves this cost. The algorithm uses a greedy, minimum-cost-first strategy to find the first solution and then uses the cost of this solution to prune out other solutions. A partial solution, or node, consists of a partial itinerary, which is a list of cities already traveled, and a list of cities remaining to be added to the itinerary. New candidates are generated from a given partial solution by choosing the next city from the list of remaining cities, and inserting it in all of the possible places in the partial itinerary. The first path is found by expanding a node into all of its possible next nodes, choosing the best (least-cost) node and expanding that node with a mandatory task, and spawning speculative tasks to expand the remaining nodes. As each complete route is found, a shared variable is updated atomically with the new path length, if it is shorter than the previously found shortest solution. Branches are pruned whenever the partial cost exceeds the shortest path found so far.

Figure 11.10 shows the ParVis display of the traveling salesman program run with 12 cities. There are two parts to the program: the first initializes the data structure, and the second does the work of finding the shortest path. For simplicity in presentation, the data structure initialization code is run separately, and only the path searching code is monitored. At this magnification, it is difficult to find any correspondences between the display and the source code.

A generally useful strategy for comprehending a complex display generated by a program with futures in multiple places, such as this program, is to use the `doc-string-search` operator to highlight those tasks generated by a specific occurence of `future`. Figure 11.11 shows a blowup of the portion

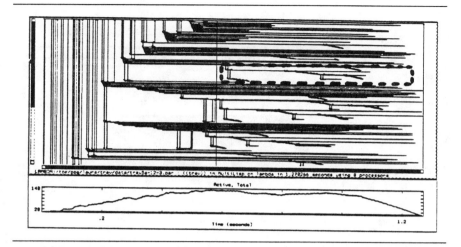

FIGURE 11.10
ParVis display of traveling salesman program.

of Figure 11.10 indicated by a dashed rectangle. The filter expression (doc-string-search "expand-candidate") has been applied to the display, highlighting the tasks that expand new candidates, and deemphasizing the other tasks. The relevant section of code for expanding candidates is given in Figure 11.12. From the display in Figure 11.11, we can see that expand-candidate recursively calls itself, occasionally spawning other tasks along the way. Those other tasks are generated when the cost of the new node is smaller than that of the best solution found so far, in which case that path will be searched further. When the cost of the new node is greater than the best solution, that branch is pruned. Looking at the length of the expand-candidate tasks when the node is pruned, we can see that the work done by the individual tasks doesn't justify the overhead of spawning a new task. Rearranging the definition so that the recursive call to expand-candidate is evaluated in a new task only when the node is to be expanded leads to the definition in Figure 11.13. Running the traveling salesman program again with this modification results in a speedup of roughly 15%.

11.6.4 Suggested Improvements

In this section we have seen how the filter facility is useful in improving understanding and performance of the traveling salesman program. The ability to selectively highlight tasks let us pick out detail from complicated displays while

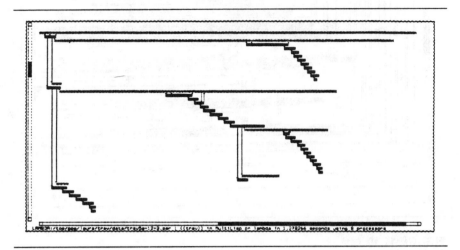

FIGURE 11.11
Enlargement of Figure 11.10.

```
(define (expand-candidate before after)
  (let ((rest-candidates
          (future (expand-candidate
                    (cdr before)
                    (cons (car before)
                          after)))))
    (if <condition>
        <code involving rest-candidates>
        rest-candidates)))
```

FIGURE 11.12
Original definition of expand-candidate, an internal procedure of
search.

the ability to gather statistics let us gather summary information. However, the
examples presented also pointed out some places where the filter language could
be improved.

While the long-queue filter in Section 11.6.1 allowed us to find all
tasks which at some point are queued for longer than 30 milliseconds, there is

```
(define (expand-candidate before after)
  (if <condition>
      (let* ((rest-candidates
               (future
                 (expand-candidate
                   (cdr before)
                   (cons (car before)
                         after)))))
         <code involving rest-candidates>)
      (expand-candidate
        (cdr before)
        (cons (car before) after))))
```

FIGURE 11.13
New definition of `expand-candidate`.

presently no way to find the average length of time that tasks remain on the queue. This suggests the need for a more general statistics gathering facility, allowing the calculation of averages, standard deviations, and the like.

In the presentation of the traveling salesman program, the program was manually separated into two parts and events were recorded for only one part, in order to simplify the display for expository purposes. One can imagine other situations in which it would be desirable to suppress the display of part of a program, but where it would be more difficult to do the separation. This suggests another use for filters, which is to use them to specify a portion of the display to make "invisible", rather than simply deemphasizing those tasks.

We were limited in the analysis we could do with the traveling salesman program because a certain amount of its behavior depended on information related to speculative parallelism, to which we didn't have access. Suggested extensions to the event format include adding priority information to `create` events, and adding a new `change-priority` event that records priority changes of tasks. These extensions would require changing ParVis to display the new information, and adding to the filter language to manipulate the new events.

Finally, although this wasn't brought up by the examples, it is a common phenomenon that novice users prefer interfaces such as menus that provide a lot of syntactic and semantic support, while expert users get impatient with such tools and prefer the ability to enter as much information as possible via the keyboard. A more flexible interface that would give users a choice of defining filters either with the menu interface or by typing them in directly would support both classes of users. The trick is to retain the ability to input data from the display in both systems. One suggestion would be to provide an editor command that allows the user to specify the desired type of input, which would then set up the appropriate sensitivity in the display.

11.7 Limitations to ParVis

At the start of this project, my goal was to build a system that was capable of analyzing datasets of approximately 10,000 futures. In practice, ParVis turns out to be useful for datasets of up to approximately 1000 futures. I don't believe that this is due to a fundamental limitation of the design. Rather, it is the slowness of the implementation, in particular the time it takes to load a dataset and create the data structures necessary for the display, and the time it takes to refresh the display, which makes manipulating datasets larger than approximately 1000 futures unpleasant. However, while there are a number of changes that could be made to the implementation that would allow ParVis to reach the goal of roughly 10,000 futures, there are reasons to believe that fundamental design limitations preclude it from analyzing datasets much larger than that.

10,000 still isn't very many futures, given that Mul-T can generate as many as 2000 futures per processor per second. To make matters more difficult, we're still dealing with relatively coarse-grained parallelism. In an environment where there are larger numbers of finer-grained processors, it doesn't seem feasible to take the approach of recording information for each and every task created. Finer-grained tasks lead to two problems (1) too many futures might be impossibly unwieldy to analyze and (2) the act of recording traces may change the timing of the program under test. The first problem may be addressed by using other performance analysis techniques to narrow down performance problems to particular places in a program, and then use a ParVis-like tool to analyze the bottlenecks in that place.

Another fundamental limitation is the assumption that there is a direct correspondence between user-inserted parallel directives and created tasks. As the Quicksort exercise showed, it can be too much work to optimize Multilisp programs by hand, even with the help of ParVis. In particular, since optimal performance depends on the balance of time to execute `future` and time to execute other operations, the user can't reasonably be expected to do this optimization, even with the aid of ParVis. This sort of thing should be left up to the compiler. At this point, the question to ask is how does ParVis interact with code that has been modified by the compiler, once there is no longer a one-to-one relationship between parallel branches specified by the user and those actually taken by the program.

11.8 Related Work

In this section I discuss related work in parallel program understanding, a spectrum ranging from correctness analysis (i.e. debugging) to performance analysis. Table 11.5 lists the systems summarized in this section. The various systems surveyed are designed for two categories of programming models, loosely-coupled distributed message-passing systems and tightly-coupled shared-memory systems. Some of the issues addressed include program execution reproducibility, interactive versus post-mortem debuggers, program monitoring, and graphic versus textual displays.

TABLE 11.5
Summary of surveyed approaches taken to debugging parallel programs.

Distributed, message-passing systems		
1982	BugNet	Curtis and Wittie [4] SUNY
1985	Idd	Harter, Heimbigner and King [10] U. of Colorado
1985	Radar	R. LeBlanc and Robbins [5] Georgia Tech.
1986	ECSP	Baiardi, De Francesco and Vaglini [9] U. of Pisa
1987	Belvedere	Hough and Cuny [11] UMass Amherst
Shared-memory, tightly-coupled systems		
1986	P-sequences	Carver and Tai [6] N. Carolina State U.
1986	Instant Replay	T. LeBlanc and Mellor-Crummey [7] Rochester
1986	WHICH	Clamen [12] MIT
1988	Toolkit	Fowler, T. LeBlanc, Mellor-Crummey [8] Rochester

11.8.1   Reproducible Program Execution

Nondeterminism is a fundamental issue in the debugging of parallel programs. This means that the behavior of a process may be determined by the ability to exchange information with other processes. Nondeterminism implies that the same program run successively might not exhibit the same behavior. There are two approaches that can be taken to address this problem. The *one-shot* approach gathers as much information about the program the first time around, whereas *reproducible program execution* provides facilities to rerun the program and guarantee the same behavior.

Five of the papers surveyed provide reproducible program execution facilities, namely Curtis and Wittie's BugNet [4], LeBlanc and Robbins' Radar [5], Carver and Tai's P-sequences [6], LeBlanc and Mellor-Crummey's Instant Replay [7], and Fowler, LeBlanc and Mellor-Crummey's Toolkit [8]. Both BugNet and Radar record the contents of messages between loosely-coupled processes in an event log during program execution. The user can then *replay* a single process with simulated communications from the event log. In addition, BugNet allows replaying of selected subset of processes, rather than just one. Note that both BugNet and Radar are designed to work in a distributed, loosely-coupled, message-passing environment where the communications between processes are likely to be less frequent than in a tightly-coupled shared-memory system. The higher frequency of communication in the latter case would make this approach impractical.

P-sequences provide repeatable execution for concurrent programs whose processes interact via semaphores. A P-sequence is a total order of all synchronization operations that occur in the program. P-sequences may be created by the programmer to test a specific sequence, or recorded in a program run and used to reproduce that run. Instant Replay takes the more general approach of modeling all interactions between processes as operations on shared objects, and represents a series of modifications to a shared object as a totally ordered sequence of versions. The partial order of accesses to each object is recorded by maintaining the current version number for each object and the number of readers for that object. This ensures that a total order of writers is maintained with respect to each shared object, a total order of readers with respect to the writers of each shared object, and a partial order of readers with respect to each shared object. During program replay, this partial order is maintained.

11.8.2   Behavioral Abstraction

The Behavioral Abstraction approach to the reproducible execution problem, exemplified by ECSP [9] and the Interactive Distributed Debugger (Idd) [10], requires the user to formally specify the expected behavior of the program. Because multiple executions of parallel programs are indeterminate, all information necessary to diagnose program errors must be collected during a single execution. An event recognition tool monitors the stream of primitive events that occur during execution, and either detects inconsistencies between these events and the formal specification, at which point it halts the program and returns control the user, or presents the user with an abstract view of the program's behavior in terms of a sequence of hierarchically-defined events.

11.8.3 Interactive Versus Post-Mortem Tools

Another axis along which program analysis tools are divided is whether they are designed to be used during or after program execution. Among the interactive tools, some continually monitor the program during execution, and others are only intended for use when the program halts due to a breakpoint or an error. Like ParVis, both Belvedere [11] and Radar are intended for post-mortem use and record events during program execution that are then used to generate a graphic display. In addition to the systems discussed in this section, Toolkit, discussed in Section 11.8.4, fits the same pattern of post-mortem tools.

Idd is a system designed for use in a distributed, message-passing environment. It monitors message traffic, displays the messages graphically as the system proceeds, and saves a history file of messages for later viewing. If a program signals an error during execution, the programmer may examine the message history accumulated so far to determine the source of the error. At this point, breakpoints may be inserted into the program, by selecting a message event and having the system restart and halt when that time point is reached.

WHICH [12] is essentially an extension to the existing sequential debugger for MultiScheme, a parallel dialect of Scheme similar to Multilisp. WHICH addresses several limitations of the sequential debugger, including the possibility of another process mutating a value that the user is currently examining, and the inability to examine the thread of computation other than the current one. WHICH provides a textual display of the spawning tree (which tasks created which other tasks), and the data-dependency graph (which tasks are waiting for results from which other tasks), plus commands to move between different processes.

11.8.4 PPUTTs Toolkit

The Toolkit system done by the Parallel Program Understanding Tools and Techniques (PPUTTs) group at the University of Rochester [8] is similar enough to the work described in this report to warrant a section to itself. The Toolkit is based on the Instant Replay work reported earlier [7], and is intended for tightly-coupled shared-memory multiprocessors. The basic idea is that the execution history is used both for reproducible program execution *and* for generating an interactive graphic display (called Moviola) for post-mortem analysis. Moviola's display is quite similar to that of ParVis, with time displayed on one axis and processes on the other. Arrows joining events in different processses reflect temporal relationships resulting from synchronization. In a shared-memory model, the relationships are between the processes that write a value and processes that subsequently read the value. In a message-passing model, the relationships are between the processes that send a message and the processes that receive them. The display is interactive, with facilities for zooming, panning, and interrogating individual events for more detailed information. As in ParVis, the interactive graphic display runs on a graphics workstation, while parallel programs run on a target multiprocessor.

A major difference between Toolkit and ParVis is that Toolkit's execution history is based on a partial order of accesses to shared memory, whereas in the future model tasks communicate by returning values. Toolkit supports a variety of programming models including direct shared memory, message passing, and remote procedure call, by modeling all interactions between processes as operations on shared objects, and by providing a customizable instrumentation facility.

11.9 An Integrated Parallel Programming Environment

As we have seen, ParVis is very useful in tuning performance of Multilisp programs. However, the ParVis system has a number of limitations to its usefulness in this task, and doesn't address a number of other issues that arise in parallel programming. In this section I discuss an integrated parallel programming environment that addresses some of these issues.

The primary change that I envision to ParVis for the integrated environment is making it interactive, not in the sense of a continually updating display during a program run, but rather having ParVis available to display the accumulated state when the program signals an error or breakpoint. In particular, I would like a parallel debugger similar to WHICH, but with its incomprehensible textual displays of the spawning tree and data-dependency graph replaced by the graphical display of ParVis. When the user wishes to move from examining one process stack to another, she can simply use the mouse to point at the task of interest. This will require interactive communication between ParVis running on a graphics workstation and the target multiprocessor. Additionally, we may borrow the idea from Idd and Moviola of using the graphic display to insert breakpoints at a certain event, and then restarting the program and halting when the event is reached.

The Idd paper doesn't address the problem of program reproducibility when inserting breakpoints and restarting. If we wanted ParVis to be completely general, we would require a scheme such as Instant Replay. Instant Replay requires that the user explicitly state which objects are shared, due to the overhead introduced for each accessed object. It would be prohibitively expensive to assume that *all* objects in shared memory are potentially sharable. Currently, Multilisp doesn't provide explicit for declaring shared objects. However, it can be argued that it's a good idea to explicitly state which objects are being used to share information between processes, since such objects should have some locking mechanism associated with them anyway. Also, the compiler may come to our aid by figuring out which variables may be shared and which are strictly local. Along with constructs for declaring shared objects, future research on Multilisp may come up with additional higher-level language constructs for structuring parallelism. In this event, the ParVis display should be augmented so as to distinguish the use of these constructs.

Although there are drawbacks to the Behavioral Assertion model for debugging parallel programs, perhaps the idea of monitoring the program during execution may be used to specify those tasks that are of interest to the user, so that only the relevant events may be saved into a dataset. This would alleviate the problem of overly large datasets, and allow the analysis of larger program runs.

11.10 Conclusion

In addition to the examples provided in this report, ParVis has been used extensively by another member of our group, Randy Osborne, to investigate speculative parallelism [3,13]. With this new tool, he was able to discover a number of things about his programs that were opaque to him before. More work needs to be done to overcome limitations to the size of programs that can be analyzed, and to extend ParVis to be useful for debugging as well as performance analysis.

The problem area addressed by ParVis is that of parallel program understanding. In the range from performance analysis to debugging, ParVis is more useful for the former. When analyzing parallel programs, the focus shifts from the internal state of individual processes to interaction between processes. Traditional profiling tools such as those that give the total amount of parallelism over time, or the total number of instructions executed, are inadequate for understanding, since they don't provide sufficient information to explain *why* a parallel program behaves in a certain way.

The key contribution of ParVis is providing the programmer with an understanding of relationships among individual tasks. It accomplishes this by displaying the state of individual tasks over time, the dependencies between tasks, and the relationship between statistical information and detailed task information. Additionally, it provides a filter facility which aids in the analysis of complex displays.

References

1. Robert Halstead, "Multilisp: a language for concurrent symbolic computation," *ACM Trans. on Prog. Languages and Systems*, pages 501–538, October 1985.

2. Robert Halstead, "An assessment of Multilisp: Lessons from experience," *International Journal of Parallel Programming*, 15(6), December 1986.

3. Randy Osborne, *Speculative Computation in Multilisp: A Model and its Implementation*, PhD thesis, Mass. Inst. of Technology, Dept. of E.E.C.S., expected in August 1989.

4. R. Curtis and L. Wittie, "BugNet: a debugging system for parallel programming environments," In *The 3rd International Conference on Distributed Computing Systems*, pages 394–399. IEEE Computer Society, Computer Society Press, October 1982.

5. Richard LeBlanc and Arnold Robbins, "Event-driven monitoring of distributed programs," In *The 5th International Conference on Distributed Computing Systems*, pages 515–522. IEEE Computer Society, Computer Society Press, May 1985.

6. Richard Carver and Kuo-Chung Tai, "Reproducible testing of concurrent programs based on shared variables," In *The 6th International Conference on Distributed Computing Systems*, pages 428–433. IEEE Computer Society, Computer Society Press, May 1986.

7. Thomas LeBlanc and John Mellor-Crummey, "Debugging parallel programs with Instant Replay," Technical Report TR 194, Computer Science Department, The University of Rochester, Rochester, New York 14627, September 1986.

8. Robert Fowler, Thomas LeBlanc, and John Mellor-Crummey, "An integrated approach to parallel program debugging and performance analysis on large-scale multiprocessors," In *Proceedings, ACM SIGPLAN/SIGOPS Workshop on Parallel and Distributed Debugging*, pages 163–173, May 1988. Special issue of SIGPLAN Notices, 24(1), January 1989.

9. Fabrizio Baiardi, Nicoletta Derancesco, and Gigliola Vaglini, "Development of a debugger for a concurrent language," *IEEE Transactions on Software Engineering*, SE-12(4):547–553, April 1986.

10. Paul Harter, Jr., Dennis Heimbigner, and Roger King, "Idd: An interactive distributed debugger," In *The 5th International Conference on Distributed Computing Systems*, pages 498–506. IEEE Computer Society, Computer Society Press, May 1985.

11. Alfred Hough and Janice Cuny, "Belvedere: Prototype of a pattern-oriented debugger for highly parallel computation," In *1987 International Conference on Parallel Processing*, pages 735–738, August 1987.

12. Stewart Clamen, "Debugging in a parallel Lisp environment," Bachelor's thesis, Mass. Inst. of Technology, Dept. of E.E.C.S., June 1986.

13. Randy Osborne, Personal communication.

12

Reflective Memory Instrumentation Issues

Blaine Gaither
Jeff Hardy

Reflective memory is a mechanism for providing shared memory communications at high speed between homogeneous or heterogeneous systems at distances of up to 120 feet. This paper discusses the architecture and applications of reflective memory, the performance issues particular to reflective memory systems, and finally the instrumentation designed into the Gould NP1 reflective memory.

12.1 Applications

The principle application of reflective memory is to connect systems without the overhead of operating system intervention. It is also used to connect heterogeneous networks of computers. Typically real-time frontend systems, running proprietary operating systems, are connected to a backend system, which in the case of NP1 runs UNIX.[1] The frontend systems often are doing data acquisition, or real-time control, while the backend systems are doing significant number crunching. An example might be multi-dome flight simulation or payload simulation.

[1] UNIX is a trademark of AT&T Bell Laboratories.

12.2 NP1 Overview

The NP1 is a vector mini-supercomputer based on the vector register approach [1, 2]. It consists of one to four processors, sharing a 153 megabyte per second (MB/s) bus. I/O devices supported on this bus include a >100 MB/s supercomputer channel.

Access to memory for CPUs and I/O channels is through the bus. The CPUs use cache write-through with bus watching to assure cache consistency.

12.3 Reflective Memory

Up to eight systems may be connected on a single reflective memory bus over distances with a maximum of 120 feet. Reflective memory allows for a maximum of 32 NP1 CPUs to share memory.

The NP1 reflective memory hardware consists of two boards that sit on the NP bus. This set of boards is connected to the reflective memory boards in other systems by a set of cables in a series arrangement. There is no "backplane" for the reflective memory, but the network of interconnected reflective memory boards is called the reflective memory bus (RM bus).

In a reflective memory system each system declares one or more regions of memory as reflected. Within the UNIX environment applications gain access to the shared (reflected) memory region through a "map-refl" system call. Applications on different systems communicate as if they were in the same processor sharing the memory region. Each system has its own copy of the reflected region in its local memory. Thus, reads are at local speeds without contention; writes also occur without contention on the local copy of the data. A delay may occur between the time the write occurs on the local system, and when other systems' memories are updated.

A description of the mechanisms for sharing memory across several buses follows. Whenever a write is made to a reflected region of the local memory, the reflective memory interface for that system consults an on-board page table that translates the physical address on the originating system's bus to a virtual address on the reflective memory bus. In addition to address mapping, the translation table contains information as to whether stores to this virtual address are to be sent out on the reflective memory bus (whether or not the page is reflected), and also whether interrupts, or other external signals should be generated whenever stores are made to this page. Should the translation table so indicate, the local reflective memory boards translate the address and broadcast the write on the reflective memory bus.

When a write is broadcast on the reflective memory bus, each system's reflective memory boards translate the address from a reflective memory bus address to a local physical address. The translation also produces information as to whether stores to this page are to be repeated in local memory (reflected), and instrumentation information pertinent to the page. If the translation table indicates that the local system is to "reflect" this write, a write is performed by the reflective memory boards to the local memory.

12.4 Performance Issues

The speed of the NP bus is 153 MB/s , while the speed of the reflective memory bus is 26 MB/s . In order to match the speed of these two busses, substantial queueing is provided on the reflective memory boards. Queueing for a maximum of 1024×128 bit transactions is provided on the reflective memory boards in the outgoing (NP $\rightarrow$ RM Bus) direction, while queueing for a maximum of 32×32 bit transactions is provided in the incoming direction. The outgoing buffer size was chosen based upon a study of the typical amounts of data exchanged by large real-time systems using reflective memory.

The size of the buffers is very important because if the output buffer is full, the CPUs on the local bus are blocked (by making memory look busy) until the buffer is empty. In the opposite direction, if the reflective memory boards are unable to write to NP memory for an extended period, and a full buffer condition exists, the reflective memory bus is blocked, preventing any further transmissions until the buffer has free space.

It is conceivably very easy for an NP1 processor to fill the buffer when doing writes to a shared area of memory. The CPU can issue writes at the full 153 MB/s of the NP bus, while the reflective memory bus operates at a maximum of 26 MB/S. After the CPU has queued 1024 writes, the output buffer is filled and thereafter the NP bus is effectively slowed to RM bus speed. Thus the system slows to about 17% of its peak speed.

12.5 Instrumentation

In order to help monitor the status of an NP1 on a reflective memory network, instrumentation was built into the reflective memory board pair. The following events are available as probe points or for external monitoring, or the events can be strapped to cause interrupts.

Output Buffer Overflow - NP to RM Bus

Input Buffer Overflow - RM Bus to NP

Write by RM to a page - Each page has a flag that can cause an event to be signaled when a write to that page comes across the RM Bus.

Write by NP to a page - Each page has a flag that can cause an event to be signaled when the NP writes to that page in reflective memory.

Additional instrumentation is available to show how many of the buffers are in use, RM bus busy, bidding for the RM bus which node got the RM bus, RM bus bidding for NP bus access, and RM-granted NP bus access.

12.6 Application Level Monitoring

Several strategies are possible for monitoring reflective memory based systems. Much of the instrumentation discussed in the previous section is at a low level. A framework for software monitoring is needed to fill out the reflective memory application development environment.

Since heterogeneous systems are supported, a low end real-time processor can be economically dedicated to monitoring the state of data stored in the shared region. This processor can perform sampling, error detection, and dumping trace buffers written in memory by application processors. Note that since reads are answered out of local memory, the act of monitoring shared data does not impose any artifact on the system under test. In addition, event-driven monitoring could be supported by tying some of hardware instrumentation to interrupt lines.

A reflective memory design could easily support the sampling of network delay by a monitoring processor. Since the page tables for translating local writes to RM bus addresses is distinct from that used to translate addresses coming from the reflective memory to local addresses, they may be set up to be noninvertable. That is, a local store to page 10 gets translated to RM page 20, while RM page 20 is translated to local page 11. Essentially the RM boards could be set up to send a write back to the system that originated it but at a different address. The time delay noted on the originating system would be the same as that on all the receiving systems, discounting local buffer delays. This same technique could be used to implement semaphores using backoff locks.

The critical factor to the above design (not implemented on the current NP1 implementation) is to permit the RM boards to re-reflect outgoing data to a different address in local memory. This re-reflection must normally be inhibited to prevent infinite loops in the normal case.

12.7 Conclusions

As the demand for shared memory parallel processing exceeds the capacities of single bus systems, interconnection schemes like reflective memory will be increasingly important. The instrumentation mechanisms presented in this paper are a starting point for developing a measurement environment for these systems.

References

1. D. Vianney and S. Heffner, "An Overview of the Gould NP1 Parallel Multicomputer System," Proceedings of the Second International Conference on Supercomputing, Vol. 1, 1987, pp. 29-34.

2. D. Vianney and S. Heffner, "The Gould NP1 Architecture," Proceedings of the Second International Conference on Supercomputing, Vol. 1, 1987, pp. 35-43.

13

Performance: The Need For An In-depth View

Harry F. Jordan

13.1 Introduction

Many of the studies of parallel processor performance have been stimulated by scientific computing tasks that are compute bound. For such tasks, the utilization of processors is most important, and use of other resources, such as I/O facilities, can be safely neglected. For these tasks, the best performance implies the smallest execution time. In parallel programs it is not the total number of processor cycles that is to be minimized but the time to completion of the job. Minimum processor cycles would probably imply sequential execution on a single processor, making parallelism unnecessary. Thus execution time can be taken as the direct indicator of performance for compute bound parallel programs, and it remains to determine what factors determine the minimum execution time for a particular program run on a particular parallel computer system.

Although the execution time is the most direct indicator of performance, it is influenced by a wide variety of things. At the bottom is the hardware technology, which has a uniform scaling influence on all processors in the system. Processor architecture and system architecture come next, followed by the operating system, which is often characterized as an extension of the architecture.

The language used to write the program, its compiler and run time support libraries separate the program from the operating system extended architecture. The program structure, based on language and programming style can have a strong impact on performance and has the advantage of being accessible to the user. Finally, the mathematical algorithm selected can have impact on the available parallelism, and thus the execution time, in a significant way. The execution time measurement potentially combines influences from all these levels, and experience shows that it is seldom attributable to only one of them.

One approach to separating the influences of the various levels on parallel program performance is to measure different quantities to characterize the different influences. Vector unit idle time and interprocess communication traffic would be examples of such quantities. The approach taken in this paper is to rely only on the total execution time measurement. To supply the additional information needed to separate influences on time to completion, the execution time is measured more than once, under variation of some parameter of the parallel program and system pair. Program parameters might be vector length or synchronization granularity, while system parameters could be number of processors or operating system time slice.

It will be shown by example that parametrized measurements of execution time can give detailed insight into various system and program features which influence performance. Combined with analytical modeling, such measurements can be used to identify important aspects of the interaction of program with system. The information obtained can help to extrapolate the performance of a program scaled up for a production run, aid in restructuring the program for improved performance, or indicate the characteristics of a better system for running the program.

13.2 Levels of the Computation Influencing Performance

The pair consisting of a program and a computer system constitutes a computation. Performance is influenced by system features, program features, and the interaction between them. Table 13.1 lists six different levels of the computation that may impact performance. The user can influence these levels to varying degrees. He has total control over the program and algorithm but none at all over the hardware implementation. Limited control over the architecture might involve using fewer than the maximum number of processors in a multiprocessor system.

At the root of the hardware implementation is the digital logic technology used, but other factors, such as the degree of integration, circuit interconnections and cooling, play a role in determining speed. The hardware influences can

TABLE 13.1
Levels that impact performance

Level	Notes
Hardware	Establishes fundamental speed scale
Architecture	Both individual unit and system level
Operating system	As an extension to the hardware
Language	Includes compiler and run-time support
Program	Control structure and synchronization
Algorithm	Data dependency structure

usually be summed up by stating the clock period of the machine. This is not entirely divorced from the architecture, since a RISC microprocessor with a 10 nanosecond (ns) clock period is not the same as a supercomputer with the same clock rate.

Parallel systems attempt to use the architecture to achieve a higher performance than would result from a sequential machine with the same clock rate. Architecture is often the target for performance studies, either for selecting a system or optimizing a design. The arithmetic unit, control unit and memory hierarchy all have an impact on the performance of each processor in the system. The total system performance is also influenced by the synchronization and data movement among processors. Any of these architectural features can set an upper limit on the performance of a particular program. Perhaps a litmus test for a well balanced architecture is the ability to find different programs whose performance is limited by each of these factors in turn.

The operating system is often characterized as an extension of the hardware, but it also shares resources among multiple users of the system. As an extension of the role of sharing resources among users, it may also be involved in sharing resources among multiple processes belonging to one user's parallel program. Thus process control, synchronization and interprocess data movement may involve the operating system. Input/output is managed by the operating system in more or less traditional ways.

The programming language influences performance through the primitive operations made available to the programmer and through the efficiency of their implementation. Though based on the machine instruction set, the language influence on performance is strongly determined by the compiler and the run-time package system. The important compiler features include not only the basic implementation of the language primitives but also global optimization and automatic parallelization, if used. A sizable run-time system often supports the language. Frequency and cost of linkages to the run-time package are often important performance influences. The degree to which the run-time package relies on the operating system for support is also important. For example, it is possible that no low-cost synchronization whatever is available in a multiprocessor as a result of a two level linkage through the run-time and operating systems, along with a possible context switch for one or more processors.

The organization and style of the program has an important impact on performance, and almost all programmers make some degree of effort to structure their program to run fast on what they perceive to be the abstract model of the computer system. The choice of data structures, the program control structure, type of synchronizations used and the management of I/O can all have a strong influence on performance. The result of many performance studies is to suggest modifications of program structure which will lead to better performance. Also, the ability to change parameters of the program can be used to advantage in studying the performance implications of lower levels of the computation.

While programming style can be considered the tactics of the computation plan, the algorithm constitutes the strategy. Aspects of the algorithm which relate directly to performance include the depth of the dependence graph, its size or number of operations, the maximum, minimum and average parallelism, and the fraction of the operations forming a strictly sequential chain. Different algorithms may be more vectorizable or parallelizable, and this may or may not trade off against the size of the computation. Although the choice of algorithm may be determined by an understanding of the system performance, algorithm variation does not usually play a direct role in performance studies.

13.3 Parametrized Execution Time

Two reciprocal measures of performance have been most frequently used in characterizing computations: execution time and speed. Speed has the disadvantage that it can suppress the number of operations needed to do the job. An algorithm and program can exhibit a very high rate of executing operations while, at the same time, requiring far more operations than a better algorithm, data structure or program organization. Even more questionable is the use of speedup, or the ratio of operation rate on a parallel computer to the operation rate of a "similar" sequential machine. Imagining a sequential machine that forms a meaningful basis for the denominator of the ratio is extremely tenuous. The utility of speedup curves is a result of the fact that they characterize performance over a range of variation in a system parameter, yielding much more information than a single value of the (suspect) ratio. This idea of tracking a performance measure over the variation of a parameter of the computation is very powerful when applied to the execution time to completion, which is the direct characterization of the performance.

A significant advantage to execution time as a measure of performance is that it is non-invasive. Measuring start and stop times does not change program performance. Its disadvantage is that it represents a combination of influences from all the levels of the computation listed in Table 13.1. Taking a hint from speedup curves, considerably more information can be obtained if the execution time is measured as a function of the variation in some significant parameter of the computation which changes the influence of one or more levels on the performance. Examples of parameters that can be varied to give significant information about performance include:

□ vector length - on a pipelined or SIMD vector machine;

□ number of processes - on a multiprocessor;

□ address stride - on a machine needing regular access patterns;

□ data placement - in private or shared memories;

□ virtual process ratio - on the Connection Machine.

Things that can be seen from such parametrized execution time curves include the effectiveness of the architecture in handling a particular kind of program parallelism, the effectiveness of the compiler in exploiting the architecture to best advantage, and the efficiency of the run-time/operating system in handling a particular control or synchronization structure in the program.

Perhaps the most familiar example is the characterization of the performance of pipelined vector computers by giving time to complete a simple vector operation as a function of vector length. Bucher [1] gave a clear exposition of this in characterizing the operation of the Cray 1. Following her discussion, assume that vectors of length N are processed in strips consisting of R components each. The strips can arise from the existence of vector registers or a limitation on the size of a vector length specifier.

A vector operation can be characterized by the parameters of Table 13.2. Using these parameters, the execution time can be expressed as:

$$T(N) = T_S + N\left(\frac{T_r}{R} + T_e\right) + T_r\left(1 - \frac{N \bmod R}{R}\right)\left(\left\lceil\frac{N}{R}\right\rceil - \left\lfloor\frac{N}{R}\right\rfloor\right) \quad .(13.1)$$

The first two terms represent the behavior of an ideal pipeline that takes strips into account only in an average way. The last term can be seen as a "granularity correction" that characterizes the detailed effects of starting new strips. If the parameters of Table 13.2 are taken as the hardware values for the Cray 1 when performing a vector equals vector plus scalar operation, the resulting curve appears as in Fig. 13.1, where division of the execution time by N makes the curve approach an asymptote of $T_r/R + T_e$. This asymptotic rate is clearly the maximum pipeline delivery rate with the strip start up time amortized over the R vector components in a strip. Bucher's measurements show that the model describes the Cray 1 operation very well.

TABLE 13.2
Parameters characterizing a vector operation

N	-	Vector length
T_S	-	Time to start a full vector operation
T_r	-	Time to start a strip
T_e	-	Time to deliver one result at full pipeline speed
R	-	Length of strip (size of vector registers)

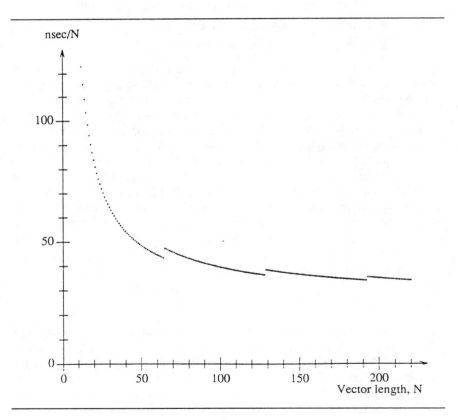

FIGURE 13.1
Execution time per Component for $V = V + S$ operation.

The parameters characterizing a vector operation are influenced by two different levels. Bucher's paper was devoted to studying the hardware effects coming from the vector unit design. In only slightly more complex situations the software, in particular the compiler, may have a significant influence. A vector operation is specified by the user either as a sequential loop for an auto-vectorizing compiler or as an explicit vector operation, say, in Fortran 8X. The compiler produces code that strip mines the operation and attempts to recognize any special cases where code more efficient than the general case can be used. T_S and T_r are influenced by the type of code produced, as well as by the vector unit hardware.

The use of such a parametrized execution time measurement, along with its describing model, can give good insight into system performance. Even in a complex program, it is possible that the strip character of a major vector operation will have a visible effect on the overall execution time. A measurement of the height of the discontinuities at the strip boundaries can give a good estimate of T_r, which is relatively insensitive to other effects and the positions of the discontinuities yields the strip length. This can help in evaluating overall vector performance or, if the hardware parameters are known, in understanding the quality of compiler generated vector code.

13.4 Multiprocessor Examples

In characterizing multiprocessors, execution time versus number of processors is a useful measurement. This is the inverse of the much used, and much misused, speedup curve. The oldest model for this measurement is Amdahl's law [2]. This simple characterization of multiprocessors has been modified and extended by numerous authors to include the effects of things such as synchronization overhead, interprocessor communication, process management, memory size, etc. In its simplest form, Amdahl's law assumes that code is either sequential or parallel and that the two do not overlap. In this respect, it is best suited to describing SIMD computers. Properly extended and applied, however, it can help give insight into various aspects of multiprocessor performance.

Some execution time versus number of processes measurements that illustrate well the influences from a broad range of factors were carried out on a HEP system at the U. S. Army Ballistic Research Laboratory [3]. The computer is an MIMD system that is partially pipelined and partially parallel. The processing is spread over 4 process execution modules (PEMs), each of which is a pipelined multiprocessor in which instructions execute at maximum rate if about 15 processes are simultaneously active. The 4 PEMs connect to 4 pipelined memory modules through a pipelined switch to form a multiprocessor system with about 60-fold parallelism.

To see the large number of effects that can be deciphered from the time versus processes curve, we start from the analysis of the performance of a single PEM [4]. This analysis considered four effects extending the simple Amdahl's law model: limited parallelism in part of the program, effect of critical section synchronization, granularity of parallel tasks, and the hardware limit on degree of pipelined parallelism. The first three effects apply to any multiprocessor system while the fourth only exists in pipelined MIMD systems.

The complete execution time model for a program whose structure involves a parallel loop and a critical section which must be executed by one process at a time is:

$$T(P) = T_S + t_c + \max\left(\frac{Nt_u}{\min(P,U)}, (P-1) \times t_c\right) + \delta(P), \qquad (13.2)$$

where:

P - number of processes,

T_S - amount of sequential work,

N - range of the parallel loop,

t_u - work for one instance of the loop body,

U - average length of multiprocessor pipeline,

t_c - work for single critical section execution, and

$\delta(P)$ - "granularity" correction for $N \bmod P \neq 0$.

The first term of Eq. (2) represents the strictly sequential work from Amdahl's law. The second is the amount of critical section executed by one process. The third term changes depending on whether the parallel work or the sequentialized critical section dominates. The parallel work part of the term has a denominator exhibiting the limit, U, on the amount of parallelism available from the multiprocessing pipeline. The "granularity" correction $\delta(P)$ has the form:

$$\delta(P) = t_u\left(\frac{(N \bmod P)}{\min(N \bmod P,\ U)} - \frac{(N \bmod P)t_u}{\min(P,U)}\right) \qquad (13.3)$$

In its use of the mod function it resembles Eq. (1) and arises from the same phenomenon of dividing N units of work over a number of hardware units which does not divide N evenly. Reference [4] shows that this model corresponds very accurately to the measured execution time for the above type of program on a HEP computer consisting of a single pipelined multiprocessor unit, or PEM.

The overall shape of the measurements, first reported in [3], for a four PEM HEP system is quite similar to the above model, as shown in Fig. 13.2. The program is a simple 200 by 200 matrix multiply, parallelized over rows of the

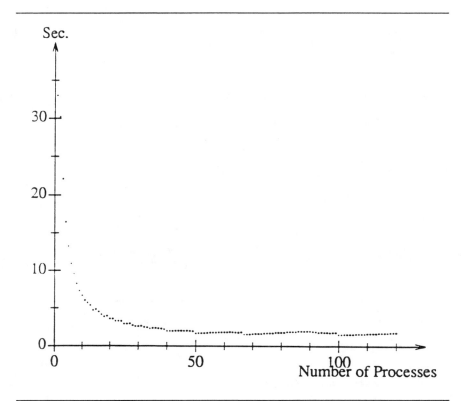

FIGURE 13.2
200×200 matrix multiply on a four PEM HEP.

product matrix. The critical section effects are missing, since matrix multiply is ideally parallelizable, but the granularity discontinuities can be seen at divisors of 200. A least squares fit to Amdahl's law suggests a sequential code size of $T_S = 0.55$ sec. and parallel work of 60.93 sec., which for $N = 200$ means $t_u = 0.30$ sec.

In Fig. 13.3 the granularity discontinuities can be clearly seen, but some rather complex looking fine structure starts to appear. It is tempting to dismiss the fine structure as measurement inaccuracy, but Fig. 13.4 makes it clear that it contains some intriguing regularity. In fact, the fine structure represents some important information about the architecture of the system and, to a lesser extent, the program structure. In order to understand the fine structure quite accurately, three new aspects must be added to the basic understanding of a single PEM

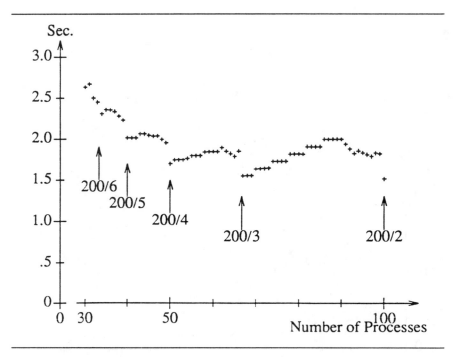

FIGURE 13.3
Granularity discontinuities and fine structure.

operation from reference [4]:

1. the four PEM nature of the system,

2. the program's distribution of processes to PEMs, and

3. the concept of lookahead in a PEM.

   Figure 13.5 shows the architecture of the four PEM Ballistic Research Laboratory HEP system. The four pipelined multiprocessor units are connected to the data memory modules by the nodes of a pipelined switching network. A separate program memory is included in each PEM and does not affect performance since it can deliver instructions at the maximum rate required. The independent processor parallelism of the four PEMs, superimposed on the pipelined parallelism of each one, has what is perhaps the most obvious effect. Varying the number of independent processors executing a parallel program shows the same granularity effects expressed by Eq. (3). But because the parallelism limit, U, does not appear in this case and P is the number of physical processors, the

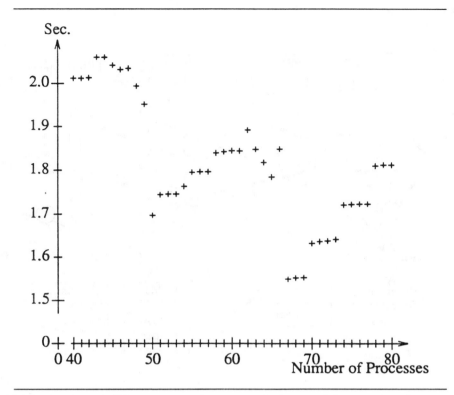

FIGURE 13.4
Details of the fine structure.

granularity discontinuities are between plateaus in the execution time. The execution time does not change until a change in the maximum execution time among the processors. It seems clear that this effect is related to the groups of four identical data points for successive numbers of processors.

The parallel processes of a single job in this system are managed by the program rather than the operating system, and this matrix multiplication program divides them evenly among the four PEMs. After the pipelined parallelism limit has been reached for a PEM, adding a process to the pipeline leaves the aggregate number of instructions per second over all processes the same, and thus decreases the execution rate per process proportionally. So for a single PEM, the execution time will increase until the addition of a process reduces the maximum number of units of work, $\lceil N/P \rceil$, per process. With four PEMs starting with processes evenly distributed among them, only the addition of a process to the first one

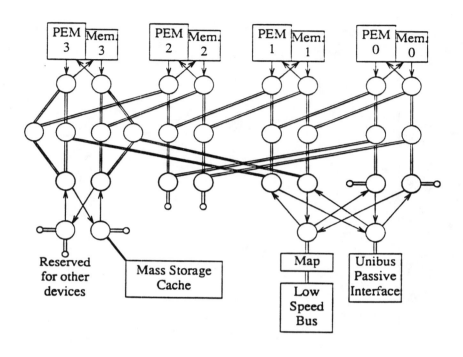

FIGURE 13.5
Architecture of a four PEM HEP computer.

of the four increases the total execution time, which is the maximum over the
PEMs. This effect is clearly seen in Fig. 13.4 between 70 and 80 processes.

The observing reader will have noticed that the above argument predicts a
jump in execution time for each P such that $P[\text{mod}4] = 1$ and that a jump occurs
at 70, not 69. This is a result of the way this version of the program does process
management. It does actually divide processes evenly among PEMs. The initial
process, running on PEM0, divided the remaining $P - 1$ processes evenly and
then proceeded to help with the matrix multiply, thereby yielding one too many
processes on PEM0. When $P[\text{mod}4] = 1$, PEM0 should have exactly one more
process than the other PEMs, so the allocation comes out as expected in this
case. The increases in execution time therefore occur at $P[\text{mod}4] = 2$, where
the program divides $P - 2$ processes evenly but gives both of the remainder
processes to PEM0.

The fine structure in Fig. 13.4 can almost be explained by a superposition of the above four PEM effect on the granularity correction of Eq. (3). However, there are some unexpected decreases in execution time, most obvious between 62 and 65 processes, that are not accounted for. To explain this final feature of the execution time versus processes curve, it is necessary to understand the lookahead feature installed on each of the four PEMs of the BRL HEP.

The primary use of the execution pipeline in a pipelined multiprocessor is to overlap the execution of instructions from independent streams. Figure 13.6a shows the situation for a four stage pipeline executing the jth instruction of four independent instruction streams, I_0, I_1, I_2, and I_3. If more instruction streams are active than there are stages in the pipeline, then the time between instruction issues from the same stream increases by the ratio of the number of active processes to the length of the pipe, as shown in Fig. 13.6b. Finally, some successive instructions in a single process may be independent. A limited amount of simultaneous execution may be obtained by placing such instructions together in the pipeline. The lookahead feature of a HEP PEM only takes effect if the process queue is empty at issue time. In that case it checks some simple sufficient conditions for independence of the next instruction in the just serviced stream and, if they are satisfied, issues that instruction immediately. Figure 13.6c shows this situation for one process executing in a four stage pipeline.

In a HEP PEM, the execution pipeline is eight stages long and lookahead does not apply to the memory access pipeline. Thus lookahead has an effect only when fewer than eight processes are active on a PEM and is very sensitive to the actual instruction sequence. This feature affects the matrix multiplication when a small number, $200[\bmod P]$, of rows of the product matrix remain to be done after $\lfloor 200/P \rfloor$ parallel steps with all of the processes. When fewer than eight processes are active on a PEM in the remainder phase, lookahead is used more and more efficiently as the number that are active decreases.

Specifically, between $P = 62$ and $P = 65$ in Fig. 13.4, the number of processes active in the remainder phase decreases by three for each increase of P by one. The allocation of processes to PEMs and the assignment of remainder work to processes implies that the PEM having the most work, PEM0, executes 5, 4, 3 and 2 processes in the remainder phase for $P = 62$, 63, 64 and 65, respectively. The speedup that results from increasing use of lookahead on this PEM accounts for the decreasing execution time.

With the final addition of the lookahead understanding, the nature of the fine structure becomes completely explained. Its apparent randomness comes from the superposition of effects with an underlying period of $P[\bmod 4]$ on effects related to the remainder of 200 divided by P. The detailed management of processes by the program also had an effect that confused the issue by making an explanation based only on the architecture incomplete in subtle ways.

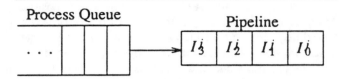

a. Single process instruction rate is $r = \dfrac{1}{\text{pipe latency}}$.

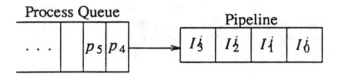

b. Single process instruction rate is $\dfrac{4}{6} r = \dfrac{1}{6/4 \cdot \text{pipe latency}}$.

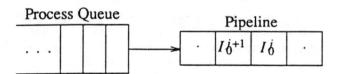

c. Instruction rate is $f_l r$, where f_l = average # instructions in pipe.

FIGURE 13.6
Load cases for a multiprocessor pipeline.

Another example of a major performance effect and corresponding execution time model comes from the class of multiprogrammed multiprocessors.
Multiprogramming involves the operating system in process management in order to optimize the use of system resources, primarily I/O devices and memory
occupancy. If multiple processes are used within a single job, the operating
system often becomes the mechanism chosen to manage process interactions
unique to parallel programming: process creation, termination and synchronization. Even if the operating system is not directly involved in synchronizations,
process management by the operating system for the purpose of multiprogramming may interact strongly with the process control involved in parallel process

synchronization. Such an effect was measured [5] on the Encore Multimax [6] and Sequent Balance [7] multiprocessors. It constitutes an interesting example of operating system interaction with parallel programs.

The example involves barrier synchronization. In this case the barrier is defined as a point in the code of all processes cooperating in the execution of a parallel program which every process must reach before any process may pass. This simple characterization of barrier operation can be implemented in many different ways [8] using either the identification of a master process or a simple lock/unlock mechanism if it exists in the system [9], but the understanding of the effect is virtually independent of the implementation given the relation of instruction execution times to swap overhead. The basic effect results from the tacit assumption that parallel processes working on a single job are coscheduled and the multiprogramming assumption that processes are independent of one another, except in so far as they compete for resources.

If the number of processes assumed for the execution of a parallel program is fixed, then it is possible that the multiprogramming load will prevent their coscheduling on physical processors, even if the system contains that many physical processors. The nature of a process barrier demands participation of all processes in reporting that they have reached the barrier and in acknowledging the barrier release signal. If some processes are swapped out at any given time, and if the operating system does not take explicit account of the barrier synchronization in its scheduling, the barrier may take several process swap times to complete. In order to remove the complications introduced by an arbitrary multiprogramming load, Fig. 13.7 shows the situation when a parallel program, run alone on a 20 processor Encore Multimax, uses more processes than there are physical processors.

The specific program is a barrier-synchronized Gaussian elimination on a 200×200 matrix. Three barrier synchronizations are performed in processing each of the 200 pivots. Using more processes for the program gives the expected drop in execution time up to 19 processes. The Umax[1] operating system keeps one processor occupied with system functions, so 20 processes is already more than can be coscheduled on a 20 processor system. The sharp rise in execution time beginning at 20 processes is qualitatively the result of adding to the barrier delay caused by small variations in process arrival times, the effects of operating system process management, which involve a much larger time scale.

To model the effect, assume that P processes are running on a smaller number Q of physical processors. Assume an operating system scheduler which runs processes for a time quantum T_q before making a new scheduling decision in the absence of other explicit operating system interaction by the program. It is also assumed that the barrier is implemented directly with hardware-supported

---

[1] Umax is a trademark of Encore.

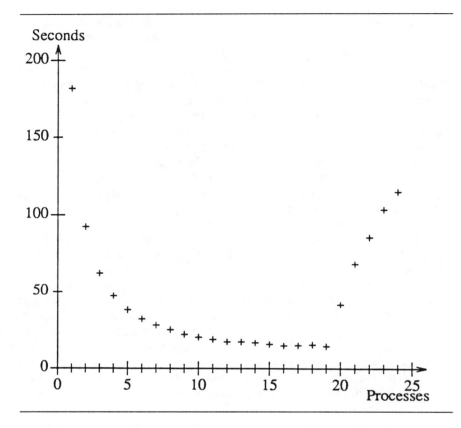

FIGURE 13.7
Barrier sychronized Gaussian elimination on a 20 processor Multimax.

lock/unlock to make it efficient in the normal coscheduled case. When a barrier is reached, $P - Q$ processes will be swapped out. After an expected wait of T_q/Q, one of the Q running processes will reach the end of its time quantum and be swapped out, thereby starting one of the suspended processes which will quickly satisfy its part of the barrier synchronization. When this has happened $P - Q$ times, assuming first-come, first-served scheduling, the barrier will be satisfied. The expected wait at a barrier resulting from the lack of coscheduling is thus:

$$\hat{W_b} = \frac{P - Q}{Q}T_q \quad .$$

(13.4)

If the time to execute the program with coscheduled processes is T_{prog} and the number of barriers in the program is N_b, then the total execution time with $P > Q$ processes is:

$$T(P) = T_{prog}(Q) + N_b \hat{W}_b = T_{prog}(Q) + N_b \frac{P - Q}{Q} T_q \; . \tag{13.5}$$

With 600 barriers in the measured program and 19 processors, a linear fit to the rising tail of the graph of Fig. 13.7 gives an operating system time quantum of about 0.6 second. The fit is not particularly good, since the extra time per process decreases as $P - Q$ increases. Since the operating system is a derivative of Unix, and since Unix policies usually reduce the time quantum when more processes are waiting for processor resources, this decrease is not unexpected. The example thus shows that parametrized measurements of execution time can give insight into operating system parameters and policies as well as architecture and program structure.

13.5 Conclusions

We have shown several examples of the impact on performance arising from different levels of the computation. In each case, a parametrized performance measure can be related to a model that gives insight into policies and characteristics of the architecture, operating system, language or program. The real power of parametrized execution time measurements comes from the identification of the correct model in a specific case. The case of the matrix multiplication fine structure shows, however, that even very complex-seeming variations in measurements yield to this kind of analysis.

Some performance effects are, of course, specific to individual systems. But if a sufficiently general model is developed, it can give insight into all systems of a general class. The classes of pipelined vector processors, parallel/pipelined multiprocessors and multiprogrammed multiprocessors were explicitly covered here. The combination of parametrized performance measurement with models based on the parameters offers a powerful mechanism for understanding performance for the purposes of extrapolating the performance of long production runs, discovering beneficial program modifications, optimizing architectural parameters, and determining operating system policies.

References

1. I. Y. Bucher, "The computational speed of supercomputers, *Performance Evaluation Review: Proc. ACM Sigmetrics Conf. on Measurement and Modeling of Computer Systems*, pp. 151-165 (Aug. 1983).

2. G. M. Amdahl, "Validity of the single processor approach to achieving large-scale computing capabilities, *AFIPS Conf. Proc.*, V. 30, AFIPS Press, Reston, VA, pp. 483-485 (1967).

3. H. F. Jordan, "Performance and program structure in a large shared memory multiprocessor," in *New Computing Environments: Parallel, Vector and Systolic*, Arthur Wouk, Ed., pp. 201-217, SIAM, Philadelphia, PA, 1986.

4. H. F. Jordan, "Interpreting parallel processor performance measurements," *SIAM J. Sci. Stat. Comput.*, V. 8, No. 2, pp. s220-s226 (March 1987).

5. M. S. Benten and H. F. Jordan, "Multiprogramming and the Performance of Parallel Programs," *Proc. 3rd SIAM Conf. on Parallel Processing for Scientific Computing*, Los Angeles, CA (Dec. 1987).

6. Multimax Technical Summary, Encore Computer Corporation, Marlboro, MA (1986).

7. Balance 8000 System Technical Summary, Sequent Computer Systems, Beaverton, OR (1985).

8. T. Axelrod, "Effects of Synchronization Barriers on Multiprocessor Performance," *Parallel Computing*, V. 3, No. 2, (1986) pp. 129-140.

9. N. S. Arenstorf and H. F. Jordan, "Comparing Barrier Algorithms," *ICASE Rept. No. 87-65*, NASA Langley Res. Ctr., Hampton, VA (Sept. 1987) to appear in Parallel Computing.

14

A VLSI Chip Set For A Multiprocessor Performance Measurement System

A. Mink
R. Carpenter

14.1 Introduction

Our premise is that MIMD multiprocessor performance measurement tools must be hybrid tools, thus requiring some level of hardware support. This hardware support is necessary to reduce perturbation of the executing processes to a tolerable level [1-7]. The cost, size, and implementation technology of this hardware must also be reasonable in comparison to the cost, size, and implementation technology of the machine being measured.

Basic elements of performance measurement are event detection (triggering) and data capture (sampling). A trigger is the mechanism that detects a predefined event and causes a data sample to be taken. Taking a sample consists of collecting the set of measurement data that describes the event and storing it for analysis. Performance measurement tools are classified as either hardware, software, or hybrid, depending on the implementation of the triggering and sampling mechanisms [8].

Software tools can perturb the execution characteristics of programs beyond tolerable levels. Perturbation is caused by extra instructions executed by the measurement tool embedded in either the process or the operating system. Extra instructions require longer execution time and more memory space. If sampling is done by software, then additional memory is required for the storage of the measurement data. Secondary perturbation is caused by translation look-aside buffer and cache invalidations, as well as additional bus traffic.

Hardware tools do not cause any perturbations to the execution characteristics of programs, but suffer from signal access and recognition problems [9]. Hardware tools do not have an "internal view" of the executing process and due to high levels of VLSI integration, may not have access to memory management unit (MMU) activity, cache activity, or virtual addresses.

In our research we have pursued two classes of measurement data; timed event trace data and resource utilization data. Timed event trace data are concerned with program execution activities, while resource utilization data are concerned with the activity of the architecture. We have designed and implemented two separate tools to acquire these classes of measurement data.

Our hybrid tool, TRAMS [10,11], is illustrated in Figure 14.1. The TRAMS is a memory mapped device capable of collecting and storing measurement data when triggered. Triggering is done in software, by having the user embed code in the program. This trigger code consists of a simple write instruction to the TRAMS address. Sampling is done in hardware. The data written to the TRAMS are user specified, and normally identifies the writing process and the event in the process. The TRAMS stores these data along with a timestamp and the identity of the CPU into its own (sample) memory. These data are then read out of the sample memory, usually after the experiment, and are used for performance analysis.

Our hardware tool, REMS [12,9], is illustrated in Figure 14.2. The REMS trigger mechanism and sampling mechanism are both hardware. The trigger mechanism is a non-intrusive pattern matcher, which watches processor signal lines such as virtual addresses. A set of counter pairs, called preprocessors, facilitates the collection of resource utilization data samples. One REMS device is required for each processor. When the pattern matcher detects one of a set of user specified patterns, it causes a trigger. When a trigger occurs, the timed event trace data (a timestamp and the virtual address – representing the event), and the resource utilization data (the counter contents) are then captured by the REMS and stored in a local sample memory. These data are then read out of the dual ported sample memory, either during or after an experiment, by another processor and are used for performance analysis. The general applicability of passive pattern matching triggering is limited due to cost, signal accessibility, and the inability to externally distinguish between different processes.

In the course of our experimentation we have concluded that a tool such as the TRAMS does a good job of acquiring timed event trace data while its software trigger mechanism introduces a tolerable level of perturbation through its use of a simple memory write, provided events are separated by some tens

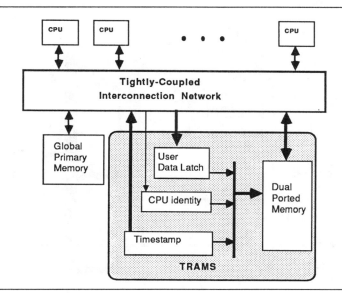

FIGURE 14.1
The TRAMS performance measurement tool on a tightly coupled MIMD
architecture.

of machine instructions. Our evaluation of the REMS indicates that it does
a good job of acquiring resource utilization data, but as mentioned above it
has problems with sampling timed event trace data and its hardware triggering.
Although pattern matching triggering introduces no perturbation to the processes,
it is expensive instrumentation. Even though our implementation of the TRAMS
is only a single circuit board, in today's technology this is considered large
and potentially too costly to replicate as an option for microprocessor based
multiprocessors. As a result we have designed a VLSI chip set that will integrate
the TRAMS functions of software triggering and hardware sampling of timed
event trace data, with the hardware REMS counter pairs, which provide resource
utilization data. The integration is to be compact and economical and can easily
be interfaced to a wide range of different MIMD multiprocessors. The result
consists of two integrated circuits (IC), the uTRAMS and the uREMS.

14.2 Measurement System Design

The uTRAMS chip handles the data capture and processor interface in a similar
manner to that of the TRAMS. Two previous implementations of the TRAMS

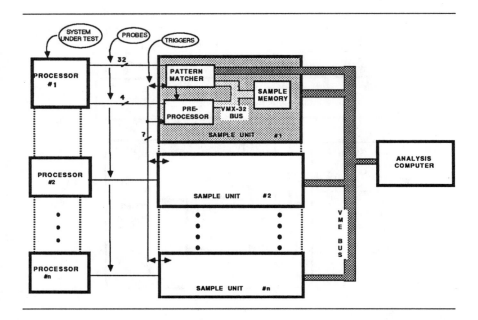

FIGURE 14.2
The REMS performance measurement tool on an MIMD architecture.

concept kept the data capture and data storage together on a single board. A tightly-coupled multiprocessor system with a single shared bus requires only a single TRAMS board placed on that central bus. In a loosely-coupled multiprocessor system with an interprocessor communication network, no such central location exists. Thus a loosely-coupled system requires that the data capture function be distributed (replicated for each processor), while the data storage function can be either distributed or centralized. For our initial implementation, distributed storage was easier due to the similarity to the tightly-coupled TRAMS design. But centralized data storage offers less complexity of the measurement device at each processor and the space to store much more measurement data before memory overflow occurs. Use of centralized data storage involves re-placing the local TRAMS memory with a FIFO and an interface to a separate, dedicated collection network. Since the local memory accounted for the majority of the TRAMS real estate, this new design for the uTRAMS device, one for each processor, is reduced to IC proportions.

Both the uTRAMS and uREMS VLSI chips contain three largely-independent sections. (1) The data capture section captures measurement data when activated by a memory write trigger from the program being measured. (2) The output section places the captured data on a dedicated collection network. (3)

The FIFO section that allows capture of bursty data and speed-matching between the data capture and the network interface.

The overall design of a single measurement node is shown in Figure 14.3. Application for various architectures is as follows: in a loosely-coupled system one node per processor is expected; in a tightly-coupled system with a single shared bus a single node located on the shared bus is sufficient; in a clustered system one node per cluster is anticipated if there is a convenient central location, otherwise one node per processor is required. The measurement node is designed for both centralized or distributed data storage. For central data storage the measurement node interfaces to a dedicated, simple collection network, Figure 14.4. For distributed data storage the measurement node interfaces to a local memory, Figure 14.5.

As can be seen from Figure 14.3, this chip set requires a little front-end logic to interface to a processor. The uTRAMS is intended to be able to operate with a number of different processor interface protocols (80x86, 680x0, 32x32, ...) with few external components, for address recognition and signal selection. The uTRAMS is mapped into a number of contiguous locations in the memory (or I/O) space of the measured processor, see Appendix A. To decrease the complexity of the uTRAMS, the address decoding is done externally. Separate addresses are allocated to write to the control register, to read the status register, to trigger a uTRAMS sample, and to trigger both a uTRAMS and a uREMS sample, etc. It is anticipated that this address recognition can be implemented in a single programmable logic device LD.

The uREMS chip requires an input signal for each counter. In an operational environment the potential set of signals that one may wish to count will exceed the number of counters, so a means of conveniently selecting the desired signals from among the set should be provided. A set of multiplexors is needed that can be programmed by the user. The alternative would require the user to connect individual leads to the desired signals. If the desired signal to be counted does not exist, additional logic (either combinational or sequential) may be necessary to compute the desired signal from a number of other available signals. Manufacturers could assist by providing a conveniently accessible set of relevant signals for measurement.

14.3 uTRAMS Data Capture Section

The uTRAMS data capture section of Figure 14.6, provides two modes of data capture, time trace and raw trace modes. In the time trace mode, writing to the normal uTRAMS address causes capture of a data sample consisting of the lowest sixteen bits of written data, a sample ID, a processor identification, and a timestamp; 64 bits in all, see Figure 14.7. The sample ID is necessary to

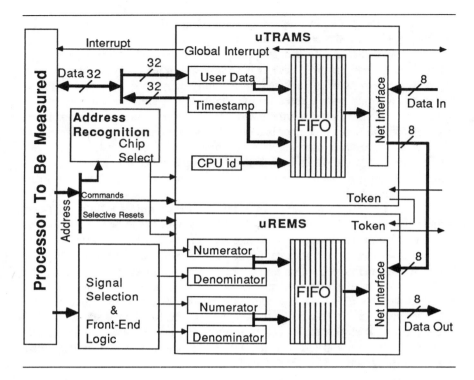

FIGURE 14.3
Block diagram of a measurement node.

distinguish between a timed trace sample, a raw trace sample, and a uREMS sample. Mode selection is implicit in the trigger address and requires no additional overhead.

In the raw trace mode, the user directly writes 48 bits to the uTRAMS through separate measurement addresses, while the top 16 bits are allocated to sample type and processor identification, see Figure 14.7. The raw mode allows the user to send software-collected data over the network, which will generally qualify the preceding event. For example, in a message passing environment, the timestamped event "process 23 sending a message at <time>" may require additional information such as source node, destination node, message size, and message identification. Since the 16 bit user field of a time trace sample is not large enough to include all this, a raw trace sample following a time trace sample would be used to qualify the event. The uTRAMS can be configured to accept either 16 or 32 bit data. Writing the activating word of the sample signals the FIFO that its input rank has been filled.

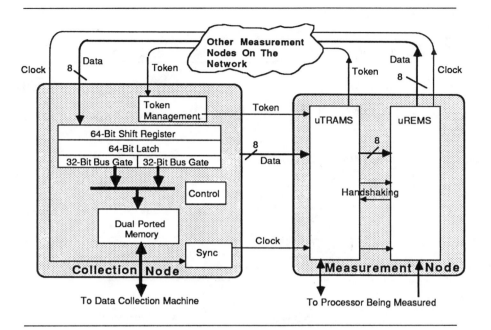

FIGURE 14.4
Measurement nodes organized with a central data collection node via a
dedicated token ring network.

Both modes of data capture provide a sample filtering capability. Associated
with a trigger is both a data capture mode and a filter level, the data capture
mode being either time trace or raw trace. If the trigger filter level (see Appendix
A) is below a user specified threshold, then the data are not captured and thus
filtered. This filtering is useful so that both the operating system and the user
code can be extensively instrumented and at execution time the user can select
the level of the desired set of measurements by selecting the appropriate filter
threshold level. No code changes are required between related measurement
experiments, which yields consistent results, and also no overhead conditional
statements are needed to skip unwanted measurements. There are eight separate
filter levels for the user and eight for the operating system. The thresholds for
both are specified by the user during initialization. The memory mapped address
that the user writes to specifies both the data capture mode and the filter level.
For example, address xxxx23 (octal) could specify time trace capture (mode 2)
and filter level 3. Thus each capture mode has a block of addresses that specifies
a filter level.

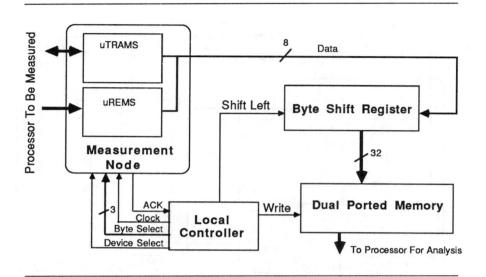

FIGURE 14.5
Measurement node organized with a local memory and directed by a local
controller.

The uTRAMS chip contains a 36-bit timestamp counter that is included in
each time trace sample to indicate relative time. The timestamp counter in all
uTRAMSs is synchronized via two common signals that are generated at some
central location and distributed to the uTRAMSs. One signal is the Timebase
Clock that causes all the timestamp counters to advance at the same rate. The
other signal is a Reset that will simultaneously set all timestamp counters to zero
when it is received. Since the Timebase Clock and the clock of the processor
being measured are not synchronized, a buffering latch must be provided. This
assures that the timestamp data can remain stable for an extended period while
being read by the measured processor. The 36-bit timestamp counter can operate
up to at least 10 MHz.

Processor identification can be obtained in one of two ways, external pins or
an internal register. When the uTRAMS is associated with a single processor, the
processor identification is written into a register of the uTRAMS on initialization.
The contents of this register is then used each time a sample is captured. In a
centralized configuration, when the uTRAMS is attached to a common bus of
multiple processors, the processor identification is dynamic and must be supplied
as an input to the chip at the same time as the user data. This information must
be available on the bus, or external logic must compute it.

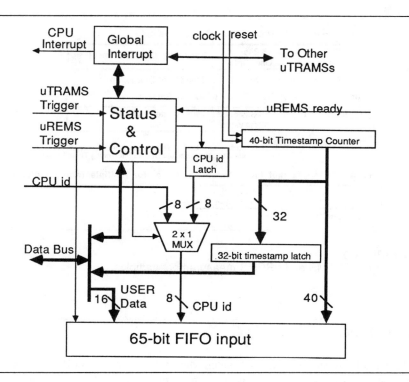

FIGURE 14.6
uTRAMS data capture section.

A Global Interrupt is provided by uTRAMS [11]. The local processor for any uTRAMS chip can cause this line to be asserted, causing an interrupt at all other uTRAMS/processors that are accepting this interrupt. Once accepted, each uTRAMS asserts this interrupt. The processor associated with each uTRAMS can sense the state of the Global Interrupt line. After performing the assigned interrupt task, each processor commands its uTRAMS to de-assert the Global Interrupt line, but does not resume normal processing until all other nodes have released the Global Interrupt line.

Interaction with the uTRAMS is accomplished via a configuration register, and a control and status register as shown in Appendix A. The configuration register contains the static CPU identification (if it is dynamic it is obtained externally with each sample), the sample filter threshold levels (one for both user and supervisor mode), and the number of wait states to use when responding to the processor. The control and status register contains information on the Global Interrupt, sampling, and the FIFO.

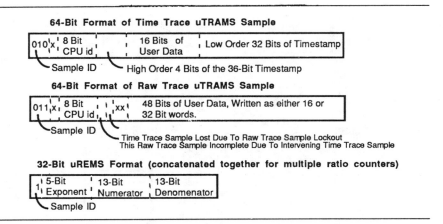

FIGURE 14.7
Format of uTRAMS and uREMS measurement samples.

14.4 FIFO

The sample generation rate is nonperiodic and bursty. The collection network can only accept samples at some maximum rate (limited by its bandwidth and the activity of other uTRAMS nodes) that is less than the maximum potential sample generation rate. A first-in, first-out (FIFO) memory is placed between the data capture (input) and output sections of both the uTRAMS and uREMS to smooth out peaks in the data collection rate. This is an asynchronous, fall-through FIFO, see Figure 14.8. The uTRAMS FIFO is 65 bits wide, 64 of uTRAMS data and a 65th bit (uREMS flag) that indicates an associated uREMS data sample. The present uREMS FIFO is 64 bits wide, containing the contents of two ratio counters. When a trigger causes a sample (see Figure 14.7) to be taken, the data are placed in the FIFO. A sample is discarded if the input rank of the FIFO is full or if the filter level is below the specified threshold.

14.5 Output Section

The Output section, see Figure 14.9, has two modes of operation. In the network mode, a dedicated token ring network will connect a group of measurement nodes to a central collection node, see Figure 14.4. The non-network mode can be used for testing and for a local RAM, see Figure 14.5.

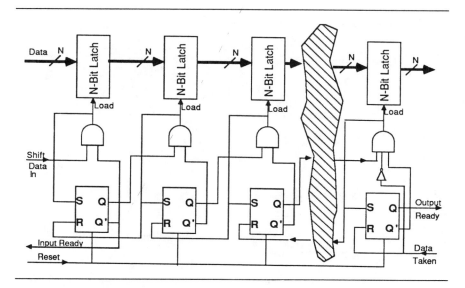

FIGURE 14.8
Asynchronous, fall-through FIFO.

The ring network uses a simple token arbitrated protocol with a single master (the collection node) as the destination for all data on the ring. Until a uTRAMS receives the token, it regenerates the network input data and passes it on to its output. When a uTRAMS node receives the token, it places one sample of its data on the network and then passes the token. If the uTRAMS node has no data to send, it immediately passes on the token. If the accompanying uREMS also has data to send, as indicated by the uREMS flag bit (the 65th bit of the uTRAMS sample data), then the uTRAMS passes the token to the uREMS. The uREMS places its data on the network and passes the token back to the uTRAMS, which then passes the token onto the next uTRAMS node in the network. Multiple uREMS chips can be associated with a single uTRAMS. In this case the token is passed from the uTRAMS through each uREMS in a daisy chain fashion back to the uTRAMS. The collection node is the only originator of tokens, and will detect the loss of a token by a timeout mechanism.

Since the network bandwidth is a concern, the network data path is designed for byte serial rather than bit serial operation. This requires eight data lines rather than one line. Internal control logic sequentially selects each byte for output. In addition to the data lines, three control lines are needed for a token signal, a synchronizing clock signal, and a reset signal. Thus a total of 11 signal lines are required to implement this network.

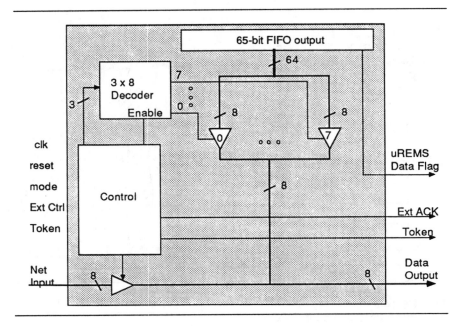

FIGURE 14.9
uTRAMS and uREMS network section.

In the non-network mode a local controller directs the operation of the output section. When the output of the FIFO indicates that data are present, the external controller sequentially selects each data byte for output.

14.6 uREMS Data Capture Section

The uREMS data capture section collects data from resource utilization counters. When a trigger indicates that uREMS samples should be taken along with the uTRAMS sample, the contents of these counters are loaded into the FIFO.

Our research has indicated that short-term averages and ratios are an important class of resource utilization measurements. Examples of these are cache hit ratio (successful cache accesses ÷ all cache accesses) and bus utilization or duty cycle (busy bus cycles ÷ all bus cycles). A ratio counter circuit should compute these values by counting the two related events and then dividing the two numbers. Real-time calculation of the division of two numbers, on-the-fly, is too expensive. As a compromise, we collect both the numerator and denominator counts and do the division later during the measurement data analysis processing.

Experimental *accuracy* in the computer measurement field is rather poor due to all of the unquantifiable perturbations. Thus, one is justified in compressing the ratio counter data by use of a reduced-precision format. Since the numerator and denominator are related, such a format can be achieved by representing the numerator and denominator counts as two truncated mantissas with a common exponent, see Figure 14.10. The total number of bits required to represent this pair is dependent on the accuracy required of the ratio; if a 3.0% error is acceptable, a 64 bit ratio counter can be truncated to a total of 15 bits (5 bit numerator, 5 bit denominator, and 5 bit exponent). A .01% error can be achieve by truncating a 64 bit ratio counter to a total of 31 bits (13 bit numerator, 13 bit denominator, and 5 bit exponent). Our uREMS can be configured for either of these representations.

Our ratio counters are designed to directly represent this truncated mantissa format. The numerator and denominator counters are structured such that the radix point is floating. As a result, the least significant bit of the count is not in a fixed position of the counter, while the most significant bits of the count are fixed in the most significant bits of the counter. To increment the numerator or denominator counters, a one has to be added to the least significant bit of the count. The function of the increment register is to indicate the current position of that least significant bit, which is common to both the numerator and denominator. When a numerator or denominator carry-out occurs, the exponent counter is incremented and the contents of the other counters and the increment register are shifted to the right, thus making room for the new most significant bit. The purpose of this design was to make the readout of the counters, in our reduced-precision format, easy and quick. The result is that the "n" truncated bits of each counter are always in the "n" most significant bits of that counter, no further manipulation of the data is required. Thus our ratio counter is a pair of counters, accumulating related hardware events in full precision, and reporting them in a truncated-precision format.

Resource utilization data need not be captured at every trigger. Thus, associated with a trigger, is the option to indicate whether or not resource utilization data should also be captured (the 65th bit in the uTRAMS FIFO). This helps to alleviate some storage and transfer requirements. When a trigger occurs with the option to take resource utilization data, the contents of all the ratio counters are placed in the FIFO. An additional option indicates which of the ratio counters, if any, are to be reset after reading. Independent resource measurements for different parts of the executing program are improved by resetting these ratio counters.

Some front-end logic to the uREMS is necessary for user convenience, see Figures 14.3 and 14.11. A number of resource measurement signals should be

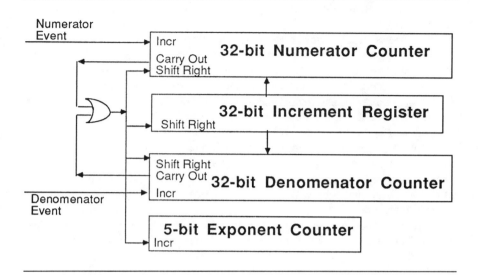

FIGURE 14.10
uREMS ratio counter.

made available to the uREMS so that any one of them can be programmably selected. Some resource measurement signals may not exist, requiring combinational or sequential logic to compute them.

14.7 Testing

Test facilities have been incorporated into the design of each functional section. These test facilities are based on a "linear scan" concept, in which information is serially shifted into or out of the IC under external control. The serial I/O is used to minimize pin requirements. A linear scan facility has been built into the FIFO that allows a number of testing operations. In the linear scan mode, the input rank and output rank of the FIFO are organized as one long shift register. An external bit stream can be serially loaded into or extracted from the input rank and/or the output rank of the FIFO, and the contents of the input rank can be propagated through the FIFO. Thus a known external bit pattern can be loaded into and propagated through the FIFO, and then extracted to verify the operability of the FIFO. Also, the information from the data capture section can be extract without propagating through the FIFO, and known values can be supplied to the output section.

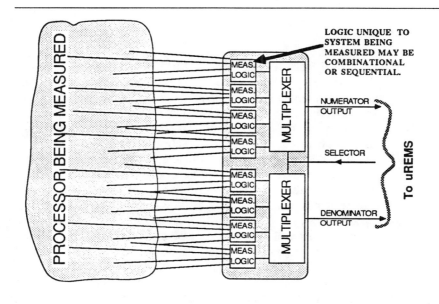

FIGURE 14.11
Signal selection and front-end logic for the uREMS.

Once the operability of the FIFO is verified, it can be used to provide the output section with a known input. This can be done by loading the FIFO output rank with a known bit pattern, as input for the output section. The normal output of the output section can then be compared against the known input data to verify the operability of the output section. In addition, selective read out of the output section under the direction of a local controller can further probe any suspected output path.

Each ratio counter in the data capture sections of the uREMS has its own "linear scan" test facility. The contents of the numerator counter, increment register, denominator counter, and exponent counter can be serially shifted out for examination.

The data capture sections of the uTRAMS can be tested in two ways. First, by having the processor set the configuration register and the control and status registers to known values and then read back their contents, for comparison. Second, by writting known samples to the uTRAMS and then extracting the resultant sample from either the FIFO (via its linear scan facility) or the output section once they have been tested.

14.8 Conclusions

A hybrid performance measurement tool for MIMD multiprocessors, as described in this paper, using software (embedded code) triggers and hardware sampling introduces a minimal amount of perturbation to the executing program. This perturbation can be as small as a single memory write instruction per measurement sample. This design, using two VLSI chips, requires as little as two LDs, for address recognition and signal selection, as interface to a multiprocessor. Manufacturers could assist by providing a conveniently accessible set of relevant signals for measurement. This generic interface design provides for a wide range of applicability among many different MIMD multiprocessors. The small footprint of this measurement tool makes it attractive to incorporate on processor boards and will have very little impact on cabinet space and power. Our object is to provide a useful measurement tool at a reasonable cost and size. This design is in the public domain, and fabrication costs to replicate this tool are quite low. A CMOS implementation of these chips is sufficiently fast for the current crop of non-supercomputer multiprocessors. For higher-end multiprocessors another, faster (and possibly more costly) implementation is appropriate, based on the cost of these machines.

Acknowledgement

This work was partially sponsored by the Defense Advanced Research Projects Agency.

References

1. R. Carpenter, Performance Measurement Instrumentation for Multiprocessor Computers. In *High Performance Computer Systems*. E. Gelenbe, Ed. Elsevier Science Publishing Co, New York, NY, 1988.

2. H. Fromm, et al. Experiences with Performance Measurement and Modeling of a Processor Array. *IEEE Trans. on Computers, Vol. C-32*,1 (January 1983) 15–31.

3. F. Gregoretti, F. Maddaleno, and M. Zamboni, . Monitoring Tools For Multiprocessors. *Euromicro Journal: Microprocessing and Microprogramming, Vol. 18*,1–5 (December 1986) 409–416.

4. U. Hercksen, R. Klar, W. Kleinoder, and K. Kneibl, Measuring Simultaneous Events in a Multiprocessor System. In *Proceedings of 1982 ACM*

SIGMETRICS Conf. on Measurement and Modelling of Computer Systems, (August 1982), pp. 77–87.

5. J. Hughes, Diamond: A Digital Analyzer And Monitoring Device. *ACM Performance Evaluation Review, Vol. 9,* 2 (May 1980) 27–34.

6. R. Klar and N. Luttenberger, VLSI-based Monitoring of the Inter-process-Communication in Multi-Microcomputer Systems with Shared Memory. *EUROMICRO Journal: Microprocessing and Microprogramming, Vol 18,*1-5 (December 1986) 195–204.

7. S. Mitchell, SySM Functional Requirements Description. Harris Corp., P.O. Box 98000, Melbourne, Fl. 32902, Feburary 1986.

8. D. Ferrari, *Computer System Performance Evaluation.* Prentice-Hall, Inc., Englewood Cliffs, N.J., 1978.

9. G. Nacht and A. Mink, A Hardware Instrumentation Approach for Performance Measurement of a Shared-Memory Multiprocessor. In *Proceedings of the 4th International Conference on Modelling Techniques and Tools for Computer Performance Evaluation,* Palma de Mallorca, Spain (September 1988), Vol. II, pp. 321–339.

10. A. Mink, J. Draper, J. Roberts, and R. Carpenter, Hardware Assisted Multiprocessor Performance Measurements. In *Proceedings of The 12th IFIP WG 7.3 International Symposium on Performance: Performance 87,* Brussels, Belgium (December 1987), pp. 151–168.

11. J. Roberts, J. Antonishek and A. Mink, Hybrid Performance Measurement Instrumentation for Loosely-Coupled MIMD Architectures. In *Proceedings of The Fourth Conf. on Hypercube Concurrent Computers and Applications,* Monterey, CA. (March 1989).

12. A. Mink and G. Nacht, Performance Measurement of a Shared-Memory Multiprocessor Using Hardware Instrumentation. In *Proceedings of The 22nd Hawaii International Conf. on System Sciences,* (January 1989), Vol. I, pp. 267–276.

Appendix A

Register Formats and Memory Mapped Addresses

The measurement node is mapped into a block of 256 addresses, thus 8 address bits are used to specify intended actions. These bits are formatted as follows:

2 bits	1 bit	5 bits
uREMS selective resets	uREMS trigger	encoded uTRAMS commands

The uREMS selective reset is used to selectively clear any of the uREMS ratio counters, after a sample (if any) is taken. The uREMS trigger causes all of the uREMS attached to this uTRAMS chip to take a sample, if the uTRAMS successfully takes a sample. The uTRAMS cannot take a sample if it is not in sampling mode, its FIFO is full, or if the filter level of the sample is below the threshold level.

The 16 bit configuration register format is:

8 bits	3 bit	3 bit	2 bits
CPU identifier	user mode filter threshold	supervisor mode filter threshold	encoded number of wait states

The 16 bit status and control register format is:

Bit	Ctrl Reg (write)		Status Reg (read)
15	R/O	Sense Global Interrupt status	
14		Set/Clr Global Interrupt	
13		Enable/Disable Global Interrupt	
12	C/O	Global Interrupt request to CPU	
11	—	N/A	—
10		Raw trace priority over Time trace	
9	R/O	In raw trace mode	
8	—	N/A	—
7	R/O	FIFO full	
6	R/O	FIFO overflow (data lost)	
5	—	N/A	—
4		Enable/Disable sampling	
3	—	N/A	—
2	R/O	32-bit (vs. 16-bit) mode	
1	R/O	Dynamic (vs. static) CPU id	
0	—	N/A	—

R/O - Read only, writes ignored
C/O - Clear only on write

The encoded uTRAMS commands are as follows:

Octal	Binary	Command
00	00000	Reset uTRAMS
01	00001	Status and Control register
02	00010	Configuration register
03	00011	N/A
04	00100	Timestamp (low order 16 bits or all 32 bits)
05	00101	Timestamp (high order 16 bits)
06	00110	N/A
07	00111	N/A
10	01000	Raw trace data (bits 16-31 for 16-bit mode)
11	01001	Raw trace data (bits 32-47)
12	01010	N/A
13	01011	N/A
14	01100	N/A
15	01101	N/A
16	01110	N/A
17	01111	N/A
20	10000	Time trace sample at level 0
21	10001	" " " level 1
22	10010	" " " level 2
23	10011	" " " level 3
24	10100	" " " level 4
25	10101	" " " level 5
26	10110	" " " level 6
27	10111	" " " level 7
30	11000	Raw trace sample at level 0, activating word (bits 0-15/0-31 in 16-bit/32-bit mode)
31	11001	" " " level 1 "
32	11010	" " " level 2 "
33	11011	" " " level 3 "
34	11100	" " " level 4 "
35	11101	" " " level 5 "
36	11110	" " " level 6 "

15

Performance of Parallel Applications on a Shared-Memory Multiprocessor System

Shreekant S. Thakkar

15.1 Introduction

Sequent's Symmetry Model A and Model B systems are variations of a shared-memory multiprocessor using up to 30 Intel 80386 microprocessors. The significant difference between the two machines is in the cache coherency protocol they use. Model A machines support a write-through cache protocol. Model B systems support a copyback protocol. There are small hardware differences, but Model B systems can support either protocol by selecting appropriate cache control software.

This situation presents a unique opportunity to study and compare the performance of two different multiprocessor cache protocols on identical hardware. The system is also instrumented to allow detailed measurement of hardware and system software behavior. We were able to evaluate and compare the performance of several different applications on Symmetry systems using both write-through and copyback modes.

The major observation was that cache miss-rate dominates the performance of the system. If the miss-rate gets higher than some number, the processor accesses can saturate the bus. The copyback system performance shows significant reduction in the cache miss-rate compared to the write-through system.

This allows significantly higher scaling of the system than is possible for a write-through system. The write-sharing is not a problem in a system such as Symmetry since the parallel programming model used here is a medium or large grain process model. In this model, the real hot-spot is locks and not the shared data structures.

15.2 Symmetry Multiprocessor Systems

Sequent's Symmetry Series is a bus-based shared-memory multiprocessor system [1]. A diagram is shown in Figure 15.1. A machine can have from two to thirty CPUs with a total performance of around 120 MIPS. Each processor subsystem contains a 32-bit microprocessor, a floating-point unit, optional floating-point accelerator, and a private cache.

The system features a 53.4 Megabyte/second (MB/sec) pipelined system bus, up to 240 MB of main memory, and a diagnostic and console processor. Symmetry systems can support five dual-channel disk controllers (DCCs), with up to 8 disks per channel. Each channel can transfer at 1.8 MB/sec.

The DYNIX operating system is a parallel version of UNIX, designed and implemented by Sequent for their Balance and Symmetry machines. It provides all services of AT&T System V UNIX as well as Berkeley 4.2 BSD UNIX.

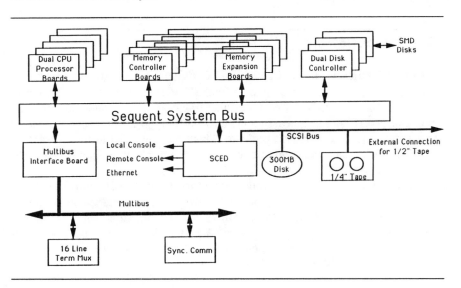

FIGURE 15.1
Symmetry functional block diagram.

We evaluated the performance of applications on three different configurations of Sequent Symmetry systems: on standard processor subsystems using
write-through cache mode; standard processor subsystems using copyback cache
mode; and on a system using the copyback cache protocols with larger processor
caches and a faster processor clock rate.

Model A Symmetry systems use the Symmetry write-through cache coherency protocol. Model B Symmetry Systems use the Symmetry copyback
cache coherence protocol. Each processor in Model A and B system has a 64
Kbyte two-way set associative cache.

We also evaluated performance of several applications on a variant of model
B (called Model B' here) that has a cache that is twice as large and a 25% faster
processor.

15.3 Symmetry Cache Coherence and Bus Protocols

The Symmetry cache and bus protocols work together to support cache coherency in the system. The cache coherence protocol is a write invalidate and
ownership-based protocol. That is, a write by a processor will first invalidate
all copies in the systems before the write is completed. To complete a write the
cache must first gain ownership of the cache block in question. This action is
described below.

15.3.1   The Protocols

The Sequent System Bus (SSB) in Symmetry Model A systems used the following cycles to support the write-through protocol:

RA	Read Address cycle
WAI	Write Address with Invalidate cycle
RDF/RDL	Read Data First and Last cycles
WDF/WDL	Write Data First and Last cycle.

The SSB protocol was extended in Model B to support the copyback cache
coherency scheme by adding the following cycles:

RAI	Read Address with Invalidate
WA	Write Address
IA	Invalidate Address cycle

Two additional cycle type bits were added to the Symmetry bus to extend
the bus protocol to support the Symmetry copyback cache coherence protocol.

The first bit is used to identify transactions using the extended 64-bit width of the bus. The second bit allows an address to be tagged to show whether or not it should cause an invalidation. This can be used with a read address if a cache needs to ensure that it holds the only copy of a block (i.e., gain ownership).

In addition, in Model B systems two status lines were added to the bus to support the protocol. They are SHARED and OWNED. The first, SHARED, indicates that an RA cycle on the bus has hit a block that exists in another cache. This lets a requester know whether to install a new block as PRIVATE or SHARED. The second, OWNED, indicates that an RA or RAI cycle on the bus has hit a block that is held MODIFIED by another cache. This lets the memory subsystems know that a cache will respond to the request.

The Symmetry copyback cache coherence protocol [1] makes use of four cache states: INVALID, PRIVATE, SHARED, and MODIFIED.

These states are defined as follows:

INVALID   Block is not currently valid in the cache.

PRIVATE   Block has been read and does not exist in any other cache in the system.

SHARED   Block has been read and may exist in another cache.

MODIFIED   Block has been modified and does not exist in any other cache in the system.

The coherence protocol, in general, works as follows:

READ HIT.   No bus activity is required and requested data are supplied to the processor.

READ MISS.   An RA type cycle is issued on the bus. If any cache has a copy of the block of data in PRIVATE or SHARED state it changes the state of the block to SHARED, and asserts the SHARED line on the backplane.

If any cache has the data in MODIFIED state it asserts the OWNED line, responds to the request, and changes its local state to INVALID. The state could have been changed to SHARED instead of INVALID, but our implementation does not allow this. The memory subsystem observes this transaction, noting the assertion of the OWNED signal, and takes a copy of the data as they are being passed from one cache to the next (called "implied" copyback operation). This process allows the responding cache to relinquish ownership.

If no cache signals ownership then the memory responds to the request with its copy of the requested block. The receiving processor sets his tags to PRIVATE, if SHARED was not asserted, or SHARED otherwise.

WRITE HIT.   If the block is in MODIFIED state, this implies that this cache already owns the block and can complete the write. No bus activity is necessary.

If the block is in the PRIVATE state, then the cache changes the state to MOD-- IFIED and completes the write. If the block is in the SHARED state then the cache issues an IA cycle on the bus, causing all other caches to invalidate their copies (i.e. write invalidate operation), and changes its state to MODIFIED.

WRITE MISS.   An RAI cycle is issued on the bus to obtain the current copy of the block and to signal all other caches to invalidate their copy. If any cache has the copy of the block in MODIFIED state then it responds to the request. Any cache that holds the block in PRIVATE or SHARED state invalidates its copy. If no cache holds the block MODIFIED then memory will respond to the request. The receiving cache installs the block as MODIFIED and completes the write.

15.3.2   Response Latency

In general, caches in multiprocessor systems serve two masters, the processor and the bus. A cache has to respond to bus requests when it owns a dirty block, and also to processor requests. The memory only responds to a single processor access at a time, hence it can respond much faster. Thus a cache-to-cache transfer is usually slower than a memory-to-cache transfer. The Symmetry multiprocessor system follows this pattern.

The Sequent System Bus is an unpended (split-transaction) bus. A fixed number of requests are allowed on the bus, and responses to requests are strictly ordered. Responses to earlier requests have to come back before responses to later requests can be allowed on the bus.

The number of requests allowed on the bus is optimized for the number of cycles required by a memory response, because memory responds to the majority of bus requests. Cache responses, having longer latency, require more bus cycles than memory responses. The additional bus cycles spent waiting for non-optimal, slower-than-memory responses are wasteful of bus bandwidth because they prevent further requests from being put on the bus. These additional cycles can be classified as "hold" cycles. Thus if a cache responds to a bus request, potentially useful bus cycles are wasted as hold cycles. One of the performance characteristics discussed in this evaluation is the effect of cache traffic on bus utilization.

15.3.3   Synchronization Mechanism

The synchronization mechanism on the Symmetry Model A uses global inter- locks. Only one processor is allowed to access the bus with locked access. Other processors subsequently read the locked variable after failing to complete their atomic access. These processors continuously read this value waiting for it to change. This action is called spinning in cache since it does not involve any bus accesses. The write on the bus of the atomic access invalidates copies of the lock variable the other processors are spinning on. The whole activity of accessing a locked variable restarts after this invalidation. This mechanism is costly in terms of bus utilization beyond 10 processors [2].

The synchronization mechanism on the Symmetry Model B uses cache-based locks. The locks are ownership based. That is, the cache controller treats a locked read from a processor like a write operation.

Assuming a cache miss, the cache controller performs an exclusive read operation on the bus to gain ownership of the block. The atomic lock operation is then completed in the cache. These locks are optimized for multi-user systems where locks are lightly contested and the critical sections are short. They do not work well in some parallel applications where a lock is heavily contested. The heavy contention for locks produces lot of cache-to-cache transfers. On Symmetry Model B systems these transfers generate hold cycles as mentioned earlier.

Several software synchronization schemes can be used to reduce contention for the locks in the hardware [2,3]. These schemes are orthogonal to the hardware based locks and are implemented using them. The queue-based software synchronization scheme reported by Graunke and Thakkar [2] eliminates the contention entirely for these locks. Thus the cache-to-cache traffic in Model B systems due to these locks is eliminated. They also work well in Model A systems.

15.4 Performance Monitoring

Symmetry systems incorporate performance monitoring hardware that can be accessed by special system software. The hardware includes counters, masks and multiplexing logic. The mask can be set and appropriate events of interest selected before the counters are started. The counters can be stopped and read by system software. This action is non-intrusive on system performance.

The types of events that can be measured include all types of accesses to the cache controller by the processor, accesses from the bus to the cache controller (i.e owned and invalidate operations), and state changes. This allows us to detect the accesses to shared blocks, etc. Other events that can be measured include the different types of bus cycles and other aspects of bus protocol. These features give us a unique opportunity to study this architecture and its behavior under different applications.

A software tool called System Perforamance Monitor (SPM) was developed to monitor and display performance of the system in real-time. The tool runs on X-window stations. The user interface allows one to select different aspects of the system to be monitored including the hardware, operating system and the application. The monitoring is non-intrusive and does not have any significant affect on the bus traffic. SPM allows a user to select and display various probe points in the system. The tool allows visual correlation of information from various parts of the system. System performance was evaluated in terms of bus utilization, miss-rate, and application speed.

15.5 Performance Evaluation

We have evaluated performance of more than 12 different parallel applications on Symmetry systems using both cache coherence modes. We are reporting here on the most interesting of these applications. We will discuss two parallel applications: the Butterfly Network Simulator and Parallel Linpack.

The parallel applications we examined are all based on medium- and large-grain parallelism. These types of applications run efficiently on shared memory system such as the Symmetry because they exhibit less write-sharing. The contention is for the lock rather than a medium or large data structure. This attribute has been observed for all the parallel applications we have monitored. We will also discuss the performance of a multiuser workload in an engineering environment.

15.5.1   Butterfly Network Simulator Application

The Butterfly Network Simulator [4] is an integer intensive application. It is the one application that used team splitting to improve load balance for small problem sizes. The network simulated has two concurrent halves of exactly the same size, so team splitting is particularly effective. Each half of the network being simulated has roughly **N log N** transfers between the switch nodes on each step of the simulation.

The communication pattern between the switch nodes resembles the FFT butterfly pattern, so locality is minimized and the decoupling of the processors performing the simulation is very slow (logarithmic) as the problem size N is increased. It is expected that this sort of communication behavior is the worst case for real applications, that is applications that are not contrived benchmarks designed specifically to stress the memory subsystem. As long as N is not much larger than the processor count of the machine used to perform the simulation, the entire data set of the application will fit in the individual processor caches and the cache-to-cache data traffic will be high.

We evaluated the performance of the Butterfly Simulator using write-through cache mode and copyback cache mode. Two problem sizes were used; we will distinguish these by small (order 7 network) and large sizes (order 10 network) for our explanation. A thirty processor Symmetry system was used for monitoring the behavior of this application.

Speedup. In write-through mode, the speedup achieved as processors were added reached about 7.5x with 14 processors, then decreased with addition of more processors (Figure 15.2).

In copyback mode, the speedup of this program is dependent on the problem size. The speedup for problem size 1 is over 14 with 30 processors. The speedup for problem size 2 is around 20 with 30 processors (Figure 15.3).

The single processor Model B performance is around 22% better than the single Model B$'$ processor. This shows that the overhead of parallelization is high. This overhead has to be overcome by the parallelism in the application.

The degradation in performance of this application is due to the application behavior and not due to operating system behavior. The user time is a major contributor to the loss in performance for the application both in write-through and copyback system. However the user time rises much more in the write-through system than in the copyback system (400% as opposed to 40%). This indicates that there is significant overhead in the write-through system. This overhead on Model A is due to the synchronization mechanism.

An experiment was conducted in copyback mode to see if resident set size and operating system paging mechanisms played any role in limiting the performance of this code. The results indicated that these factors had no significant impact on the performance of this program.

Bus Utilization.   In write-through mode, the bus utilization (Figure 15.4) goes up rapidly to 8 processors. At 8 processors the bus is about 65% utilized. The bus utilization increases to 73% for 16 processors and then goes down to 63% with 28 processors. This fall of bus utilization is related directly to the synchronization mechanism on the write-through system. The synchronization mechanism on the write-though system inhibits bus utilization as the number of processors participating for this application increases. Unfortunately the number of cycles lost due to synchronization on the write-through system cannot be measured directly. The roll-off starts to happen around 10 processors.

The **write invalidates** dominate the bus utilization (Figure 15.5) in the write-through system. The roll-off results because of synchronization activity inhibiting the bus utilization. Read cycles continue to increase at a slow rate and are caused by normal cache miss and synchronization activity. The bus holds are asserted as processor writes swamp the bus write pipes.

The bus utilization (Figure 15.4) in copyback mode with 28 processors is 40% less than in write-through mode. The write-through system's peak traffic goes over 70% with 14 processors. For the same number of processors, copyback system bus traffic is less than half of the write-through system.

In copyback mode, the bus traffic is dominated by non-exclusive reads cycles (Figure 15.6). These read cycles increase with the number of processors. The read cycles increase for three reasons. First, there are cache misses due to the cold start by each processor, and these contribute to the read cycles on

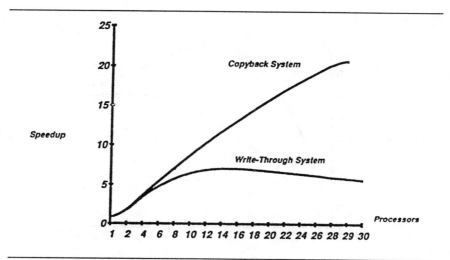

FIGURE 15.2
Butterfly Simulator—speedup (Order = 9, Vector Length = 4096).

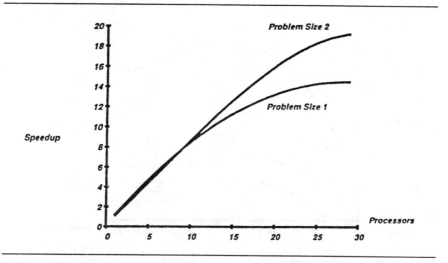

FIGURE 15.3
Butterfly Simulator—copyback system.

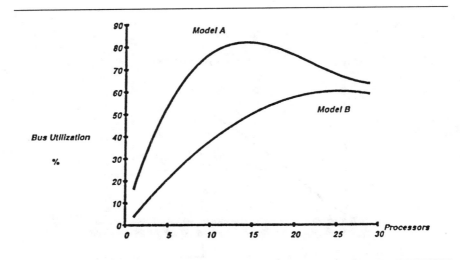

FIGURE 15.4
Butterfly Simulator—bus utilization (Order = 9, Vector Length = 4096).

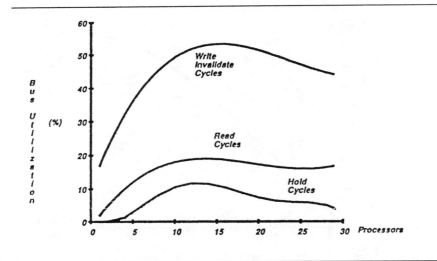

FIGURE 15.5
Butterfly Simulator—write-through system (Order = 9, Vector Length = 4096).

the bus. Second, the **read invalidate** cycles cause invalidation in other caches and these processors' later requests will be cache misses. These misses also contribute additional read cycles. Third, the read misses caused ·by the size of the cache; as the cache size increases these reads will decrease.

The cache miss-rate decreases per cache in copyback mode as more processors are added because of the increase in total cache space. This is indicated by the decrease in write (copyback) cycles beyond 18 processors for large problem size. The miss-rate is measured per second instead of per reference. The reason for this is that only sampling of performance counters for a given period is possible with the present instrumentation. The miss-rate per second and per reference are similar for the parallel application since the miss-rate has been observed to vary by little over the execution of the application.

The IA cycles on the bus in copyback mode are less than 1% of the traffic with a 28-processor system. This indicates that there is little write sharing activity. This confirms what we have seen on the Balance [5] and what other researchers have reported since then [6,7].

There are hold cycles (Figure 15.7) on the bus caused by the synchronization or by other cache-to-cache traffic. The cause of these hold cycles has yet to be determined. This degradation in bus performance will contribute to the loss in speedup for this application. The hold cycles rise exponentially, which fits the roll-off seen in the speedup.

Cache Miss-rate.   In write-through mode for the small problem size, the cache miss-rate (Figure 15.8) is around 13% (these numbers include all the processor writes) with a single processor. The miss-rate falls to under half that with 28 processors. The read miss-rate is low, as the number of read cycles on the bus show small increases with addition of more processors.

In copyback mode the cache miss-rate is about 1.9% with a single processor and falls to around 1.3% with 14 processors. The miss-rate stays around 1.3% beyond 14 processors.

The copyback miss-rate for large problem size (Figure 15.9), as expected, is much higher than for small problem size. The miss-rate for large problem size decreases when a larger cache is used as in Model B' (Figure 15.9). This corresponds to the reduction in the bus utilization between the two systems (Figure 15.10).

Coherence Protocol Traffic.   The Symmetry cache coherence protocol behavior indicates the amount of read sharing, owned and memory traffic. Figures 15.11 and 15.12 show that the percentage of owned traffic doubles when the number of processors is increased from 10 to 24. The amount of read sharing shows a 3% increase when the number of processors is increased from 10 to 24. The memory to cache response ratio is around 3:1. Increasing the cache size has

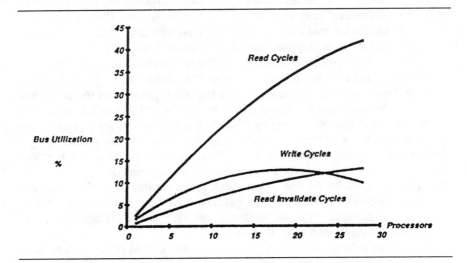

FIGURE 15.6
Butterfly Simulator—copyback system (Order = 9, Vector Length = 4096).

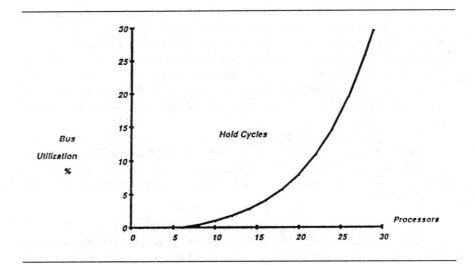

FIGURE 15.7
Butterfly Simulator—copyback system (Order = 9, Vector Length = 4096).

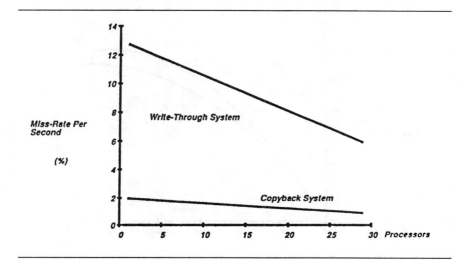

FIGURE 15.8
Butterfly Simulator—miss rate (Order = 7, Vector Length = 1024).

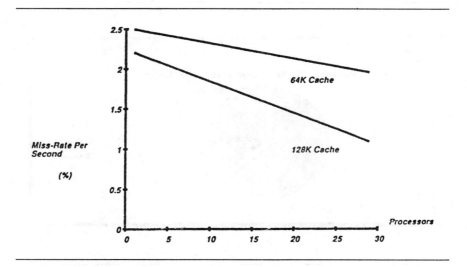

FIGURE 15.9
Butterfly Simulator—copyback system (Order = 9, Vector Length = 4096).

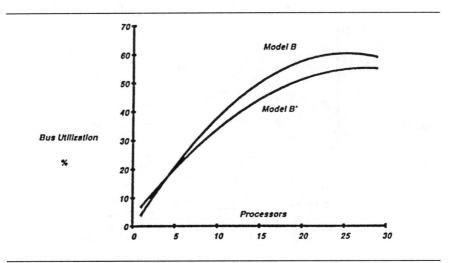

FIGURE 15.10
Butterfly Simulator—copyback system (Order = 9, Vector Length = 4096).

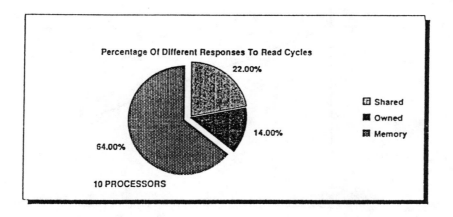

FIGURE 15.11
Butterfly: Symmetry Model B copyback system.

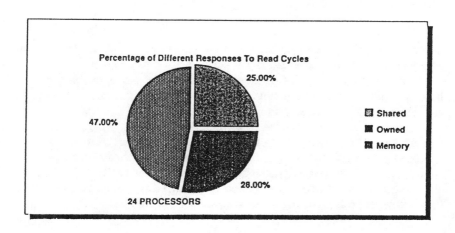

FIGURE 15.12
Butterfly: Symmetry Model B copyback system.

results similar to increasing the number of processors, that is, the owned traffic doubles.

Summary.   The write pipe in the write-through system is a limiting factor for most applications that use more than 8-10 processors. This application suffers from the system degradation caused by the write-pipe filling up. The application also suffers from degradation caused by the global bus synchronization scheme when the number of processors participating increases beyond 10 processors.

In copyback mode there seem to be several slopes in the speedup curves. These slopes indicate roll-off in the speed-up. Some of the roll-off can be attributed to the increase in cycles lost through ownership-based locks. However another component in the roll-off is the problem size, the grain size of computation.

15.5.2 Parallel LINPACK

LINPACK is a library package used for comparing the performance of different computer systems solving dense systems of linear equations [8]. LINPACK is a floating-point intensive benchmark. It measures the performance of two subroutines SGEFA and SGESL. SGEFA factors a matrix by Gaussian elimination.

SGESL solves the real system

$$Ax = b$$

using the factors computed by SGEFA. Both subroutines call a third subroutine, SAXPY, which computes a constant times a vector plus a vector.

There are two versions of LINPACK, a single and a double precision floating-point version. The double precision version of the above subroutines are called DGEFA, DGESL and DAXPY.

This study used a C-version of the parallel LINPACK program written by Jack Dongarra. The program uses static allocation of work using the Sequent microtasking library. The purpose in this study was to understand the behavior of the architecture rather than get the best performance for LINPACK. The study also used a dynamic allocating version of parallel LINPACK. However, very little difference was observed in the behavior of the architecture.

Speedup.   Figure 15.13 shows the speedup of parallel LINPACK on write-through and copyback systems. The speedup is just under 5 for both systems. The reason for this small speedup is that the problem size is too small. The overhead of parallelization overwhelm the parallelization. However, the speedup for the write-through systems rolls-off more than speedup on copyback system. This can be attributed to the writes generated in the write-through system as described below.

Figure 15.14 shows that speedup improves considerably in the copyback system as the problem size is increased. The roll-off in this version is attributed to large cache miss-rate since the problem no longer fits in the cache. The routines can be restructured in LINPACK so that a better miss-rate can result. This has been done at Sequent and other places. However, the objective here was not to pursue tuning effort.

Bus Utilization.   The bus utilization for the small problem size on the write-through system is 4 times that of the copyback system (Figure 15.15). The write-through system bus utilization is dominated by write invalidates (Figure 15.16). The copyback system bus utilization is dominated entirely by read cycles. It is interesting to note that the read cycles for both systems are similar (Figure 15.17).

Figure 15.18 shows how the bus utilization increases as the problem size increases. This increase is caused by increase in the cache miss-rate (Figure 15.22) because the problem cannot be contained in the cache. The bus utilization includes both non-exclusive read and write (copyback) cycles (Figure 15.19). Both types of cycles increase as problem the problem size increases. Like the previous application, there are very little **Invalidate Address** cycles. This indicates very little write sharing.

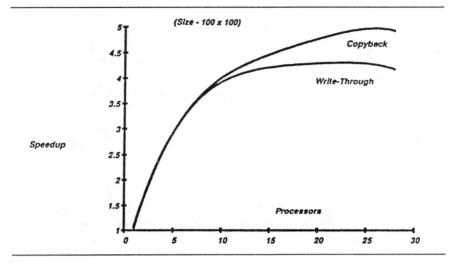

FIGURE 15.13
Parallel Linpack—speedup.

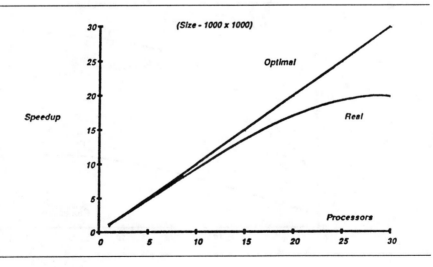

FIGURE 15.14
Parallel Linpack—copyback system.

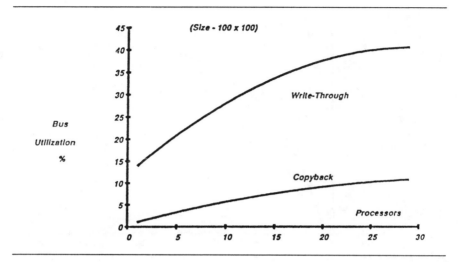

FIGURE 15.15
Parallel Linpack—bus utilization.

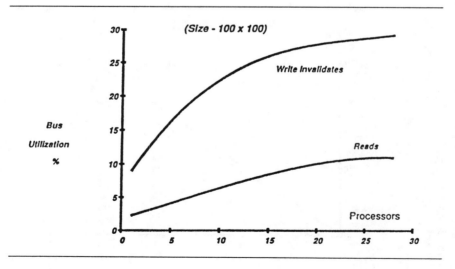

FIGURE 15.16
Parallel Linpack—write-through system.

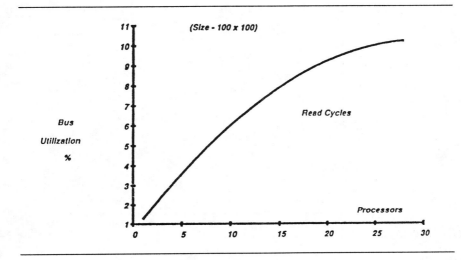

FIGURE 15.17
Parallel Linpack—copyback system.

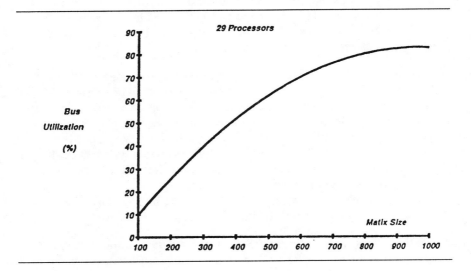

FIGURE 15.18
Parallel Linpack—copyback system.

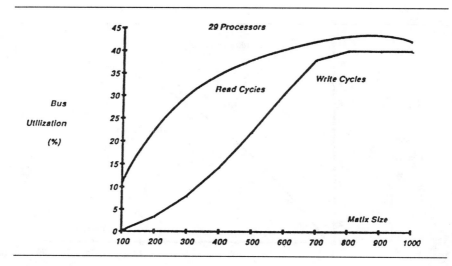

FIGURE 15.19
Parallel Linpack—copyback system.

There is degradation in performance due to synchronization mechanism. The hold cycles rise as more processors are added. They consume less than 18% of the bus bandwidth for the large problem size with 29 processors (Figure 15.20). These cycles can be eliminated by using queue-based locks that the new version Sequent Parallel Library supports.

Miss-Rate.   The write-through system for the small problem size has a significantly large cache miss-rate since it also includes all the writes (Figure 15.21). Symmetry uses a non-allocating policy on write misses in a write-through system. The miss-rate for a write-through system drops significantly as the number of processors participating is increased. The cache miss-rate also drops in the copyback cache system. The bus utilization for a copyback system is small since the cache miss-rate is small. This miss-rate is essentially due to cold start since the data for the small problem fit in the cache.
    The cache miss-rate (Figure 15.22) rises as the problem size is increased. It increases by 6 times for a 10-fold increase in the problem size.

Cache Coherence Traffic.   Figure 15.23 shows that 99% of the responses for a read request come from memory in a 24 processor copyback system. There is little read sharing (10%). Only 1% of the responses come from the caches.

Summary.   The speedup for parallel Linpack in both the write-through and copyback system is small for the small problem size. This is entirely due to the

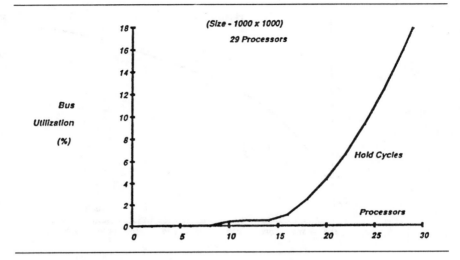

FIGURE 15.20
Parallel Linpack—copyback system.

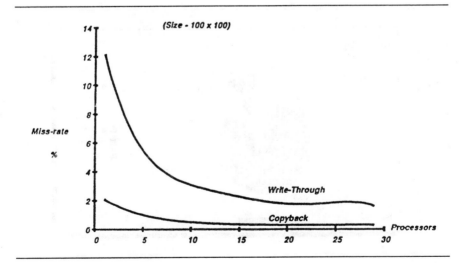

FIGURE 15.21
Parallel Linpack—miss-rate.

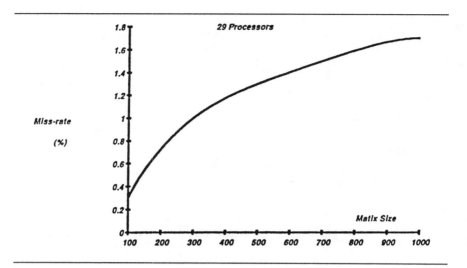

FIGURE 15.22
Parallel Linpack—copyback system.

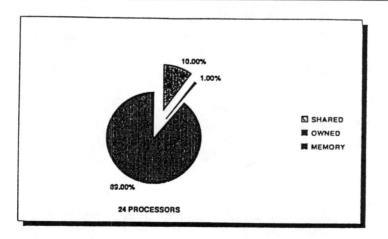

FIGURE 15.23
Parallel Linpack—Read request responses.

high overhead of parallelization. As the problem size is increased the speedup gets better until the traffic cause by a high miss-rate and the hold cycles caused by the synchronization mechanism saturate the bus. The miss-rate can be reduced by restructuring the computation. The hold cycles due to the synchronization mechanisms can be eliminated by using the queue-based locks.

15.6 Conclusions

The performance of Symmetry Multiprocessor System has been presented for parallel environments. The Symmetry copyback cache coherence and bus protocol have been shown to perform well for both parallel applications.

The copyback systems have significantly superior performance over the write-through systems. The copyback policy allows the scaling of systems that would otherwise be impossible. This scaling is primarily achieved through the reduction in bus writes generated by each processor. Further reduction in the bus traffic is also achieved through reduction in miss-rate by the adoption of the copyback policy.

All the application environments show that they would benefit if the cache size were increased. However, a balance has to be reached here. The size of the cache should not be increased so as to make it the primary responder. This can have detrimental affect on the performance as the observations indicate.

The traffic due to write sharing is almost non-existent on the system. This is because the parallel applications on this type of system use a medium or large grain parallelism process model. The real hot-spot in this type of environment is the synchronization mechanism and not the shared data structures.

References

1. T. Lovett and S. S. Thakkar, "The Symmetry Multiprocessor System," Proceeding of ICPP, 1988.

2. G. Graunke and S. S. Thakkar, "An Analysis of Synchronization Algorithms for Shared-Memory Multiprocessors," Sequent Computer Systems, Submitted For Publication.

3. T. Anderson, "The Performance Implications of Spin-Waiting Alternatives for Shared-Memory Multiprocessors," Technical Report, Department of Computer Science, University of Washington, 1989.

4. E. D. Brooks, III, T. S. Axelrod, and G. A. Darmohray, "The Cerabus Multiprocessor Simulator," G. Rodrigue, Editor, Parallel Processing for Scientific Computing, SIAM, 1989, pp. 384-390.

5. S. S. Thakkar, "Performance of Shared Memory Multiprocessor System," Proceedings of ICCD, 1987.

6. S. Eggers and R. Katz, "The Effect of Sharing on the Cache and Bus Performance of Parallel Programs," Proceedings of ASPLOS II, 1989.

7. W. Weber, and A. Gupta, "The Effects of Sharing on the Cache and Bus Performance of Parallel Programs," Proceedings of ASPLOS II, 1989.

8. J. J. Dongara, "Performance of Various Computers Using Standard Linear Equations Software in a Fortran Environment," Technical Report, Argonne National Laboratory, September 1988.

16

Graphical Aids to Constructing Parallel Programs Summary

David Bailey

Parallel computer programs, like the computer systems they run on, are complicated entities. Constructing, characterizing, analyzing, and debugging such programs currently presents a daunting challenge to application scientists, so much so that many of them simply decline to try them. It is clear that effective visualization tools can greatly decrease the pain of programming on such systems and accordingly increase their usability, particularly by non-expert users. Graphics tools that can aid in debugging parallel programs have particularly great potential in this regard.

Experience with existing prototypes of such tools indicates that a truly effective production tool of this sort would require the following general features:

1. Easy to use.

   It must be simple enough that it can even be used by scientists with no prior background in parallel computing. This implies in particular that the performance information needs to be closely related to the original source code (i.e. subroutines, loops, data variables, etc.).

257

2. Extensible and customizable.

A common experience of users of prototype systems is that different programs and different parallel environments require entirely different presentations of data.

3. Available on a variety of hardware and software systems.

Ideally, such a system could be used for any parallel computer and for any application language. However, given the current vacuum of systems that are usable in different environments, a system that works over even a narrow range of different systems (for example, just for the Fortran language on modestly parallel systems) would be a notable advance of the state of the art.

4. Encourages rapid prototyping.

A system that can be brought up quickly in at least a basic demonstration mode will likely gain wide acceptance and therefore be more successful.

5. Effectively manages complexity.

A usable system must have an extensive interactive capability to select and to analyze the enormous amount of data such a system could generate. It seems likely that a good system would need to impose a hierarchy on such data, and to pre-filter and post-filter this information.

6. Integrated into programming environment.

It is essential for ease of use that the system be integrated into all levels of the programming environment, from the instruction level up to the source code level, and that information be shared between different pieces of the programming environment including the graphical subsystem, the debugger, etc.

The system may be divided into two subsystems: an event language and a graphic language. The event language is used for describing the primitive events that we wish to monitor, while the graphic language consists of a toolkit of "widgets" that support both static (timeline) and dynamic (animated) displays. Some specific capabilities required by each subsystem include the following:

Event Language.

1. Indicate task events, such as start, stop, wait, etc.

2. Monitor the value of an individual variable, array, or other data structure.

3. Detect instances of a certain variable or array element whose value exceeds a predefined threshold.

Graphic Language.

1. Display the current processor utilization.

2. Display the current subroutine calling tree.

3. Display the source code corresponding to the current location of an individual processor's activity, at various subroutine levels.

4. Display in some compact form the contents of an array (i.e. display the nonzero elements of a matrix in a 2-D variable intensity plot).

5. Indicate the expansion or contraction of an abstract data structure such as a tree.

6. Indicate resource utilization, such as memory usage, cache hits, etc.

A parallel computing visualization system that can work across several different application languages appears to be a particularly difficult goal. For example, one would have to define for each language what language objects need to be tracked in a multiprocessing system. Some underlying events, such as task creation, deletion, cache hits, data breakpoints, etc., should be common. However, some sort of standard event description system needs to be developed to facilitate the development of such a multilingual tool. Thus, the solution to the goal must involve a hierarchy of standards, with the standard event description system at the base of the hierarchy, with language-specific standards on top of that, and finally the means to allow the developer to specify events that are specific to his application.

Even within a single language, a visualization system needs to have considerable flexibility in specifying objects to be monitored. In some cases it may be most useful to view the current subroutine calling tree. In other cases, one may need to monitor the activity of individual variables. Flexibility is required because viewing objects at too low a level frequently has substantial impact on the performance of the program. In addition, an excessively invasive level of monitoring can frequently mask the phenomenon that the user wishes to study, analogous to the quantum measurement effect.

It is clear that considerable compiler support would be required for a really effective visualization system. For one thing, at execution time the visualization system would need to have access to the symbol table, so that data objects such as arrays, common blocks, or scalar variables can be monitored. Additionally, it seems clear that compiler generation of performance data collection would be the least invasive of execution performance. Even so it will likely be necessary for the user to specify before execution, probably at compile time, what objects may need to be monitored. In this way, the performance impact can be minimized.

As mentioned earlier, such a system is likely to generate vast quantities of data that need to be analyzed. In order to manage these data, filtering must be done both before and after the data are collected. The prefiltering is done at the event language level and the postfiltering at the graphic language level. The problem with the collecting of event data is that collecting every event gives us too much information, yet it isn't useful to filter events at the primitive event level. For example, it isn't useful to look at memory addresses when we're interested in collecting events that are associated with particular lines of source code. The solution is to provide a hierarchy of events defined both at the language and application level. Information for this hierarchy may be obtained both from the compiler and the user. Events may then be filtered according to this hierarchy.

At the graphic language, or postfiltering stage, we need to provide a hierarchy of "views," ranging from individual events (e.g. single instructions) to a high-level program view. It is also necessary to provide the ability to link summary information (e.g., processor utilization over time) to detailed individual events (for example, which processes were running at a given time). Finally, filtering must be available within each level within the hierarchy.

In considering the features of an effective parallel computation monitoring tool, it is instructive to examine other software tools that have been successful. Examples mentioned by the group include the UNIX[1] operating system, the GNU emacs editor, the X-windows and NeWS[2] graphics systems, the PHIGS+ rendering system, and the Pacific Sierra VAST-2 automatic vectorizing/parallelizing system. Each of these products features high quality, ready availability on a wide range of advanced systems, a simple user interface, and a compact, straightforward connection with other software components. It is likely that an effective parallel computation tool will need to possess these characteristics too.

[1] UNIX is a trademark of AT&T Bell Laboratories.
[2] NeWS is a trademark of Sun Microsystems.

17

Standards Working Group Summary[1]

Allen D. Malony
Kathleen Nichols

17.1 Introduction

Traditionally, the development of standards in any discipline is a result of two organizational needs. First, to promote modular thinking and to merge advances in different technological areas of a discipline, standard interfaces are required. The second need is to avoid duplication of effort by providing common foundations upon which new developments can take place. With performance instrumentation and visualization for parallel computer systems becoming an important area of research and development, the discussion of alternative techniques in an attempt to characterize common approaches is a worthwhile endeavor.

Standards have been adopted for computer systems in many different areas: bus interfaces (e.g. Multibus, VME), communications protocols (e.g. Ethernet, TCP/IP), and computer graphics (e.g. GKS), to name a few. In the area of performance instrumentation and visualization (PIV) the only possible de facto

---

[1] Working group was entitled "Standards in Performance Instrumentation and Visualization for Parallel Computer Systems."

"standard" is the UNIX[2] profiling methodology adopted by most UNIX-based systems. Although this is adequate for single processor systems, performance measurement of parallel computers necessitates new approaches and tools. Early discussion of standards for parallel computer performance instrumentation and visualization will help orient tool developers towards a common design framework and provide tool users with a common (possibly portable) environment for performance study.

The working group on PIV standards for parallel systems addressed several topic areas including:

- Are standards in performance instrumentation and visualization possible? What are the problems with proposing PIV standards?

- What areas of PIV are candidates for standardization - e.g., performance data formats, hardware support, software support?

- Can standard formats for commonly collected data be defined - e.g., counting information, timing information, event traces?

- What standard external hardware interfaces might be proposed for support of performance measurement?

- What influence might PIV standards have on parallel computer manufacturers?

- What is a good platform for performance data visualization?

- What are some standard performance displays? Can a standard library of these visualization components be developed?

In this report, we have tried to organize and summarize the working group discussions. Key contributors to the material presented here were: Christoph Borel (LANL), Dave Cahlander (Cray Research), Joseph Carter (Intel), Tom Kitchens (Department of Energy), Daniel Reed (University of Illinois), Craig Upson (Stellar), Elizabeth Williams (Supercomputing Research Center), Michael Wozny (Rennselaer Polytechnic Institute), Mamoru Yamada (NEC), and Anthony Zilka (Intel). Every attempt was made to remain faithful to the discussions. Any errors or misrepresentations are the fault of the authors.

The first section of the report motivates the need for addressing PIV standards by briefly reviewing prior work. We will then focus attention on six areas where attempts at standards might be worthwhile: user interfaces to data collection tools, performance data exchange, hardware performance instrumentation, operating system instrumentation, performance data visualization, and performance environment architectures. Lastly, general conclusions regarding PIV standards are given.

[2]UNIX is a trademark of AT&T Bell Laboratories.

17.2 Background

The performance measurement of computer systems has a long history. However, unlike the emergence of general practices of computer systems modeling, techniques for performance measurement are still largely *ad hoc*. Granted, there are suites of programs routinely used to benchmark computers (e.g. Drystones, Whetstones, Lawrence Livermore Loops), but they provide little information useful to the hardware, system software, and application designers interested in optimizing performance. Bottleneck analysis, on the other hand, was an extension of modeling technology that has found operational use in real performance measurement and optimization. Unfortunately, the type of environment for which bottleneck analysis is appropriate restricts its general application.

Advances in parallel system design has significantly increased the number of performance-related parameters of the system that must be considered. Furthermore, due to the diversity in architectures and programming paradigms, the performance parameters between parallel systems often do not conform. This has encouraged the isolated development of tools for parallel performance measurement that typically are too narrowly focused to have broad general use. However, there does appear to be some commonality in techniques, both hardware and software, that could be promoted through standardization efforts.

17.2.1 Software Performance Measurement

The principle difference between performance analysis of parallel execution and sequential execution is the need to observe dynamic parallel operation behavior. Whereas static statistics produced by profiling sequential execution correctly directs optimization efforts to those routines accounting for the greatest execution time, the main contributor to poor parallel performance is the interaction between multiple threads of execution that reduces or slows parallel execution. This information is not guaranteed to be captured by profiling statistics alone because execution time is not synonymous with work in the case of parallel operation. Static performance measurements should not be completely discounted, but, for parallel systems, provide only one dimension of information that must be augmented to gain thorough understanding.

The need to monitor dynamic parallel events has promoted software tracing as a viable approach to parallel system performance measurement. Several environments have been built around this concept. Segall's [1] PIE system uses event tracing at the user and operating system level to observe performance. Multi-tasking libraries can be instrumented to collect information about task execution and synchronization as was done by Seager [2] for the Cray X-MP. Miller's IPS [3] and IPS-2 [4] systems, and LeBlanc's Instant Replay [5] tool have applied event tracing to the problem of parallel debugging and performance measurement. Malony [6] and Reed [7] have also used event tracing as a basis for performance environments in shared memory and distributed memory systems.

Despite the application of event tracing in several environments, there is no agreed upon standard implementational approach. Differences exist in user and system events collected, the instrumentation interface, the trace formats, and the level of performance detail. In part this is a result of programming model or system architecture variations, but many commonalities in tracing designs do exist. Further, when static measures are used, there often exists only subtle differences in the measurements taken and the instrumentation approach used. The working group addressed some of these issues; see §17.3, §17.4, and §17.6.

17.2.2   Hardware Performance Measurement

Hardware instrumentation for parallel systems has fewer real examples, primarily because of the development effort involved. Mostly these have focused on non-invasive collection of counts and event traces. The EGPA multiprocessor project [8] successfully used hardware instrumentation for tracking processor operation and memory behavior. More recently, hardware monitoring has been implemented for the Cedar machine [9] and the Intel iPSC/2 [10]. Both efforts provide some form of hardware tracing support. The National Institute of Standards and Technology (NIST) has proposed standard monitoring hardware for parallel systems [11-12]. With the increasing ease of VLSI design and the need to avoid timing perturbations in performance measurement of parallel systems, hardware monitoring will have an increasing presence. Standards proposals should help to adopt common monitors practices and to encourage parallel system manufacturers to incorporate such facilities in their machines.

17.2.3   Performance Visualization

The advantages of using graphics to present parallel system performance data can be seen in the PIE [1], Paret [13], Schedule [14], Seecube [15], and HyperView [7] environments. Although developed independently, many ideas in these environments overlap. Performance visualization can benefit significantly from the development of modular software platforms, the early adoption of standard development conventions, and the sharing of visualization software. The overriding goal here is to reduce the time required for this technology to find common application among parallel system users.

17.3 User Interfaces to Data Collection

The basic motivation for having standards in user interfaces to data collection tools is to provide for a portable instrumentation interface between parallel systems. This would help minimize the code modifications needed to make similar measurements on different systems. The approach is to define standard routine interfaces (names and arguments) that will then be supported on each system. The definition is not a functional specification; the underlying data collection facilities can be implemented very differently. Rather, it provides for a consistent syntactic interface.

By way of example, the working group concentrated on defining user level interfaces to counting and tracing facilities. The counting facility was assumed to provide mechanisms for creating, updating, and sampling user-defined counters. Thus, a user interface to the counting facility might be defined as:

Routine	Description
init_count(cid, val)	set counter *cid* to the initial value *val*
inc_count(cid)	increment counter *cid*
dump_count(cid)	take a sample of counter *cid*

Only the routine names and arguments are specified. No assumption is made on actual implementation.

We also defined a simple user interface to a tracing facility. We assumed the facility supports the recording of an event in a trace with optional data. The user interface is then:

Routine	Description
init_trace()	initialize the trace
trace_event(eid)	record event *eid* in the trace
start_trace()	start tracing
stop_trace()	stop tracing
dump_trace()	save the trace

We added routines for trace initialization and trace control although the underlying trace facility might not perform any specific function when these routines are called. Null routines would be supplied in this case.

Programs instrumented using the above counting and tracing interfaces could be executed on any machine supporting the interface standard. Although the underlying data collection facilities might differ substantially in operation, the interface specification would act as a firewall preventing system differences from showing through to the user-level instrumentation.

17.4 Performance Data Exchange

The sharing of performance data obtained from parallel systems among re-searchers is important for several reasons. In understanding a particular ma-chine, having a large performance database provides more test cases for models and avoids the replication of experiments. Researchers studying parallel system architecture also benefit from data sharing by obtaining performance results on a wide variety of parallel machines. Further, this data collection task is most fre-quently tedious and time consuming; a task better shared by many. Despite these motivating concerns, the sharing of performance data at this time is minimal.

A major impediment to performance data exchange is the lack of a stan-dard format. If one existed, it would promote the development of performance analysis software with a common interface that could then be shared among users of a particular machine. Similarly, it might help the development of more uniform performance analysis tools for different parallel machines.

The working group felt that defining a Performance Data Exchange Format (PDEF) would be a standardization effort with a good chance for success. Such an effort should initially be limited in scope and focused on a particular type of performance data. We decided to try specifying a Standard Trace Interchange Format (STIF) for event traces from multitasked parallel programs. Many paral-lel trace formats have been developed as part of specific tools (e.g., see [14]) but there is likely a significant degree of common structure that could be exploited. In general, a STIF definition should be simple to serve as a common base for trace data exchange but include mechanisms for extensibility.

We started with a basic definition of a trace. A *trace* is a time-ordered sequence of *events*. Each event is uniquely defined by an *event id*. Each oc-currence of an event is uniquely described by the event id, the id of the task that generated the event, and a timestamp. In addition, although not needed to identify an event, we added information about the physical location where the event originated, in this case, a processor id. Lastly, an optional event data field is defined. An event might appear in the trace as shown in Figure 17.1.

Given the above structure of an event in the trace, we need to define the size of the event fields and how traces from multiple tasks would be represented. A proposed event format is shown below:

Field	Size
task id	32 bits
processor id	32 bits
event id	32 bits
timestamp	64 bits
data size	32 bits
data	*data size* bytes

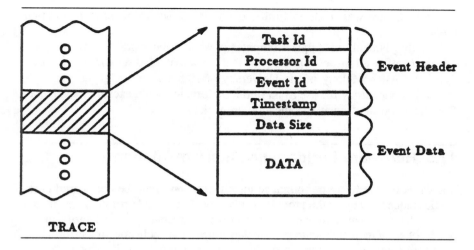

FIGURE 17.1
Trace data format.

Although this is a binary representation, there was strong opinion in the group that ASCII versions of the trace would have fewer problems in distribution. It was also observed that the event format could be separately defined; see below.

It was assumed that each program task would generate a separate trace. Our STIF specification requires that task traces be time-ordered. However, multiple task traces can either be exchanged individually or merged into a single, time-sequenced file. There is no clear reason to prefer one or the other, so in standards tradition, we allow for both.

The above description of a trace forms the basis for our simple STIF specification. It serves the purpose of defining a trace interchange format but provides no mechanisms for trace interpretation. We included as an extension to the STIF specification the provision for a configuration file where various trace-specific information could be placed such as:

- when the trace was generated
- what machine was used
- what program was traced
- event format description
- trace size (bytes and # of events)
- beginning and ending timestamps
- event definitions

No attempt was made to further define the structure of the configuration file.

Kathie Nichols of Apple Computer presented the working group with a document of a STIF description [16] that grew out of discussions with Dan Reed and Allen Malony of the University of Illinois. This STIF document is currently under study for use as an initial performance data exchange guideline. Comments on the format specification are welcome.

17.5 Hardware Performance Instrumentation

Standards for hardware performance instrumentation might be considered unrealistic. Indeed, many in the group felt this way. The attitude is mainly attributed to a realization that hardware performance instrumentation is primarily in the hands of system manufacturers and that unless the inclusion of performance hardware shows cost/performance advantages, it will not find its way to the end product. The lack of hardware instrumentation in current commercial parallel systems questions even the need for standardization. Where it exists, manufacturers may have concerns about the use of performance data by competitors and thus are not inclined toward standards efforts. Furthermore, the hope of reaching agreements on hardware instrumentation between system manufacturers is small given the degree of success of other standards attempts.

Nevertheless, there are approaches simple enough in scope and design to be considered for standardization. Clearly, there is hardware instrumentation that is system specific and, therefore, will not be universal enough to motivate a standard. The Cray X- and Y-MP monitors are, for the most part, of this nature, although comparable counting statistics might be collected on other systems. A minimal set of counts could be promoted as a standard, but beyond floating-point operations we might be hard pressed to find common measurements given the diversity of architectural designs.

The working group instead focused on hardware instrumentation to support software event tracing. For sake of discussion, we implicitly assumed software event tracing would be a common practice and that hardware support for removing the data from the system would be desired to reduce measurement overhead. This circumvented the issue of what to measure, a clear source for disagreement. Moreover, we assumed the hardware support for collecting the trace data would be external to the system. Instead we directed attention towards the interface between the system and the external hardware monitor. Basically, we wanted to define an External Hardware Instrumentation Interface (EHII) that would support hardware-assisted software event tracing.

The two approaches discussed are shown in Figure 17.2. The *address-based monitor* uses addresses seen on a memory address bus to recognize the occurrence of events. If an event is detected, event data are retrieved from the

SYSTEM INTERFACE   MONITOR ORGANIZATION

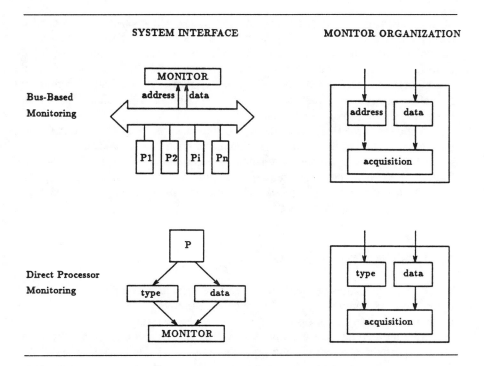

FIGURE 17.2
Hardware instrumentation alternative.

memory data bus. This approach was used in the first version of the TRAMS monitor [12]. The EHII definition in this case specifies the address and data bus interface. The external monitor is responsible for address detection and data logging.

Obviously, internal bus specifications differ between systems. In order to support the EHII specification, system manufacturers would have to provide for interface adaptors between the internal bus and the external interface. The key is to make the EHII specification extremely simple. An example specification consists of a 32-bit address port, a 32-bit data port, and one control signal to indicate that the address and data are valid. The EHII specification would also include timing characteristics. Several performance levels of the specification could be defined to allow for differences in system speeds.

The second approach differs from the first in that the external interface is from a port specifically dedicated to support external monitoring. The port could be I/O or memory mapped and ideally includes both a type field and a data field. In this respect, this *port-based monitor* approach resembles that of the address-based approach except that the type field does not represent a memory address. The EHII specification defines the type size, the data size, control signals, and timing characteristics of the external port interface. Due to differences in system hardware, some interface adaption might be required to support the specification. Again, simplicity is key. A specification similar to that above might have a 32-bit type field, a 32-bit data field, and one signal indicating that the type and data are valid.

Although these two approaches are different in terms of their internal system implementation, the EHII specifications for each can be defined to be quite similar. In fact, except for distinguishing between addresses or explicit type information, the example interface definitions are identical. Chances for adopting an EHII specification are improved if a common interface supporting each of these two approaches were adopted.[3]

17.6 OS Instrumentation

The role of standards in operating system (OS) instrumentation is to provide a common environment for performance measurement across machines. To a limited extent, the UNIX operating system serves this purpose in the way process time measurements are maintained. UNIX also assists in program profiling through periodic sampling of the program counter and the recording of timing data. However, not all parallel systems run UNIX, nor should this be required just to have a common measurement platform. Even among UNIX machines the measurement support can be implemented differently.

The working group concluded that OS instrumentation standards should not force convention in implementation but instead should only define desired measurement capabilities. To this end, the following incomplete list of standard capabilities an operating system should provide was generated:

□ basic timing support

□ process state monitoring
- context switches
- ready, blocked, idle
- tasks and threads

□ scheduler monitoring
- per job queue statistics
- total queue statistics

[3]Clearly, to complete an EHII standard specification, the electrical and mechanical characteristics of the interface connector system must be described.

❏ memory management statistics

- number of page faults

- per job memory requirements

❏ message communication statistics

- message counts

- message data volume

- per message statistics

❏ run-time support statistics

- system calls

- multitasking libraries

- programming paradigms

Clearly, there must be some facility for making timing measurements. All operating systems provide this function in one way or another but there can be differences in timing resolution and overhead. Job times are often reported as time spent in user mode and system mode. Further breakdown of system time data would provide a clearer view of the relative influences on a job while it is in the OS. This time accounting depends on the level of process state monitoring.

The ability to monitor the state changes a process (or to a finer degree a task or thread) makes in the OS is crucial for interpreting job execution. As an example, recording context switches demarcates running and non-running states. Additional states could be identified to determine if a process was ready to run, blocked for some reason, or idling. Further monitoring of scheduling decisions would allow the interaction of parallel tasks of a job at the OS level to be observed as well as providing overall scheduling statistics about system load.

How a job uses memory during execution is an important performance question. Access to this information is almost entirely through the operating system. In virtual memory systems, the number of page faults generated by a job is needed to understand whether memory requirements are satisfactory or a program is thrashing. The ability to observe memory usage over the course of a program's execution is also necessary for isolating memory allocation problems. This is especially true in the case of parallel programs on shared memory systems where combined memory requests can dynamically exceed the available resources.

In distributed memory systems, message communication can represent a bottleneck to performance. Because in these systems the OS typically manages message traffic, instrumentation to capture the number of messages generated and the message volume provides summary data about average message density. It should also be possible to monitor message communication on a per message basis. Observing dynamic message load in message passing systems is important for detecting transient bottlenecks that do not show up in summary statistics.

Lastly, there is increasing run-time support being included in parallel systems software to provide user-level interfaces to multitasking services, to offer different programming paradigm abstractions, or to serve as support software for restructuring compilers. Some of this run-time software is visible to the user, some of it is not. Instrumentation should be placed in run-time software to retrieve performance data. A simple example would be system calls where basic statistics such as the number of times a system routine was called and the cumulative time spent in the routine might suffice. Multitasking libraries encapsulate parallel execution behavior and, therefore, should also include instrumentation to measure performance. Programming abstractions can represent full-blown execution environments whose operation is completely hidden from the user. Instrumentation must be included in this software if the performance implications of using a particular programming abstraction are to be understood.

The above wish list clearly goes beyond what is provided in commercial parallel systems, although research projects have had success improving performance measurement capabilities by implementing some of these items [17-19]. As a result, several parallel system manufacturers are beginning to incorporate additional operating system instrumentation in their machines.

17.7 Performance Visualization

Although there are many possible alternatives to presenting performance data graphically, there can be an attempt to standardize on the methods used for graphics programming so that independently developed performance displays can be shared. Performance visualization is not currently at the level of scientific visualization where high-performance graphics capabilities are required. Furthermore, it should be realized that performance analysts are typically not expert graphics programmers. However, it has been demonstrated clearly that color and graphics can be used effectively in presenting performance data. Thus, a standard graphics approach to performance visualization should allow basic performance displays to be constructed easily and shared, but should not be so simple that more exotic graphics techniques cannot be explored.

The working group quickly concluded that the emerging X Windows standard [20] was presently the correct framework for performance visualization development. The rudimentary graphics capabilities of X together with user interface components available through a variety of toolkits allow simple performance displays to be built and conveniently shared. More sophisticated graphics programming is possible using X-specific interfaces to standard graphics packages such as GKS and Phigs. Since X Windows is widely available on a number of platforms, it aids the goal of portability.

An initial list of performance displays the group would like to see implemented using X is shown below:

- bargraph

- meters

- timelines

- matrix

- graphs (e.g., call graphs)

- kiviat

- pie graph

- led

- contour plot

- surface plot

- scatter plot

In fact, initial versions of many of these displays already exist; see [10].

Although not really a standardization issue, a central repository of visualization components was also encouraged by the group.

17.8 Performance Environment Architecture

Standards in performance environment architecture build on the theme of facilitating cooperation among performance analysts by providing a common foundation for performance instrumentation, analysis, and visualization. Performance environments tie these three areas together into model for performance investigation. Although implementation standards would be difficult to achieve, there are obvious corollaries in design among current performance environment prototypes. The architecture model used for the HyperView performance environment [7] was presented to the group as a possible "standard" architecture. Several additions to the model were recommended.

The general performance environment architecture proposed is shown in Figure 17.3. It is based on a trace-driven model of performance analysis where it is assumed performance data have been collected in a trace. There are four main components. The *control* component is responsible for trace management, including positioning within the trace and dispatching the next trace event to currently active performance data filters. User inputs associated with trace control and general environment configuration are also handled at this level.

The *filter* component processes trace events. The architecture supports the creation of independent filters that interpret event data differently. Each filter

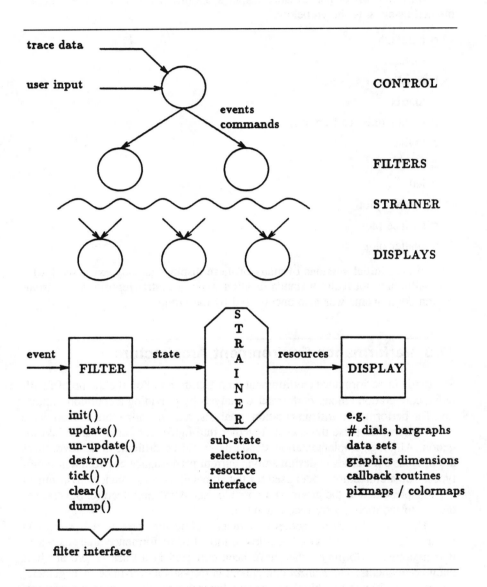

FIGURE 17.3
Performance environment architecture.

supports a common interface of routines that encapsulate filter functionality. This interface also provides for modular filter development. Each currently active filter is passed the next event for processing. Different actions are performed in response to an event depending on the filter type; e.g., the computation of a sliding window average. The architecture defines an active filter list that the control component maintains and uses to dispatch events.

Ultimately, the performance state kept by the filters will need to be displayed. A set of performance displays managed by the *display* component defines the visualization capabilities of the environment. These displays are also developed in a modular fashion. A resource interface is provided for controlling various graphics attributes of the displays, such as shape dimensions and color. The display components make no semantic interpretation of the data being presented. The displays are created and updated according to their resource interface.

Between the filters and displays is the glue for determining what part of the filter state will be shown and how. The *strainer* component supports user interaction to specify these properties. It works from a database of filter state choices and corresponding display alternatives established when the environment was built. An example of a filter-strainer-display combination is shown below:

Filter	processor state
Strainer	user time, processor 4
Display	strip chart

In general, the group thought the performance environment architecture described was flexible enough to be adapted to several performance analysis scenarios. The approach of defining standard interfaces between the filter, strainer, and display components promotes modularity in development. Other environments following a similar architecture could possibly use the same filter or display modules. The top-down organization, however, limits the style of user interaction with the environment and should ultimately be replaced by a more general scheme.

17.9 Conclusions

Performance instrumentation and visualization in parallel computer systems was found to be a multidimensional problem. A number of approaches have been taken along each dimension, thus we found that some areas were more mature than others. In addition, some areas appear more promising for standards than others. Since parallel machines and their software vary widely, we believe the most progress can be made by focusing on interfaces and formats. Even with standard interfaces and formats, a large overhead in customization is inescapable, but we urge individual researchers to attempt to conform to a standard, modular approach where possible so that performance information can be more widely shared.

Discussion centered on seven major areas. We felt that *user interfaces to data collections* would benefit by defining some standard function calls. In this way, instrumented code could be ported. *Performance data exchange* (in the form of event traces) appears to be one of the most promising areas for standardization, but the mere exchange of data fails to address whether types of events with meaning on one machine will have meaning on another. We identified standard styles of approaches for *hardware performance monitors*, but in all cases, machine-specific interfaces are required to any collection facility. The likelihood of significant action from manufacturers on this front was seen as low. *Operating System instrumentation* is seen as problematical, but we found agreement on the types of measurements and events an instrumented OS should provide. *Performance visualization* and *performance environment architectures* were also seen as fairly promising areas for standardization. Since many current and proposed visualization tools are based on the X windows standard, there appears to be a need for a set of standard X performance displays and a repository for these. We felt by defining a standard environment architecture, different sites could create custom environments more easily through sharing basic modules of the environments and creating custom modules where needed since many performance environments have similar aspects.

We felt that standards in this area and the sharing of data and instrumentation should be possible since the creation of this data and the associated tools is often a time-consuming task that does not, in itself, further the business of parallel performance research. A common data and toolbase for the research community should also allow us to make strides in reproducibility of results, since the input data and the output devices would be the same.

References

1. Z. Segall and L. Rudolph, "PIE: A programming and instrumentation environment for parallel processing," *IEEE Software 2*, **6** (November 1985), pp. 22-37.

2. M. Seager, S. Campbell, S. Sikora, R. Strout, and M. Zosel, "Graphical Multiprocessing Analysis Tool (gmat)," Tech. Rep. Lawrence Livermore National Laboratory, Computing and Mathematics Research Division, January 1988.

3. B. Miller and C.-Q. Yang, "IPS: An interactive and automatic performance measurement tool for parallel and distributed programs," in *Proc. of the 7th Int'l. Conference on Distributed Computing Systems* (September 1987).

4. B. Miller, M. Clark, S. Kierstead, and S.-S. Lim, "IPS-2: The second generation of a parallel program measurement system," Tech. Rep. CS-783, University of Wisconsin-Madison, Department of Computer Sciences, August 1988.

5. T. LeBlanc and J. Mellor-Crummey, "Debugging parallel programs with instant replay," *IEEE Transactions on Computers C-36*, **4** (April 1987), 471-482.

6. K. Gallivan, W. Jalby, A. Malony, and P.-C. Yew, "Performance analysis on the Cedar system," in *Performance Evaluation of Supercomputers*, J. Martin, Ed. North-Holland, 1988.

7. A. D. Malony, D. A. Reed, J. W. Arendt, R. A. Aydt, D. Grabas, and B. K. Totty, "An Integrated Performance Data Collection Analysis, and Visualization System," in *Proceedings of the Fourth Conference on Hypercube Concurrent Computers and Applications* (Monterey, CA, 1989), Association for Computing Machinery.

8. H. Fromm, U. Hercksen, U. Herzog, K.-H. John, R. Klar, and W. Kleinoder, "Experiences with performance measurement and modeling of a processor array," *IEEE Transactions on Computers C-32*, 1 (January 1983).

9. A. D. Malony, "Multiprocessor Instrumentation: Approaches for Cedar. In *Instrumentation for Future Parallel Computing Systems*, M. Simmons, R. Koskela, and I. Bucher, Eds. (Addison-Wesley, 1989) pp. 1-33.

10. A. D. Malony and D. A. Reed, "Visualizing parallel computer system performance," in *Instrumentation for Parallel Computer Systems*, (Addison-Wesley, 1989).

11. A. Mink and R. A. Carpenter, "A VLSI Chip Set for a Multiprocessor Performance Measurement System," in *Parallel Computing Systems: Performance Instrumentation and Visualization*, R. Koskela and M. Simmons, Eds. (Addison-Wesley, 1990).

12. J. Roberts, J. Antonishek, and A. Mink, "Hybrid Performance Measurement Instrumentation for Loosely-Coupled MIMD Architecture," in *Proceedings of the Fourth Conference on Hypercubes, Concurrent Computers, and Applications* (Monterey, CA, 1989), Association for Computing Machinery (Addison-Wesley Publishing Co.).

13. K. Nichols and J. Edmark, "Modeling multicomputer systems with PARET", *IEEE Computer 21* **5** (May 1988), pp. 39-48.

14. J. J. Dongarra and D. C. Sorenson, "Schedule: Tools for developing and analyzing parallel fortran programs," Tech Rep. ANL/MCS-TM-86, Argonne National Laboratory, Mathematics and Computer Science Division, November 1986.

15. A. L. Couch, *Graphical Representations of Program Performance on Hypercube Message-Passing Multiprocessors*, PhD. thesis, Tufts University, Department of Computer Science, 1988.

16. R. W. Hon, "A simple trace interchange format," Tech. Rep. Apple Computer, Inc., May 1989.

17. R. Barton, P. Emrath, D. Lawrie, A. Malony, and R. McGrath, "New approaches to measuring process execution time in the Cedar multiprocessor system," Tech. Rep. CSRD-744, University of Illinois at Urbana-Champaign, Center for Supercomputing Research and Development, January 1987.

18. T. Lehr, D. Black, Z. Segall, and D. Vrsalovic, "Mkm: MACH kernel monitor - description, examples, and measurements," Tech. Rep. CMU-CS-89-131, Carnegie-Mellon University, March 1989.

19. D. C. Rudolph and D. A. Reed, "CRYSTAL: Operating System Instrumentation for the Intel iPSC/2," in *Proceedings of the Fourth Conference on Hypercube Concurrent Computers and Applications* (Monterey, CA, 1989).

20. R. Scheifler and J. Gettys, "The X-Window system," *ACM Transactions on Graphics 5*, 2 (April 1986), pp. 79-109.

18

Dataflow and Hybrid Dataflow Architectures Summary

A.P.W. Bohm

18.1 Introduction

Computer systems can be characterised at several distinct levels of abstraction, at which various different modes of behaviour are apparent. The boundaries between these levels of abstraction are arbitrary, but there does seem to be some degree of consensus about where "natural" boundaries occur. The **application level** is associated with a particular application area. Here the real problem to be solved is specified in terms that relate only to the problem. Often, this *specification* will be a description of a physical problem using some form of continous mathematics. Overall, our interest lies in the *costs* of translating this description of the problem into a computational solution to an approximation of it, and the *performance* of the resulting computation. Naturally, performance measured at the application level is the most important to the end-user, but this depends in an unpredictable way on the underlying levels. The **algorithm level** is the level at which a *procedure* for solving (an approximation to) the problem is defined, independently of the vehicle that will perform the final computation. Often, the algorithm will apply to a discretised version of the real problem defined at the application level. The **programming language level** is where the procedure and discrete data domains defined at the algorithm level are expressed in a high-level

computer programming language. The **model of computation level** describes
how a computation is performed on assembly language level. Operations and
data items map one to one on the parallel computer executing this model of
computation. The **architecture level** describes the types of modules that constitute a computer and how these modules are interconnected. The **realisation
level** is concerned with the hardware implementation of the architecture.

Current techniques for using parallel computers are biased towards hardware-
oriented *paradigms*. Each application is mapped painstakingly onto one particular parallel machine architecture that has been selected for seemingly arbitrary
reasons. The mapping is specific to the selected architecture because currently
available intermediate levels of abstraction are machine-dependent. The number
of paradigms available for consideration is determined by the range of available hardware vehicles. This is a highly unsatisfactory state of affairs, because
programmers of parallel machines are forced to think machine dependently and
have to recode their programs when moving to a new machine or even to a new
machine configuration.

The *dataflow philosophy* is to free the programmer from this hardware-
oriented programming style by providing a general purpose, machine-independent
programming language and mapping this language onto a scalable, (relatively)
fine-grain multiprocessor. The model of computation, the dataflow graph, ex-
poses all parallelism available in the program. Dataflow architectures exploit
this abundant parallelism to hide latency, and provide an implicit synchronization mechanism that frees the programmer from having to explicitly specify
where processes fork and join.

A significant number of prototype dataflow computers have been constructed and documented over the past decade. Although these have evolved
from different institutions, guided by various philosophies, it is clear from the
detail of their design that they have similar internal structure and that their
instruction-sets have a number of features in common [1-3].

18.2 Dataflow Languages

Dataflow languages are based on the *single assignment rule*. There are two
versions of this rule: (1) an object gets a value assigned to it only in one place
of the program, and (2) an object (or element of a complex object) gets a value
assigned to it once during execution of the program.

We will restrict ourselves to the single assignment languages Id [4] and
SISAL [5]. Id is an expression-oriented language, supporting higher order functions, resource managers, and explicit I-structures. Id uses version (2) of the
single assignment rule. Datastructures in Id are non strict, i.e. elements of the
structure can be read before all elements have been written. Such flexibility gives
great expressive power to the language but renders difficulty for the compiler

writer because it is in general impossible to order instructions at compile time. The solution to this problem is to schedule instructions, whose order is unknown at compile time, fully in parallel. However, this now makes it hard, if not impossible to control the run-time parallelism of such programs, and consequently their resource requirements.

SISAL is an expression-oriented functional language obeying single assignment rule version (1). The language is designed such that datastructures can be implemented strictly. Elements of a strict datastructure can only be read after the datastructure is completely defined. The SISAL compiler can determine a sequential, deadlock free, execution order for each program. SISAL can therefore be implemented straightforwardly on conventional multiprocessors such as the Sequent Balance with an efficiency equal to that of Fortran or C. Moreover, when there is sufficient parallelism, near perfect speed up is achieved for a variety of applications [6]. SISAL is also implemented on the Manchester Dataflow Machine yielding highly efficient code [7]. So what SISAL may have lost in expressive power by restricting itself to strictly implementable datastructures, it may have won in implementability and efficiency.

18.3 Intermediate Forms

Both Id and SISAL are compiled into a data dependence graph form, called PG [8] and IF1 [9], respectively. Edges represent values, nodes represent operations. Both forms are recursive in that nodes can contain subgraphs. This simplifies translation into this form and analysis, but complicates optimizing code generation. Compilers for both languages perform global optimizations at a lower, non-recursive level. PG and IF1 differ in that PG assumes the underlying machine to support I-structures, introducing side-effects and consequently complications for the analysis routines. As an example, compilers based on PG do not garbage collect, whereas compilers based on IF1 do.

An important structure at this level is the static call graph in which nodes represent function and loop bodies, and edges activations. A dynamic version of this form, the process activation tree can be used to animate the behaviour of a program in execution. A first version of an program animation tool, using dynamic process trees, is described in [10]. In order for this tool to become really useful, it needs extending with source level information, such as the code executed in a certain process, the values of certain names or expressions, and the data structure access pattern of a process. Work on this is currently in progress at Colorado State University.

It is interesting to note that the hybrid machines use the process tree directly to implement matching and storage management [11,12] and it should therefore be possible for these machines to support this type of program level monitoring.

There is a complication here. The compiler may have changed the call graph of the program, for instance by inlining or partially evaluating a function. This means that there are now two call graphs: the one directly representing what the programmer wrote, and the one generated by the compiler. By switching off optimizations that change the call graph, the two forms can be reconciled, and by selectively switching the optimizations back on, the programmer can understand the effect of compiler optimizations on program execution.

18.4 Models of Computation

In terms of instruction-sets, the majority of systems implement the *tagged-token* dataflow model of computation, in which each data token carries a *tag* [2,3,10,13], in addition to its data value and the address of the successor instruction. Tags provide a straightforward means for realizing the parallelism in recursive functions and loops. A tag consists of an a number of fields, the number and type depending on the particular system. Fields include *activation name*, to separate various activations of the same function-body, *iteration level* to distinguish various loop-bodies in the same activation, and an *index*, to distinguish elements of a data structure. Four types of instruction are needed in such systems:

- □ **Arithmetic and logical operators**: These are similar to their counterparts in conventional computers, except that the output data value from an instruction is communicated directly to the successor instruction, via a token, rather than indirectly, via explicitly addressed storage locations. An output value required by several successor instructions is sent to them all, in the form of a sequence of tokens (some systems place an upper limit on the number of tokens allowed in such a sequence).

- □ **Branch operators**: These are required to implement conditional and iterative computation, and are similar to conventional branch instructions, except that they affect the routing of data between instructions, rather than the sequence of control through the program.

- □ **Tag manipulation operators**: These change the tag values (as opposed to the data values) in tokens. There are no equivalent instructions in conventional systems (nor in the so-called *static* dataflow computers [14]).

- □ **Data structure operators**: These *allocate* data structures, *read* and *write* elements of the allocated structures, and, in some systems, *fetch* complete arrays. Each of these operators invokes one or more complementary *structure storage operations* by sending token-like data packets to the appropriate structure storage module(s).

In some dataflow computers, the above operators are implemented in a strictly *fine-grain* fashion. Instructions are allowed a maximum of two or three input tokens, and are restricted to generate perhaps two or three output tokens. This both reduces the complexity of the local (cache) store and limits the size of (and time to execute) each instruction. These effects are thought to be beneficial to the implementation of dataflow computers, the former because it reduces the cost of the *matching unit store* [2] and the latter because it facilitates design of pipelined processing elements with multiple function units [15]. Recently, however, this picture has changed in that some fine-grain dataflow machines allow a small number of coarser grain *iterative instructions*, which generate a variable number of output tokens from a limited number of input tokens, have been proposed [3,7]. These have been introduced during studies of efficient code generation, with the aim of minimising the number of instructions that have to be executed (and tokens that have to be transmitted) in order to implement a particular algorithm.

Fine-grain monitoring tools on this level are based on idealized execution, and on infinite and bounded parallelism profiles [16]. It has been shown that good performance estimates can be obtained using these tools.

The new von Neumann/Dataflow hybrids [11,12,17-19] are a more radical departure from the original fine-grain dataflow approach. The tag in these systems has become simpler: it consists of an activation name only. Matching is not implemented by hardware hashing as in the Manchester and the Sigma-1 machines, but by virtual addressing, where the activation name is used as a page address and the destination (instruction address) is either directly used as an offset in the page (as in the EM-4 design) or yields the offset indirectly (as in the Epsilon design.) The nodes in the dataflow graph, are now von Neumann "threads" of code. The various designs differ in the characteristics of a thread. A thread can either be blocked and later resumed in the midst of its execution, because of e.g. a remote memory reference or it cannot block. In the latter case a remote memory reference would be the last instruction in a thread. The compiler is responsible for creating the threads in such a way that on the one hand no load balancing problems occur, i.e. threads should not become arbitrarily large, and on the other hand communication is minimized, i.e. by avoiding matching and token exchange by creating relatively large grains. The size of the threads is of course influenced by the model of computation. If, for instance, no blocking of threads is allowed, the threads will become smaller but the underlying machine will be simpler. Inside a thread the von Neumann code can refer to operands stored in conventional memory, such as registers and stack frame locations.

There is a need for monitoring tools for hybrid data-flow computation comprising threads with various semantics. These tools would provide the basis for the analysis of the efficiency of parallel program execution given certain machine characteristics.

18.5 Architecture

In terms of structure, dataflow systems contain three main types of hardware module, namely *processing elements, (structure) storage modules,* and an interconnecting *switch* that links the modules together. The switch is packet-based and communicates data packets between multiple modules of the processing and storage types. The storage modules respond to requests to allocate and deallocate blocks of store, and to access individual locations within each block. Blocks of this store correspond to high-level program data structures, and locations within blocks correspond to elements of the structures. The processing elements implement a data driven model of computation by means of data *tokens* that are passed from instruction to instruction and, hence, via the switch from processing element to processing element, since each instruction is located uniquely within a processing element and each token carries the address of its successor instruction. Processing elements contain local data storage that is akin to cache storage in conventional machines. Tokens destined for a particular instruction are cached in the appropriate local store until there is a complete, "matching" set of input tokens available, at which time the instruction is executed, thus freeing the associated set of local store locations.

For each type of hardware module there are a number of characteristics to monitor. Information can be conveniently displayed as a matrix of meters. A first version of an architecture level monitoring tool is described in [10]. The tool has been used in the design of a hardware "throttle" for the Manchester Dataflow Machine [20]. It is unclear how this tool would behave if it were directly hooked up to hardware, instead of a simulator. The sheer volume of monitoring information might change the behaviour of the hardware. This could be solved by more intelligent tracing, e.g. by reduction of the information at source. More experience with tools on this level needs to be gained.

18.6 Realization

The Sigma-1 machine is surely the most impressive dataflow multiprocessor built to date. It consists of 32 groups of 4-processing elements and 4- structure stores interconnected in a two stage network built out of 10*10 crossbar switching elements. Not all paths are used to interconnect the groups, some are used for global input output. It has demonstrated high performance on a small benchmark, e.g. 170 MFlops on an integration program, written in assembly language. The Sigma-1 machine has an independent maintenance network, that connects all SSs. Each processing element and each structure store is built on one board and has a maintenance processor, so that all modules can be tested independently. We eagerly await a thorough definition and implementation of Sigma-1's programming language DFC, a single assignment version of C, so that this impressive machine can be used more easily and compared with other parallel machines.

18.7 Conclusion

Dataflow is alive and kicking! It is still a most promising approach to parallelism and the new hybrids will make it much more easily acceptable, because off the shelf hardware can be used for their implementation. Monitoring tools have been defined and partly implemented at the various levels of abstraction, and now need to be integrated so that the user can understand model of compution phenomena such as parallelism in source code terms. Comparitive evaluation of languages and architectures is needed to understand the spectrum of possibilties in this area.

References

1. Arvind, D. E. Culler, and K. Ekanadham, "The Price of Asynchronous Parallelism: An Analysis of Dataflow Architectures," **in:** C. R. Jesshope and K. D. Reinartz (eds.), **CONPAR 88,** Cambridge University Press (1989) pp. 541-555.

2. J. R. Gurd, C. C. Kirkham, and A.P.W. Bohm, "The Manchester Dataflow Computing System," **in:** J. J.Dongarra (ed.), **Experimental Parallel Computing Architectures,** North-Holland (1987) pp. 177-219.

3. T. Shimada *et al.*, "Evaluation of a Prototype Data Flow Processor of the SIGMA-1 for Scientific Computations'," **Proceedings 13th International Symposium on Computer Architecture** (June, 1986) pp. 226-234.

4. R. S. Nikhil, K. Pingali and Arvind, **Id Nouveau** , Computation Structures Group Memo 265, MIT Laboratory for Computer Science, Cambridge MA (July 1986).

5. J. R. McGraw *et al.*, **SISAL - Streams and Iteration in a Single-Assignment Language,** Lawrence Livermore National Laboratory, M-146 (January 1985).

6. K. Aziz, M. Haines and R. R. Oldehoeft, **Purdue Parallel Benchmarks in SISAL (Revised),** TR CS-90-101, Colorado State University (1990).

7. A. P. W. Bohm and J. Sargeant, "Code Optimization for Tagged-Token Dataflow Machines," **IEEE Transactions on Computers** (January 1989) pp. 4-14. University of Manchester, UMCS-88-6-3 (June 1988).

8. K. R. Traub, **A Compiler for the MIT Tagged Token Dataflow Arch-tecture**, MIT Laboratory for Computer Science (August 1986).

9. S. K. Skedzielewski and J. R Glauert, **IF1, An Intermediate Form for Applicative Languages**, Reference Manual M-170, Lawrence Livermore National Laboratory, Livermore CA (July 1985).

10. A. P. W. Bohm, J. R. Gurd, and M. C. Kallstrom, "Monitoring Experimental Parallel Machines'," **in:** M. Simmons, R. Koskela, I. Bucher (eds.) **Instrumentation for Future Parallel Computing Systems**, ACM Press, Frontier Series, Addison Wesley (1989) pp. 121-141.

11. R.S Nikhil and Arvind, "Can dataflow subsume von Neumann computing?" **Proceedings of the 1989 International Symposium on Computer Architecture**, Eilat, ACM (1989) pp 262-272.

12. V. G. Grafe and J. E. Hoch, **The Epsilon-2 Multiprocessor System**, Sandia National Laboratories, New Mexico (1989).

13. D. A. Abramson and G. K. Egan, **The RMIT Data Flow Computer - A Hybrid Architecture**, Technical Report TR112061R, Department of Communication and Electronic Engineering, Royal Melbourne Institute of Technology, Melbourne (April, 1987).

14. J. B. Dennis, "Data Flow Supercomputers," **IEEE Computer** (November, 1980) pp. 48-56.

15. Arvind, D. E. Culler, and G. K. Maa, **Assessing the Benefits of Fine-grained Parallelism in Dataflow Programs**, Laboratory for Computer Science, Massachusetts Institute of Technology, TR-279 (March, 1988).

16. G. M. Papadopoulos, 'Program Development and Performance Monitoring on the Monsoon Dataflow Multiprocessor," **in:** M. Simmons, R. Koskela, I. Bucher (eds.) **Instrumentation for Future Parallel Computing Systems**, ACM Press, Frontier Series, Addison Wesley (1989) pp. 91-110.

17. R. Buehrer and K. Ekanadham, "Incorporating Data Flow Ideas into von Neumann Processors for Parallel Execution," **IEEE Transactions on Computers** (December, 1987) pp. 1515-1522.

18. R. A. Ianucci, **A Dataflow/von Neumann Hybrid Architecture**, TR-418, MIT Laboratory for Computer Science (May 1988).

19. S. Sakai et.al., "An Architecture of a Datflow Single Chip Processor," **Proceedings of the 1989 International Symposium on Computer Architecture**, Eilat, ACM (1989) pp 46-53.

20. Y. M. Teo, **Concurrency Control in the Multi-Ring Manchester Dataflow Machine**, Department of Computer Science, University of Manchester, UMCS-89-11-2 (November, 1989).

19

Performance Analysis of Parallel Applications and Systems Summary

Frederica Darema
Shreekant Thakker

The focus of the working group, "Monitoring the Performance of Parallel Programs," was to discuss how suitable are the various parallel, supercomputer architectures existing and proposed, to do scientific computing. Our group consisted mainly of people who were applications oriented in the respect that either they currently use computers to do their scientific computations or they have background in that area but are now involved with various design aspects of computers. Driven by our background we took the view that to understand the merits and drawbacks of architectures we would an *application driven* analysis of their suitability. Namely, we sought to derive conclusions not only based on the facility of hardware development or the economics of the hardware cost but also on the software requirements of the engineering/scientific applications. We discussed the suitability of these architectures for parallel computation of currently used mathematical approaches to the modeling of the physical world and what software environments, in terms of languages for expressing parallelism, compiler and debugger capabilities, the users would require.

There was a plethora of supercomputer architectures considered; initially we focused on which of all the architectures we should consider for our discussion. As microprocessors become more and powerful, we felt that the supercomputer systems of the future will be microprocessor based and will probably consist of large numbers of such processors. The majority of the systems will be

Multiple-Instruction-Multiple-Data (MIMD) parallel systemsneither intermediate or coarse grain. Classified according to their memory/processor interconnection, such parallel computers range from systems where the parallel processors can have access to the entire memory (*shared memory systems*), to systems where each processor has immediate access to only a portion of the memory (*distributed or message-passing systems*), with many variants in the memory hierarchy in between. Currently, it is not certain which class of architectures are more general, that is, suitable for the majority of applications. Due to a time limitation, we did not address issues regarding Single-Instruction-Multiple-Data (SIMD) parallel systems or fine-grained data-flow MIMD architectures that might be worth investigating as they could satisfy the hardware needs, at least, of specific applications.

We felt that the crucial factors in determining which architectures will dominate are the facility for mapping the applications on the parallel system and the achieved performance. Considering that the numerical solutions used in the application might differ from one architecture to another, performance is measured by the numerical efficiency of the algorithm *and* by how effectively the application can use the system resources.

There are two approaches to the issue of mapping and performance. One approach assumes that the user develops numerical techniques suitable to the architecture and optimizes the mapping to take advantage of the system features. The other approach is for the users to develop algorithms independent of the architecture and let optimizers (compilers) do the appropriate mapping to the architecture and do the optimizations. Our view is that it will be a long time until the compilers, even if they develop some sort of expert systems, will replace the human expert (the mathematician/physicist/engineer) in devising new algorithms. So we think that there will be a symbiotic relation in which the human expert devises the algorithm and does the *high-level* mapping, while the compiler does the *low-level* optimizations.

Our current experience indicates that it is conceptually and practically easy to map applications onto shared memory systems. Difficulties such as race conditions are obstacles that people seem to overcome after some initial experience with parallel programming and suitable synchronization libraries. Distributed memory systems seem to require rethinking of the numerical algorithm used and seem to require equivalent past experience in terms of programming the system. The other component in the figure of merit for running on a parallel system is how effectively the application can use the system resources, that is, what performance one achieves. At this point our experience with performance measurements that compare the relative efficiency of solving the same physics/engineering problem on a shared memory system and a distributed memory system is not extensive enough for detailed conclusions. One conjecture is that to avoid memory and network contention in a shared memory system and achieve good performance, one would have to develop numerical algorithms and make optimizations similar to the ones required to run the application on a distributed memory system. Thus, the differences of shared memory and distributed memory systems in terms of the numerical algorithm requirements might become insignificant; the issue might then be viewed from a different angle. If it is easier to build distributed memory systems, why not build only such systems. This comparative analysis of the algorithms is a key research issue in the performance experiments that will be conducted in the next few years on existing shared memory and message-passing systems. The other key issue is developing compilers will be developed that can make effective optimizations within each of the two classes.

We also felt that application-driven analysis can guide the software and hardware design characteristics within a given architectural class. In such a study of system performance one would consider a number of applications and examine the performance of specific hardware components or architectural characteristics such as the memory organization, in order to design or make incremental improvements in the software and hardware.

The last subject we addressed was performance measurement and modeling. We felt that to understand the effect of various hardware or software components, performance tools are needed that provide execution measurements. Another essential component for understanding performance is a modeling capability that enables interpretation of the results and allows predictions for subsequent algorithm, software and hardware system design. Typically performance measurements are done on small or current application problem sizes. We strongly believe that one of the features that the performance tools and modeling need to provide is a mechanism for extrapolating measurements on small problems to larger (future) problem sizes; we call this *scaling* performance methodology.